AFRICA

Prentice
Hall

Needham, Massachusetts
Upper Saddle River, New Jersey
Glenview, Illinois

Program Consultants

Heidi Hayes Jacobs

Heidi Hayes Jacobs has served as an educational consultant to more than 1,000 schools across the nation and abroad. Dr. Jacobs served as an adjunct professor in the Department of Curriculum on Teaching at Teachers College, Columbia University. She has written a best-selling book and numerous articles on curriculum reform. She completed her undergraduate studies at the University of Utah in her hometown of Salt Lake City. She received an M.A. from the University of Massachusetts, Amherst, and completed her doctoral work at Columbia University's Teachers College in 1981.

The backbone of Dr. Jacobs' experience comes from her years as a teacher of high school, middle school, and elementary school students. As an educational consultant, she works with K–12 schools and districts on curriculum reform and strategic planning.

Brenda Randolph

Brenda Randolph is the former Director of the Outreach Resource Center at the African Studies Program at Howard University, Washington, D.C. She is the Founder and Director of Africa Access, a bibliographic service on Africa for schools. She received her B.A. in history with high honors from North Carolina Central University, Durham, and her M.A. in African studies with honors from Howard University. She completed further graduate studies at the University of Maryland, College Park, where she was awarded a Graduate Fellowship.

Brenda Randolph has published numerous articles in professional journals and bulletins. She currently serves as library media specialist in Montgomery County Public Schools, Maryland.

Michal L. LeVasseur

Michal LeVasseur is an educational consultant in the field of geography. She is an adjunct professor of geography at the University of Alabama, Birmingham, and serves with the Alabama Geographic Alliance. Her undergraduate and graduate work is in the fields of anthropology (B.A.), geography (M.A.), and science education (Ph.D.).

Dr. LeVasseur's specialization has moved increasingly into the area of geography education. In 1996, she served as Director of the National Geographic Society's Summer Geography Workshop. As an educational consultant, she has worked with the National Geographic Society as well as with schools to develop programs and curricula for geography.

Special Program Consultant
Yvonne S. Gentzler, Ph.D.
Iowa State University
College of Family and Consumer Sciences
Ames, Iowa

Content Consultant on Africa
Barbara Brown
African Studies Center
Boston University
Boston, Massachusetts

Content Consultant on North Africa
Laurence Michalak
Center for Middle East Studies
University of California
Berkeley, California

ISBN 0-13-062980-4

1 2 3 4 5 6 7 8 9 10   06 05 04 03 02

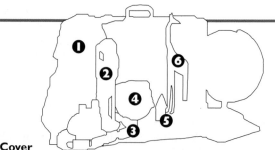

On the Cover

❶ West African batik fabric

❷ West African ebony statue of a hunter

❸ Cowrie shell belt

❹ African mask

❺ Brass model of a traditional African dwelling

❻ Wood carving of a giraffe

Content Consultants for the World Explorer Program

TABLE OF CONTENTS

AFRICA

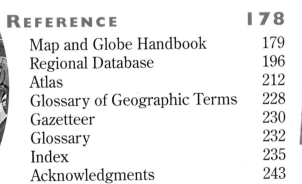

OF SPECIAL INTEREST

Maps and charts providing a closer look at countries, regions, and provinces.

A hands-on approach to learning and applying key social studies skills

Step-by-step activities for exploring important topics in Africa

Literature selections by African authors

HEROES

Profiles of people who made a difference in their country

Detailed drawings show how the use of technology makes a country unique

Maps and statistics for every nation in Africa

A view of a country through the eyes of a student artist

MAPS

CHARTS, GRAPHS, AND TABLES

READ ACTIVELY

How can I get the most out of my social studies book?

How does my reading relate to my world? Answering questions like these means that you are an active reader, an involved reader. As an active reader, you are in charge of the reading situation!

The following strategies tell how to think and read as an active reader. You don't need to use all of these strategies all the time. Feel free to choose the ones that work best in each reading situation. You might use several at a time, or you might go back and forth among them. They can be used in any order.

BEFORE YOU READ

Give yourself a purpose

The sections in this book begin with a list called "Questions to Explore." These questions focus on key ideas presented in the section. They give you a purpose for reading. You can create your own purpose by asking questions like these: How does the topic relate to your life? How might you use what you learn at school or at home?

Preview

To preview a reading selection, first read its title. Then look at the pictures and read the captions. Also read any headings in the selection. Then ask yourself: What is the reading selection about? What do the pictures and headings tell about the selection?

Reach into your background

What do you already know about the topic of the selection? How can you use what you know to help you understand what you are going to read?

WHILE YOU READ

Ask questions

Suppose you are reading about the continent of South America. Some questions you might ask are: Where is South America? What countries are found there? Why are some of the countries large and others small? Asking questions like these can help you gather evidence and gain knowledge.

Predict

As you read, make a prediction about what will happen and why. Or predict how one fact might affect another fact. Suppose you are reading about South America's climate. You might make a prediction about how the climate affects where people live. You can change your mind as you gain new information.

Connect

Connect your reading to your own life. Are the people discussed in the selection like you or someone you know? What would you do in similar situations? Connect your reading to something you have already read. Suppose you have already read about the ancient Greeks. Now you are reading about the ancient Romans. How are they alike? How are they different?

Visualize

What would places, people, and events look like in a movie or a picture? As you read about India, you could visualize the country's heavy rains. What do they look like? How do they sound? As you read about geography, you could visualize a volcanic eruption.

AFTER YOU READ

Respond

Talk about what you have read. What did you think? Share your ideas with your classmates.

Assess yourself

What did you find out? Were your predictions on target? Did you find answers to your questions?

Follow up

Show what you know. Use what you have learned to do a project. When you do projects, you continue to learn.

AFRICA

The name Africa may have come from the Latin word *aprica*, meaning "sunny." In much of Africa, the sun does shine brightly. Each morning, the African sunrise awakens one eighth of the world's population in more than fifty countries. In the chapters that follow, you'll spend the day with some of them.

GUIDING QUESTIONS

The readings and activities in this book will help you discover answers to these Guiding Questions.

1 GEOGRAPHY What are the main physical features of Africa?

2 HISTORY How have historical events affected the cultures and nations of Africa?

3 CULTURE How have Africa's cultures changed?

4 GOVERNMENT What factors led to the development of different governments across Africa?

5 ECONOMICS What factors influence the ways in which Africans make a living?

PROJECT PREVIEW

You can also discover answers to the Guiding Questions by working on projects. You can find several project possibilities on pages 176–177 at the back of this book.

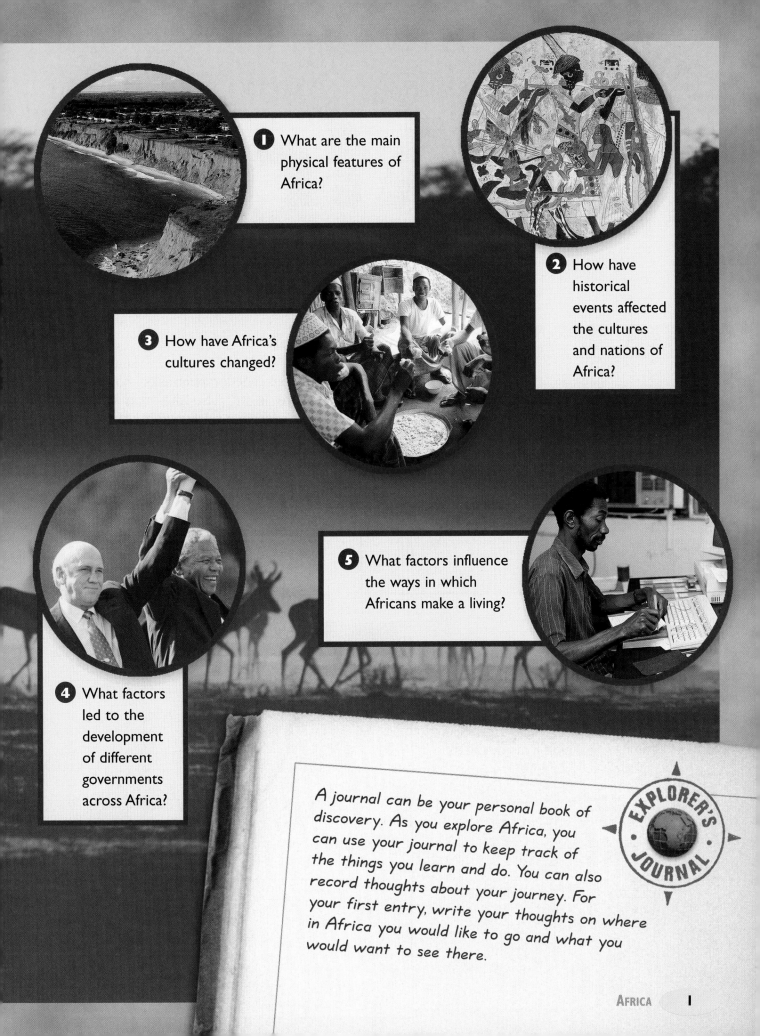

1 What are the main physical features of Africa?

2 How have historical events affected the cultures and nations of Africa?

3 How have Africa's cultures changed?

4 What factors led to the development of different governments across Africa?

5 What factors influence the ways in which Africans make a living?

A journal can be your personal book of discovery. As you explore Africa, you can use your journal to keep track of the things you learn and do. You can also record thoughts about your journey. For your first entry, write your thoughts on where in Africa you would like to go and what you would want to see there.

EXPLORER'S JOURNAL

DISCOVERY ACTIVITIES ABOUT

Africa

Learning about Africa means being an explorer and a geographer. No explorer would start out without first checking some facts. Begin by exploring the maps of Africa on the following pages.

Relative Location

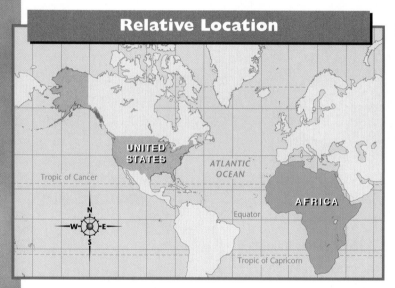

LOCATION

1. Explore Africa's Location One of the first questions a geographer asks about a place is "Where is it?" Use the map to describe Africa's location relative to the United States. What ocean lies between Africa and the United States? Note that the Equator extends through Africa. What role might the Equator play in the climates of nearby countries? How do you think climates of the United States might differ from the climates of Africa?

REGIONS

2. Explore Africa's Size How big is Africa compared to the United States? On a separate sheet of paper, trace the map of the United States and cut it out. How many times can you fit it inside the map of Africa?

Relative Size

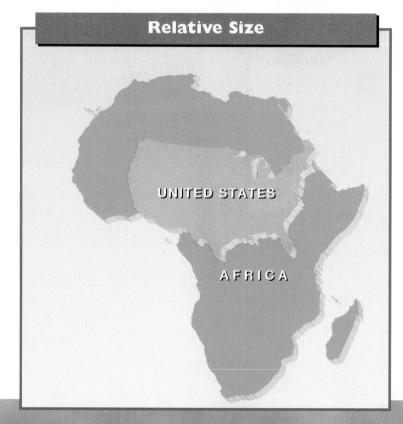

PLACE

3. Find Africa's Lakes There are several large lakes in Africa. Name four of them. What countries do they border? In what part of the continent do you find the most lakes?

MOVEMENT

4. Predict How Location Affects Economic Wealth Fifteen African nations are landlocked. That is, they do not border any ocean. Find them on the map. Landlocked nations are often poor. How do you think a landlocked location might affect a nation's economy?

Africa: Political

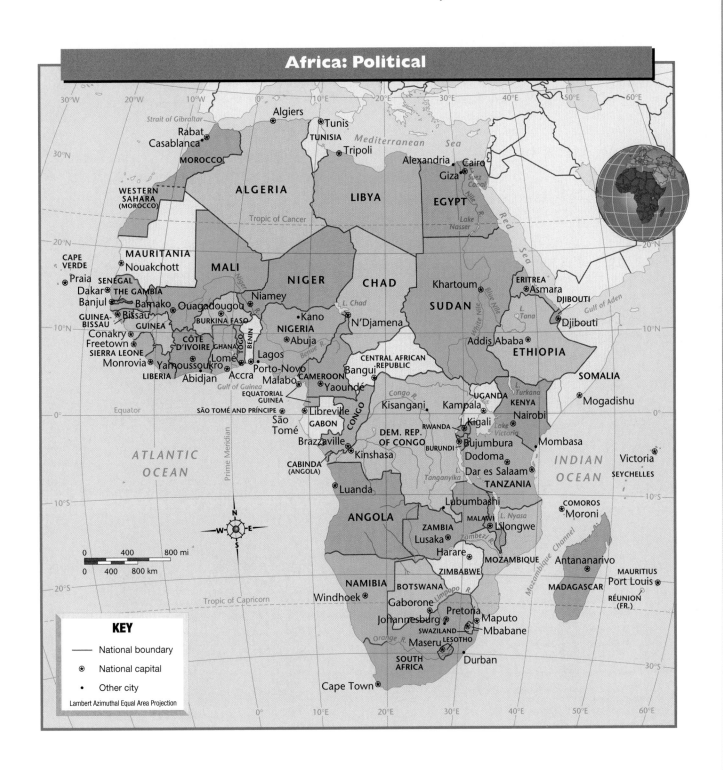

KEY

— National boundary

⊛ National capital

• Other city

Lambert Azimuthal Equal Area Projection

PLACE

5. Investigate Africa's Physical Features

Parts of Africa's coasts have very narrow strips of flat plains. Cliffs rise steeply from these plains. The interior is high and somewhat flat, forming a huge plateau. Find Southern Africa on the map below. It extends south of 10°S. The cliffs arise where the dark green areas meet the light green areas. Trace these cliffs with your finger. Note that in some places they extend nearly along the coast. Is Africa's plateau higher in the western part of the continent or the southeastern part?

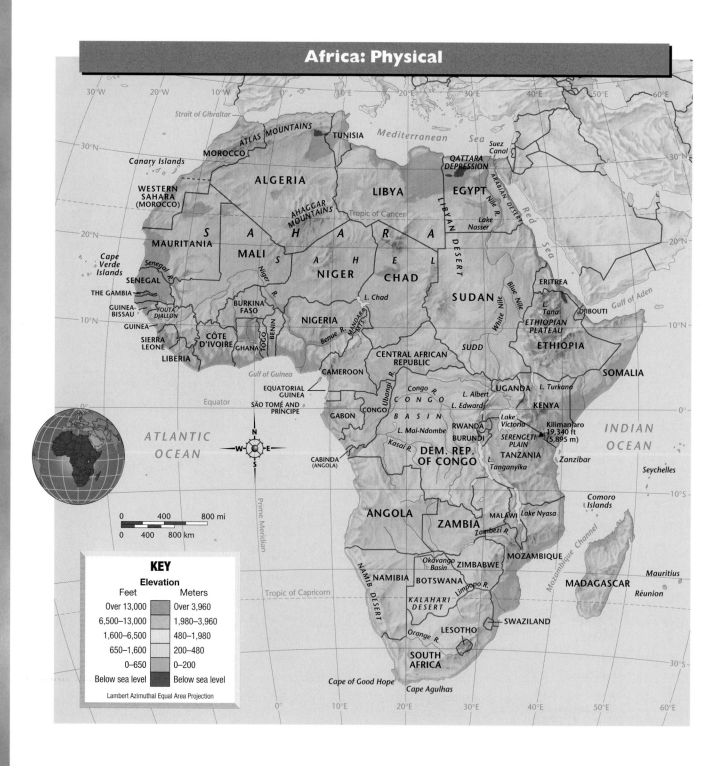

Africa: Physical

KEY

Elevation

Feet	Meters
Over 13,000	Over 3,960
6,500–13,000	1,980–3,960
1,600–6,500	480–1,980
650–1,600	200–480
0–650	0–200
Below sea level	Below sea level

Lambert Azimuthal Equal Area Projection

0   400   800 mi
0   400   800 km

6. Find Geo Cleo Geo Cleo has gone off on one of her flying trips. This time she's gone to Africa, but she hasn't told anyone exactly where in Africa she's traveling. Read the messages Geo Cleo radioed from her plane. Then use the map below and the maps on the two previous pages to locate the city described in each message.

A. I'm in a region of tall grasses and few trees, or a savanna. I've landed in a city in Ethiopia near 10°N and 40°E.

B. Not too many places in Africa have Mediterranean vegetation. And I'm not even anywhere near the Mediterranean Sea! I am flying over a city on a very narrow coastal plain. The cliffs here are really steep.

C. Today, I flew above tropical rain forests growing right along the Equator. Going north, I saw these magnificent forests change into open grasslands, or savanna. I've just landed in a city in the savanna region north of where the Benue River meets the Niger River.

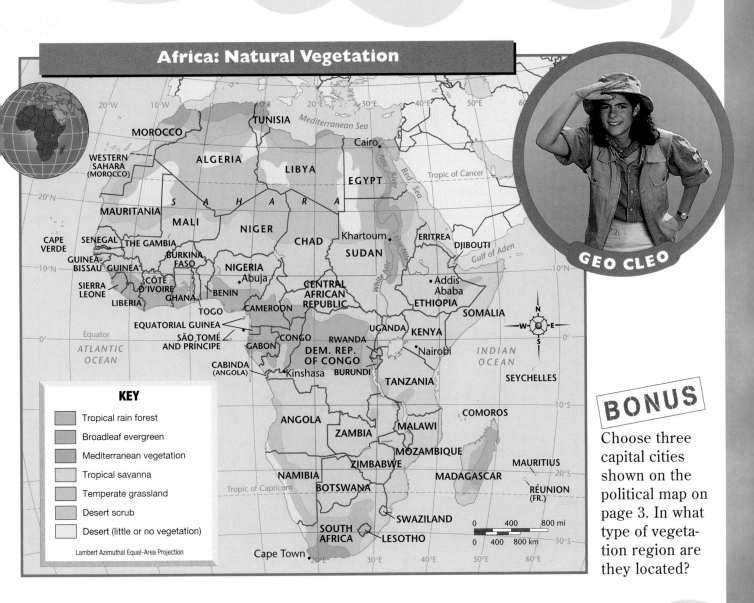

Africa: Natural Vegetation

KEY
- Tropical rain forest
- Broadleaf evergreen
- Mediterranean vegetation
- Tropical savanna
- Temperate grassland
- Desert scrub
- Desert (little or no vegetation)

Lambert Azimuthal Equal-Area Projection

GEO CLEO

BONUS

Choose three capital cities shown on the political map on page 3. In what type of vegetation region are they located?

INTERACTION

7. Estimate the Impact of Deforestation

Deforestation means a loss of trees and forest. Deforestation contributes to droughts, increased temperatures, and the loss of animal life. In already dry areas, such as lands bordering the Sahel, fewer trees and vegetation creates new desert areas. Human activity is the main cause of deforestation. Farmers and lifestock herders cut or burn down trees to make farming and grazing lands. The map on this page shows deforestation in Africa today. Which regions are most affected by deforestation? How would the loss of all vegetation, including farm crops, affect people in these regions?

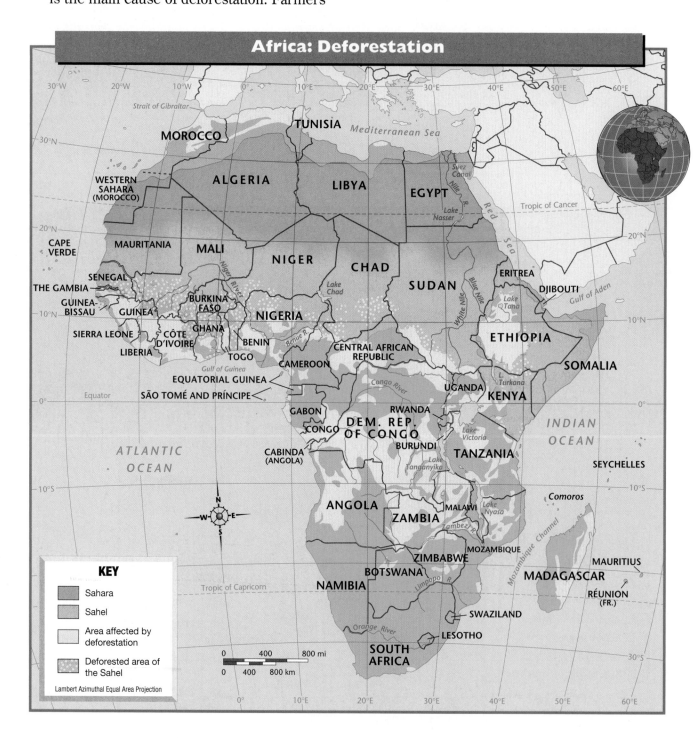

Africa: Deforestation

KEY
- Sahara
- Sahel
- Area affected by deforestation
- Deforested area of the Sahel

Lambert Azimuthal Equal Area Projection

8. **Analyze Temperatures Across the Continent** The map below shows the average temperatures on the continent of Africa. Use this map and the map on the previous page to answer the following questions. What are the average temperatures in the Sahara? In the Sahel? How do the temperatures in southern countries such as Lesotho differ from countries such as Gabon that are located along the Equator? Why do you think the temperatures in extreme northern and southern parts of Africa are similar?

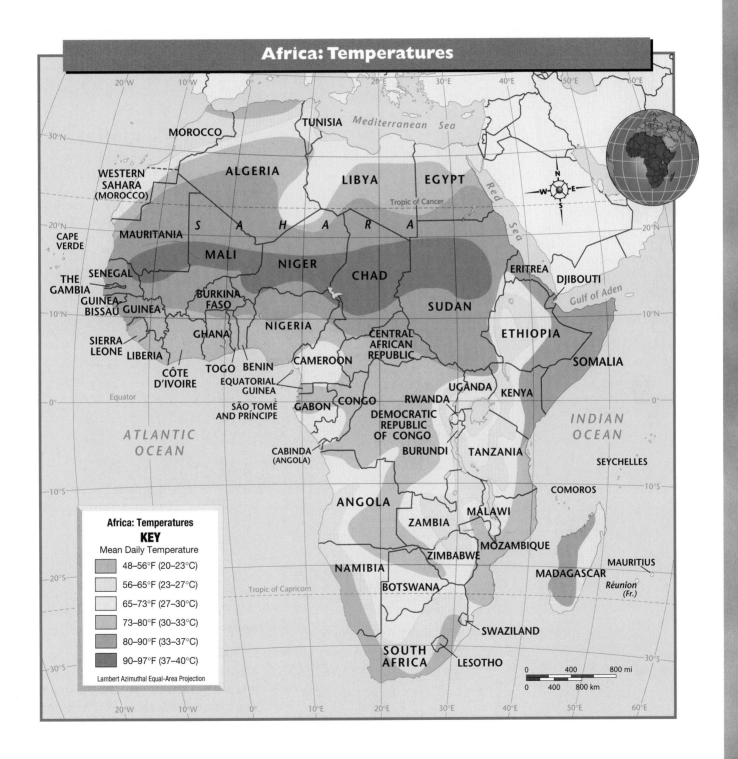

Africa: Temperatures

KEY
Mean Daily Temperature

	48–56°F (20–23°C)
	56–65°F (23–27°C)
	65–73°F (27–30°C)
	73–80°F (30–33°C)
	80–90°F (33–37°C)
	90–97°F (37–40°C)

Lambert Azimuthal Equal-Area Projection

AFRICA

Physical Geography

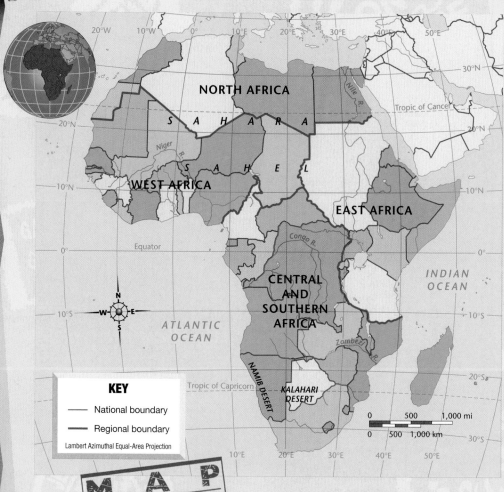

MAP ACTIVITIES

This map shows four regions of Africa. Each region contains many different landforms and climates. Start exploring the geography of Africa by doing the following activities.

Study the map
What region of Africa is the largest? Which is the smallest? Through what regions do the major rivers flow?

Consider the geography
Notice that some African nations are much larger than others. As you read this chapter, think about how landforms and climate might have affected the political boundaries of Africa.

Land and Water

SECTION 1

BEFORE YOU READ

Reach Into Your Background

Think about the state in which you live. What different landforms are in your state? Are there any mountains or valleys? How do these landforms affect your daily life?

Questions to Explore

1. Where is Africa located?
2. What are Africa's most important landforms?

Key Terms

plateau   cataract
elevation   silt
escarpment   fertile
rift   tributary

Key Places

Sahara
Great Rift Valley
Nile River
Congo River
Niger River
Zambezi River

▼ Scientists found the bones of one type of dinosaur on more than one continent. This clue made them suspect the continents were once connected.

Scientists believe that over 200 million years ago, dinosaurs easily walked from the continent of Africa to the continent of South America. That's because Africa and South America were connected. Find Africa on the world map in the atlas at the back of this book. As you can see, it would be pretty hard to walk from Africa to South America today. How did Africa and South America become separated? About 190 million years ago, forces within the Earth caused South America and Africa to move apart, forming the southern part of the Atlantic Ocean.

The Four Regions of Africa

Africa can be divided into four regions: (1) North, (2) West, (3) East, and (4) Central and Southern. Each of these regions contains many different climates and landforms.

North Africa is marked by rocky mountains and seemingly endless stretches of the world's largest desert, the Sahara. Find the Sahara, which is almost the size of the United States, on the physical map in the Activity Atlas. What countries include part of the Sahara?

West Africa, the continent's most populated region, consists mostly of grasslands. The soil in the grasslands is good for farming. Find West Africa on the map at the beginning of the chapter. What geographic features border this region to the north and south?

East Africa contains many mountains, and **plateaus,** large raised areas of mostly level land. The east also has areas of grasslands and hills. Find East Africa on the map at the beginning of this chapter. What East African countries have sea coasts?

Much of Central and Southern Africa is flat or rolling grassland. The region also contains thick rain forests, mountains, and swamps. The Namib (NAHM eeb) Desert of the country of Namibia and the Kalahari (kal uh HAHR ee) Desert of Botswana are in this region.

Africa's Major Landforms

Africa can be described as an upside-down pie. If you were to slice Africa in half from east to west, you would see that much of the continent is a plateau that drops off sharply near the sea.

The Plateau Continent Africa is often called the "plateau continent." That is because the elevation of much of the land area is high. **Elevation** is the height of land above sea level.

▼ In the Atlas Mountains of Morocco (below), some people adapt to steep slopes by building houses along the sides of the mountains. Some people living in the lush rain forests of the Democratic Republic of Congo (inset, upper left) take advantage of the tropical vegetation by gathering honey from bees' nests in the trees.

A Coastal Plain in West Africa

Most of Africa is plateaus and mountains. Africa's few plains lie mostly along its coasts, like this one at Cape Coast, Ghana. In fact, except for two basins in the Sahara, all of Africa's lowland areas lie within 500 miles (805 km) of the coast. **Critical Thinking** Based on this photograph, how do you think people living on Africa's coastal plains might make a living?

Each of Africa's four regions has mountains. The highest are in East Africa. Mount Kilimanjaro is Africa's tallest mountain. It rises to a height of 19,341 feet (5,895 m).

Coastal Plains Edge the Continent Along much of Africa's coast is a strip of coastal plain. This strip of land is dry and sandy at some points. It is marshy and moist at other places. Look at the political map in the Activity Atlas. Find the city of Accra, in the West African country of Ghana (GAHN uh). Here, the coastal strip is only 16 miles (25 km) wide. It ends at a long escarpment, or steep cliff, that is about as high as a 100-story skyscraper.

The Great Rift Valley Mount Kilimanjaro is located on the edge of the Great Rift Valley in East Africa. The Great Rift Valley was formed millions of years ago, when the continents pulled apart. A rift is a deep trench. The rift that cuts through East Africa is 4,000 miles (6,400 km) long. Most of Africa's major lakes are located in or near the Great Rift Valley.

READ ACTIVELY

Connect What part of the United States contains a deep trench?

Africa's Rivers

Four large rivers carry water from the mountains of Africa's plateaus to the sea. They are the Nile, the Congo, the Zambezi, and the Niger (NI jur). The rivers are useful for traveling. But they are broken in places by cataracts, or rock-filled rapids. Cataracts make it impossible for ships to sail from Africa's interior to the sea.

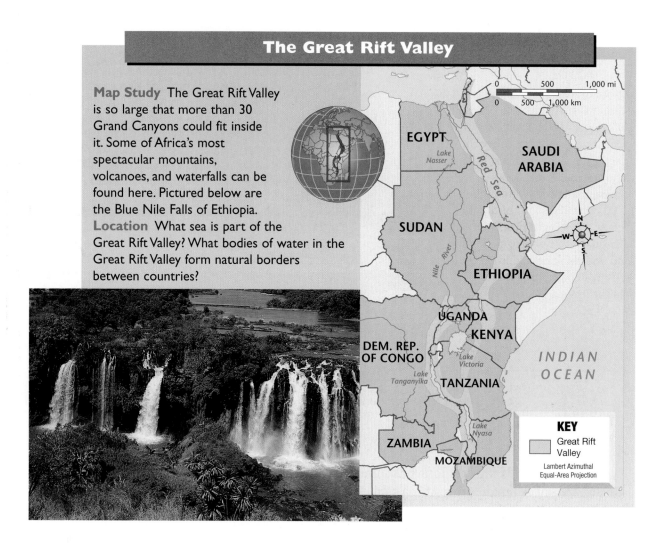

The Great Rift Valley

Map Study The Great Rift Valley is so large that more than 30 Grand Canyons could fit inside it. Some of Africa's most spectacular mountains, volcanoes, and waterfalls can be found here. Pictured below are the Blue Nile Falls of Ethiopia.

Location What sea is part of the Great Rift Valley? What bodies of water in the Great Rift Valley form natural borders between countries?

KEY
Great Rift Valley

Lambert Azimuthal Equal-Area Projection

The Nile River The Nile is the longest river in the world. Its length, more than 4,000 miles (6,400 km), is almost twice the width of the United States. The sources of the Nile are the White Nile in the country of Sudan and the Blue Nile in the highlands of Ethiopia. From these two sources, the river flows north and spills into the Mediterranean Sea.

People have farmed the land surrounding the Nile for thousands of years. At one time, the Nile flooded its banks regularly. Farmers planted their crops to match the flood cycle of the river. The floods provided water for the crops and left behind a layer of **silt,** which is the tiny bits of rock and dirt that build up on the bottoms of rivers and lakes. Silt helps make soil **fertile,** or containing substances that plants need in order to grow well.

About 30 years ago, Egypt's government built the Aswan High Dam to control the flooding of the Nile. As the water backed up behind the dam, it created Lake Nasser. Lake waters are channeled to water crops that grow in the desert. Water rushing through the dam makes electricity.

The Congo River The Congo River flows through the rain forest of the country of Congo (KAHNG oh) in Central Africa. Look at the map at the beginning of the chapter. What ocean does the Congo River flow into? At 2,900 miles (4,677 km), the Congo is Africa's second-longest river. It is fed by hundreds of **tributaries,** or small rivers and streams that flow into a larger river. People in this region grow grains and cassava to make into porridge. Cassava is a starchy plant a little like a potato. They also catch fish in the Congo with basket traps.

The Niger River   Africa's third-longest river, the Niger, begins its journey in Guinea (GIN ee). The river flows north and then bends south for 2,600 miles (4,180 km). The Niger provides water for farms in the river valley. People make a living catching fish in the river.

The Zambezi River   The fourth-longest of Africa's rivers, the Zambezi, is in southern Africa. It runs through or forms the borders of six countries: Angola, Zambia, Namibia, Botswana, Zimbabwe (zim BAHB way), and Mozambique (moh zam BEEK). The Zambezi is 2,200 miles (3,540 km) long. Boats can travel about 460 miles (740 km) of the river.

A River Without a Delta
The Congo River's current is so strong that the river does not form a delta as it flows into the ocean. Instead, the river has cut a deep, wide canyon beneath the sea for a distance of about 125 miles (200 km).

The Congo River

The Congo River flows very fast—every second, the equivalent of more than 100 swimming pools full of water flows past its mouth.

The African name for Victoria Falls means "The Smoke That Thunders." Victoria Falls lies on the Zambezi River, which crosses 2,200 miles (3,540 km) and six countries. It is broken by many waterfalls. **Critical Thinking** Based on this photo, why do you think the Zambezi River is not used as a major trade route?

People have used the Zambezi's strong current to make electricity. About halfway to its outlet in the Indian Ocean, the Zambezi plunges into a canyon, creating Victoria Falls. People can sometimes see the mist and spray of the falls from up to 40 miles (65 km) away.

SECTION 1 REVIEW

1. **Define** (a) plateau, (b) elevation, (c) escarpment, (d) rift, (e) cataract, (f) silt, (g) fertile, (h) tributary.

2. **Identify** (a) Sahara, (b) Great Rift Valley, (c) Nile River, (d) Congo River, (e) Niger River, (f) Zambezi River.

3. Why is Africa called the "plateau continent"?

4. (a) How do people use the rivers of Africa? (b) What makes them difficult to use?

Critical Thinking

5. **Drawing Conclusions** Most of the people in North Africa live north of the Sahara near the Mediterranean Sea. If the Sahara were a grassland with rivers and forests, would this change where people in North African countries live? Why?

Activity

6. **Writing to Learn** List several landforms in Africa you would like to visit. Explain why you would like to go there and what you would do on your trip.

Climate and Vegetation

Reach Into Your Background

Think about the climate where you live. What kind of weather do you have in the summer? What kind of weather do you have in the winter? What are the months when you have summer? What are the months when you have winter?

Questions to Explore

1. What types of climates and vegetation are found in Africa?
2. How do climate and vegetation affect how Africans make a living?

Key Terms

irrigate
oasis
savanna
nomad

Key Places

Sahel
Namib Desert
Kalahari Desert

A trip to Africa sounds like a great adventure. But packing for the trip might prove harder than you think. What would you pack for a two-week journey to Africa? As you read about Africa's climates and vegetation, see if you would add any items to your list.

What Influences Climate?

Look at the climate map on the following page. Find the Tropic of Cancer and the Tropic of Capricorn. As you can see, much of Africa lies between these two lines of latitude. This means that most of Africa is in a tropical climate region. Notice that the Equator runs through this midsection of the continent. These regions are usually hot.

Many parts of Africa are indeed hot. But much of Africa is not. That is because location near the Equator is not the only influence on climate. The climate of a place may depend on how close it is to large bodies of water. Major landforms also affect climate. So does the elevation of a place.

▼ If you visit Botswana during the rainy season, be prepared to get wet. Floods like this one, on the Okavango River Delta, are common.

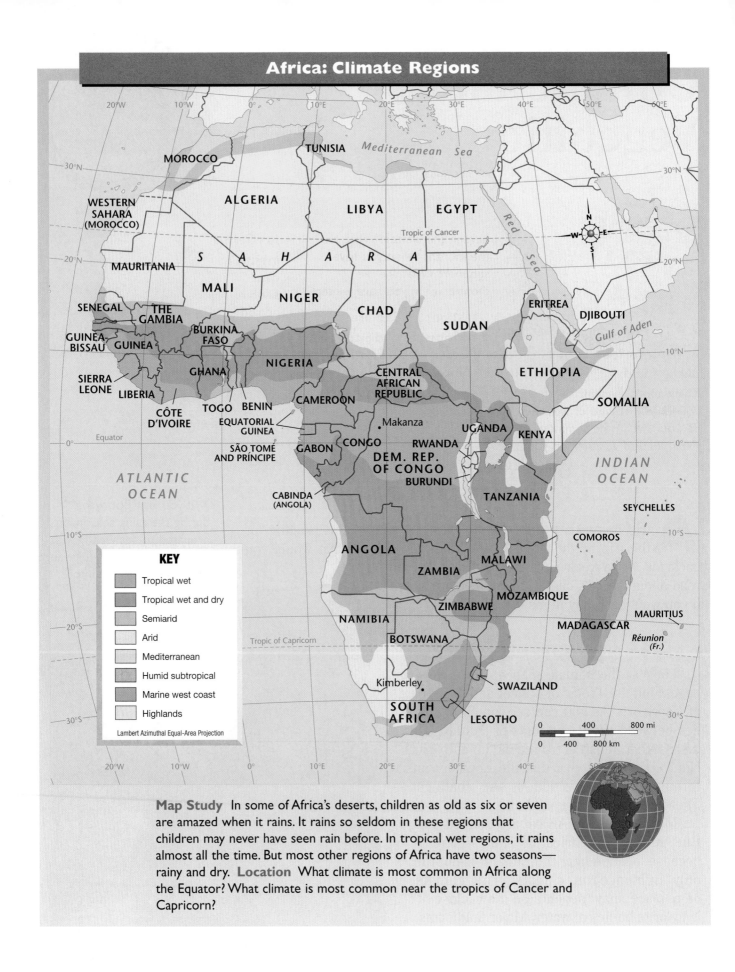

KEY

- Tropical wet
- Tropical wet and dry
- Semiarid
- Arid
- Mediterranean
- Humid subtropical
- Marine west coast
- Highlands

Lambert Azimuthal Equal-Area Projection

Map Study In some of Africa's deserts, children as old as six or seven are amazed when it rains. It rains so seldom in these regions that children may never have seen rain before. In tropical wet regions, it rains almost all the time. But most other regions of Africa have two seasons—rainy and dry. **Location** What climate is most common in Africa along the Equator? What climate is most common near the tropics of Cancer and Capricorn?

Distance From the Equator Africa's location near the Equator means that most of the continent is warm. A place's location in relation to the Equator influences the seasons. North of the Equator, winter and summer occur at the same time as they do in the United States. South of the Equator, the seasons are reversed. For example, July in South Africa is the middle of winter.

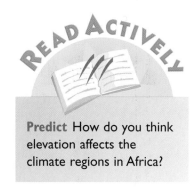

Predict How do you think elevation affects the climate regions in Africa?

Higher, Cooler: The Role of Elevation Elevation, or height above sea level, also affects climate. The higher the elevation, the cooler a place tends to be. Mount Kilimanjaro, Africa's highest peak, is located very close to the Equator. Yet ice and snow blanket the peak of Kilimanjaro year round.

The countries of Ethiopia and Somalia provide another example. They are about the same distance from the Equator, yet they have different climates. Ethiopia is on a very high plateau. Much of Ethiopia has mild temperatures and much rain. Farmers there grow a wide range of crops—including coffee, dates, and cereals. Because Ethiopia usually gets plenty of rain, many farmers there do not **irrigate,** or artificially water, their crops.

Somalia is at a much lower elevation than Ethiopia. Its climate is hot and dry. Farming is possible only in or near an oasis, where crops can be irrigated. An **oasis** is a place where springs and fresh underground water make it possible to support life in a region that gets little rain.

Unpredictable Rainfall Rainfall varies greatly from one region of Africa to another. Along parts of the west coast, winds carry moisture from the warm ocean over the land. Rainfall averages more than 100 inches (250 cm) per year. Compare that to your own height in inches. Forty inches (100 cm) of rain might fall during June alone. But in parts of the Sahara in the north and Namib Desert in the south, it may not rain at all for several years in a row.

Farmers who live in dry regions can never be sure whether there will be enough rain for their crops. Some farmers

▼ What clue in this picture shows that it is Mount Kilimanjaro's high elevation that keeps its snow from melting?

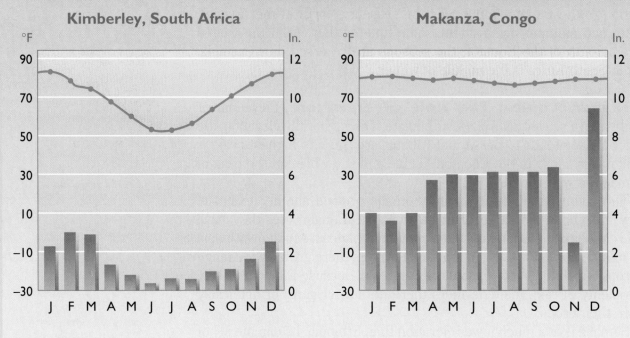

Kimberley, South Africa

Makanza, Congo

Curved lines show temperatures in Fahrenheit degrees. Bars show rainfall in inches.

Chart Study The vegetation of Kimberley, South Africa, is mostly desert scrub. Makanza, Congo, lies in a tropical rain forest. **Critical Thinking** What differences do the climate charts show that would explain why Kimberley is in a warm, dry region while Makanza is in a tropical rain forest?

choose to plant a variety of crops, each needing different amounts of rainfall. These farmers hope they will have at least one successful crop. The charts on this page show rainfall in two cities that have very different climates. Which city do you think would have the best climate for farming?

Vegetation

Look at the vegetation map in the Activity Atlas. Near the Equator are rain forests. Farther from the Equator lies a region of tall grasses, called the **savanna**.

Tropical Rain Forests Tropical rain forests are regions where it rains nearly all the time. The moisture supports a rich environment of trees, plants, and animals. Find the tropical rain forest region on the vegetation map. The tropical rain forest region used to be much larger. It covered much of Central Africa. Through the years, people cut trees from the forest to use the wood or to clear land for farming. Rain forest lands, however, do not make good farmland. Once the trees are cut down, heavy rains wash away the nutrients that make soil fertile.

READ ACTIVELY

Visualize Visualize the rain forest in the country of Cameroon. What might it look like and sound like?

Tropical Savannas Much of Africa north and south of the rain forest is tropical savanna. Tall grasses, thorny bushes, and scattered trees grow in the savanna region. Some grasses grow as high as a person's head.

The climate of the tropical savanna is tropical wet and dry. This means that the savanna has two seasons: dry and wet. During the dry season, farming is impossible. Trees lose their leaves and rivers run dry. People use the season to trade, build houses, and visit friends. In the wet season, the land turns green, and farmers plant their crops.

▲ The acacia tree produces a substance that is used in candy, glue, and ink. It grows in tropical savanna regions.

Deserts in Africa Beyond the savanna lie the deserts. The immense Sahara extends across most of North Africa. This desert covers almost as much land as the entire United States.

The southern edge of the Sahara meets the savanna in a region called the Sahel (SAH hil), which is the Arab word for shore or border. The Sahel is very hot and dry. It receives only 4 to 8 inches (10 to 20 cm) of rain per year. Small shrubs, grass, and some trees grow there.

The Namib and Kalahari deserts extend over much of Namibia and Botswana in Southern Africa. These deserts, like the Sahara, feature landscapes of bare rock, towering rock formations, sand dunes, and a few areas of small bushes and grass.

A journalist traveling in the Namib Desert described the region:

> "There was sand everywhere, an impossible amount of sand covering thousands of square miles and heaping into dunes as high as 1,200 feet. The ultimate sandpile. It was uniformly fine and found its way into everything. I blinked sand from my eyes, blew it from my nose, spit it from my mouth and throat."

Nomads make their living in the Sahara. **Nomads** are people who move around to various places to make a living. Some nomads are traders, and others hunt game and gather food. Most nomads are herders, however. They travel to places where they know they can get water and food for their herds of goats, camels, or sheep.

Some nomadic herders live mainly in the mountainous areas. In spring, they leave their winter grazing grounds in the foothills and head

LINKS
ACROSS THE WORLD

The Oldest Sunscreen In the United States, people often wear sunscreen to protect their skin from sunburn. But it is hard to get sunscreen in the Sahara. Instead, desert nomads cover themselves from head to toe in long, loose robes.

▶ These Berber nomads are traveling across the country of Morocco, through the Sahara.

up into the mountains. Other nomads live mainly in the flat desert areas. During the dry season, they set up tents near oases. When the rainy season comes, they move their goats and camels to better pastures.

Building Good Health

The climate people live in can affect their health. Throughout Africa there are regions that present health risks to livestock and humans. In rain forest regions, the moist environment is home to many disease-carrying insects. Even in the drier grasslands, disease and illness take their toll.

Nearly one fifth of Africa is home to the tsetse (TSET see) fly, a pest that makes raising cattle almost impossible. The bite of the fly kills cattle and brings a disease called sleeping sickness to humans. African researchers, together with cattle herders, have worked to find ways to control the spread of the tsetse fly. Cattle herders in Kenya are setting traps for flies. Herders in the country of Uganda use netting sewn into a tent that contains poison to catch flies.

READ ACTIVELY

Connect Do you know of any diseases that are spread by insects in the United States? If so, how do people keep the disease from spreading?

SECTION 2 REVIEW

1. **Define** (a) irrigate, (b) oasis, (c) savanna, (d) nomad.

2. **Identify** (a) Sahel, (b) Namib Desert, (c) Kalahari Desert.

3. What three factors affect the climate of Africa?

4. What most affects farming in Africa, rainfall or temperature? Explain.

Critical Thinking

5. **Recognizing Cause and Effect** If Mount Kilimanjaro were located in Canada instead of Kenya, would the climate at its peak be much different? Why or why not?

Activity

6. **Writing to Learn** Now that you know more about the climate and vegetation in Africa, make your new packing list for a two-week trip to Africa. Explain why you are bringing each item. (Hint: you may want to decide exactly which regions of Africa you will be visiting before you make the list.)

Natural Resources

BEFORE YOU READ

Reach Into Your Background

Have you ever heard the saying, "Don't put all your eggs in one basket?" What do you think this saying means?

Questions to Explore

1. What are Africa's major natural resources?

2. How are Africans developing these resources?

Key Terms

subsistence farming
cash crop
economy
diversify

"**T**ete Quarshie: I have a humble request to make of you, my noble friend. I hope you will not turn deaf ears to my cries. Here, in this load, I bear the seeds of a wonderful tree which, if cultivated in this land, will bless its sons everlastingly with wealth, and people far and near with health. These are the seeds of the cacao tree which I have brought with me from across the sea. . . . Would you, therefore, be kind enough to grant me a mere acre of land in this neighborhood to try my luck, and yours, and that of this country as a whole?"

▼ To make milk chocolate from cacao beans, shown below, chocolate makers grind the beans, and then mix them with lots of milk and sugar.

These words come from a short play, *Cocoa Comes to Mampong.* The play tells the story of cocoa in the West African country of Ghana. Cacao trees, from which cocoa and chocolate are made, used to grow only in Central and South America. As people in the Americas, Europe, and Africa began to trade with one another, they found that cacao trees could be grown in West Africa. In the play, the people granted the land to Tete Quarshie, who raised the first successful crop of cacao in Ghana.

LINKS ACROSS THE WORLD

Farming Equipment
Corn and wheat farmers in the United States often use heavy machines to work the land. Most African farmers could not use such machines. They would destroy the thin layer of topsoil on most African farms.

Agricultural Resources

Some Africans are farmers living in areas with fertile soil and much rain. But most Africans have land that is hard or impossible to farm because of poor soil or too little rain.

Farming to Live The map on the next page shows how much of Africa's land is used for **subsistence farming.** Subsistence farmers raise crops to support their families. They sell or trade a few crops for other items they need. In northern African countries such as Morocco, farmers raise barley and wheat. They also irrigate fields to grow fruits and vegetables. Farms at Saharan oases in Egypt produce dates and small crops of barley and wheat.

In countries that contain dry tropical savanna, such as Burkina Faso (bur KEE nuh FAH soh) and Niger, subsistence farmers grow grains. In regions with more rainfall, farmers also grow vegetables, fruits, and

Families Farming for a Living

Most subsistence farmers in Africa are women. Often, however, the whole family helps out. A family from Chad plows land in preparation for planting (below left). Families usually harvest crops by hand in Ethiopia (below right) and Ghana (right). **Critical Thinking** How do you think farming to provide food for your family is different from farming cash crops?

Africa: How People Make a Living

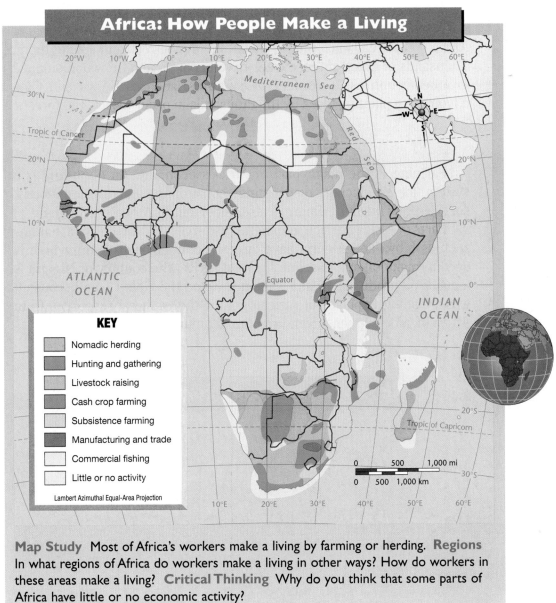

KEY

- Nomadic herding
- Hunting and gathering
- Livestock raising
- Cash crop farming
- Subsistence farming
- Manufacturing and trade
- Commercial fishing
- Little or no activity

Lambert Azimuthal Equal-Area Projection

Map Study Most of Africa's workers make a living by farming or herding. **Regions** In what regions of Africa do workers make a living in other ways? How do workers in these areas make a living? **Critical Thinking** Why do you think that some parts of Africa have little or no economic activity?

roots such as yams and cassava. Tapioca, which is used in the United States to make pudding, is made from cassava. In West Africa, corn and rice are important crops. People in many of Africa's cultures fish or raise goats or poultry.

Crops for Sale In all regions of Africa, farmers raise crops to sell. These are called **cash crops.** Farmers in Côte d'Ivoire (koht deev WAR), Ghana, and Cameroon grow cash crops of coffee and cacao. Farmers in Kenya, Tanzania, Malawi, Zimbabwe, and Mozambique grow tea as a cash crop.

In recent years, more and more farmers have planted cash crops. As more land is used for cash crops, less land is planted with crops to feed families. In some regions, this practice has led to food shortages when cash crops have failed.

Ask Questions What else would you like to know about farming in Africa?

Harvesting Trees Hardwood trees grow in all four regions of Africa. People can earn money by cutting down trees and selling them. Thousands of acres of these trees have been cut and the wood shipped to other countries. A number of countries, such as Kenya and Côte d'Ivoire, are planting trees by the thousands in order to save the forests.

Mineral Resources

Farming is the major part of Africa's economy. An economy is a system for producing, distributing, consuming, and owning goods, services, and wealth. Mining is also important to Africa's economy.

Parts of Africa are rich in mineral resources. In North Africa, nations such as Libya and Algeria have large amounts of petroleum, which is used to make oil and gasoline. In West Africa, the country of Nigeria is a major oil producer. Ghana was once called the Gold Coast because it was a leading exporter of African gold. Other mineral resources from Africa include copper, silver, uranium, titanium, and diamonds.

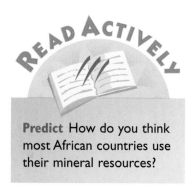

READ ACTIVELY

Predict How do you think most African countries use their mineral resources?

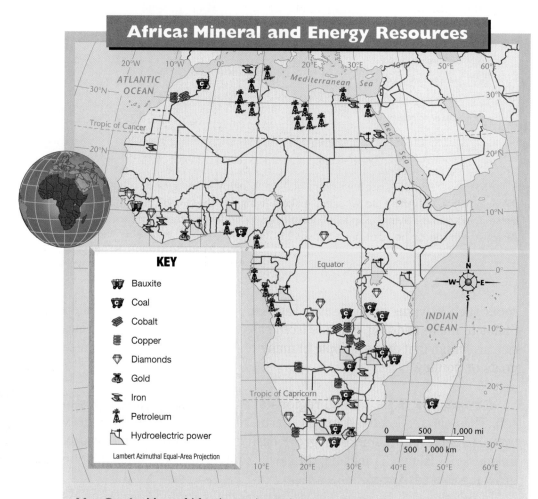

Africa: Mineral and Energy Resources

KEY
- Bauxite
- Coal
- Cobalt
- Copper
- Diamonds
- Gold
- Iron
- Petroleum
- Hydroelectric power

Lambert Azimuthal Equal-Area Projection

Map Study Most of Africa's people work in agriculture, yet most of Africa's exports are produced by miners. **Regions** Southern Africa is famous for its diamond industry. What other regions of Africa produce diamonds? **Interaction** Which resource shown on this map can be used without being used up?

Balancing Crops, Minerals, and Industry

Most of Africa's workers are farmers. When an economy of a nation is dependent on one kind of industry, such as farming, it is called a specialized economy. In Africa, specializing in just farming makes the economy sensitive to rainfall and to the price of crops. For that reason, African countries are now trying to diversify their economies. To **diversify** means to add variety. These countries are working to produce a variety of crops, raw materials, and manufactured goods. A country with a diverse economy will not be hurt as much if a major cash crop fails or if world prices for one of its major mineral exports suddenly drops.

Mining requires many workers and costly equipment. Throughout much of Africa, foreign companies mine African resources and take the profits. This system does little to help African economies. In addition, Africa has few factories to make products from its own raw materials. Therefore, many African countries want to diversify their economies to include manufacturing.

▼ All over Africa, people are moving to cities to apply for jobs in factories like this one. These men work on the assembly line at the Livingstone Car Plant in the country of Zambia.

SECTION 3 REVIEW

1. **Define** (a) subsistence farming, (b) cash crop, (c) economy, (d) diversify.

2. Why are African governments working to diversify their economies?

3. Compare subsistence farming with farming to raise cash crops. How are they similar? How are they different?

Critical Thinking

4. **Identifying Central Issues** What are some important natural resources in Africa?

Activity

5. **Writing to Learn** List some of Africa's natural resources that you and your family use. Then, write a paragraph that explains which you would miss most if you did not have it—and why.

Interpreting Diagrams

Africa is a giant. More than three times bigger than the United States, it covers close to 11,700,000 square miles (more than 30,000,000 sq km). That is about one fifth of all of the land in the world. If you drove across Africa at its widest point going 65 miles (105 km) per hour, without stopping for gas or sleep, it would take you about 72 hours. Traveling north-to-south, the trip would take about 77 hours.

A quick look at a world map will impress upon you Africa's great length and width. But the map will not show you its enormous elevations, or height.

One of the most effective ways to see Africa's elevations is to study a cross-sectional diagram of this gigantic land.

Get Ready

You already know that a diagram is a figure drawn to explain something. A *cross section* is basically a slice of something viewed from the side. For example, if you were to cut an apple in half, and look at the exposed cut, you would be looking at a cross section of the apple. If you drew a picture of what you saw, you would have a cross-sectional diagram of that apple.

You can get a good idea of a cross-sectional diagram by making one of your own—and having some fun as you do it. You'll need:

- modeling clay
- a butter knife
- pen and paper

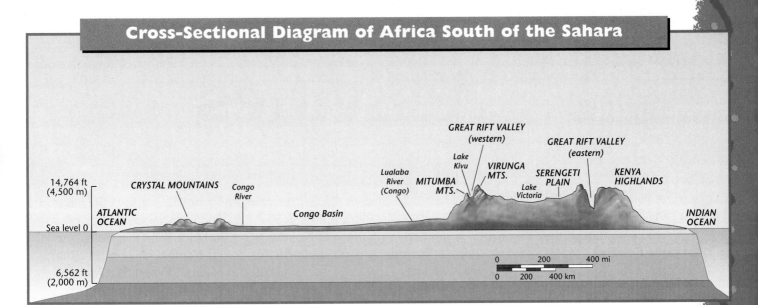

Cross-Sectional Diagram of Africa South of the Sahara

14,764 ft (4,500 m)

CRYSTAL MOUNTAINS

Congo River

GREAT RIFT VALLEY (western)

Lake Kivu

VIRUNGA MTS.

GREAT RIFT VALLEY (eastern)

SERENGETI PLAIN

KENYA HIGHLANDS

Lualaba River (Congo)

MITUMBA MTS.

Lake Victoria

ATLANTIC OCEAN

Sea level 0

Congo Basin

INDIAN OCEAN

6,562 ft (2,000 m)

0   200   400 mi
0   200   400 km

Try It Out

A. Create a continent. Take a fist-sized ball of modeling clay and shape it into an imaginary continent. First, flatten it out. Then mold the continent into any shape you want. Mold mountain ranges, valleys, plateaus, and any other landforms you wish.

B. Cut the cross section. When you've finished, put your "clay continent" flat on a table. Use the butter knife to cut it in half at its widest point.

C. Look at your result. Pick up one-half of your continent and look at the cut edge. You are looking at a cross section of your imaginary continent.

D. Sketch what you see. By sketching a side view of your model, you have made a cross-sectional diagram of your imaginary continent. How does the diagram reflect the vertical shape of the continent? Write the answer on the back of your cross-sectional diagram.

Apply the Skill

The illustration above is a cross-sectional diagram of Africa south of the Sahara. Use it to complete the following steps.

1 Understand the diagram. Just as you cut your clay continent at a certain place, the cross-sectional diagram of Africa shows the continent "cut" at a certain place. Does this cross section show Africa from east to west or from north to south? How is elevation indicated on the diagram? What geographic features are labeled on the diagram?

2 Learn from the diagram. What is the lowest point on the diagram? What is the highest point? How large a range in elevation is this? How far below the surrounding landscape does the Great Rift Valley drop?

Review and Activities

Reviewing Main Ideas

1. Why are some parts of Africa cold even though they are near the Equator?

2. List four major physical features of Africa. Choose one and describe what it is like.

3. Explain why there is little or no farming in much of North Africa and parts of Southern Africa.

4. How is subsistence farming in Africa different from farming to raise cash crops?

5. (a) List three cash crops raised in Africa. Where are they grown? (b) Name one mineral resource of Africa. Where is it found?

6. Explain why many African nations are trying to diversify their economies.

Reviewing Key Terms

Use each key term below in a sentence that shows the meaning of the term.

1. plateau
2. elevation
3. escarpment
4. rift
5. cataract
6. silt
7. fertile
8. tributary
9. irrigate
10. oasis
11. savanna
12. nomad
13. subsistence farming
14. cash crop
15. economy
16. diversify

Critical Thinking

1. **Identifying Central Issues** Explain the meaning of this statement. Give an example to support it. "People in Africa tend to live in grassland regions."

2. **Recognizing Cause and Effect** How did the yearly flooding of the Nile affect farmers in the Nile Valley? How did the building of the Aswan Dam affect the farmers?

Graphic Organizer

Copy the chart onto a sheet of paper. Then fill in the empty boxes to complete the chart.

	Amount of Rainfall	Temperature	Crops Grown
Desert	Little or none	Hot	Dates, barley, wheat in or near oases
Tropical Savanna			
Uplands and Mountain Regions			

Map Activity

Africa
For each place listed, write the letter from the map that shows its location.

1. Nile River
2. Congo River
3. Sahara
4. Namib Desert
5. Zambezi River
6. Kalahari Desert
7. Niger River
8. Great Rift Valley

Place Location

Writing Activity

Writing a Short Report
Describe some problems Africans face that are caused by Africa's landforms or climate. Give some examples of how Africans are solving these problems.

Take It to the NET

Activity Learn more about Africa's land and take a fun online quiz to test your knowledge. For help in completing this activity, visit www.phschool.com.

Chapter 1 Self-Test To review what you have learned, take the Chapter 1 Self-Test and get instant feedback on your answers. Go to www.phschool.com to take the test.

Skills Review

Turn to the Skills Activity.

Review the steps for interpreting a diagram. Then complete the following: (a) In your own words, describe what a cross-sectional diagram is. (b) What information can you find on a cross-sectional diagram?

How Am I Doing?

Answer these questions to check your progress.

1. Can I describe the location of Africa?
2. Do I understand how climate influences farming activity in Africa?
3. Can I identify some mineral resources of Africa?
4. Can I name some large landforms in Africa?
5. What information from this chapter can I include in my journal?

AFRICA

Shaped by Its History

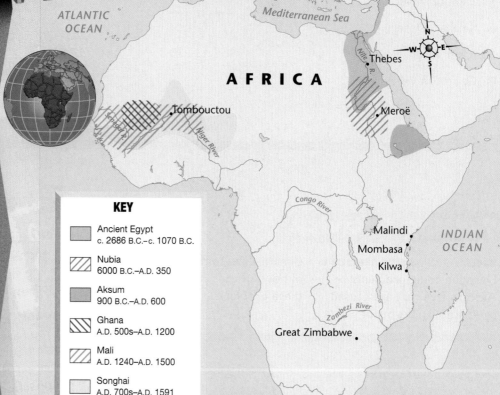

AFRICA

ATLANTIC OCEAN

Mediterranean Sea

Thebes

Meroë

Tombouctou

Senegal R.

Niger River

Congo River

Malindi

Mombasa

Kilwa

INDIAN OCEAN

Zambezi River

Great Zimbabwe

KEY

Ancient Egypt
c. 2686 B.C.–c. 1070 B.C.

Nubia
6000 B.C.–A.D. 350

Aksum
900 B.C.–A.D. 600

Ghana
A.D. 500s–A.D. 1200

Mali
A.D. 1240–A.D. 1500

Songhai
A.D. 700s–A.D. 1591

Lambert Azimuthal Equal-Area Projection

0   500   1,000 mi
0   500   1,000 km

MAP ACTIVITIES

This map shows some of Africa's great empires, kingdoms, and cities. Note that they did not all exist at the same time. Start exploring the history of Africa by doing the following activities.

Study the map
Compare this map with the political map of Africa in the Activity Atlas. Which countries took their names from early empires and kingdoms?

Consider locations
Notice that most of these empires and cities are close to rivers or oceans. How do you think the locations of empires and cities affected their development?

Africa's First People

BEFORE YOU READ

Reach Into Your Background

What are some of the things you remember from your past? Do you remember your very first day of school? What

is the earliest birthday you can remember? All those things are part of your personal history.

Questions to Explore

1. What techniques did early Africans use to get food?
2. How did important ideas and discoveries spread throughout Africa?
3. What civilizations arose along the Nile River?

Key Terms

hunter-gatherer
domesticate
surplus
civilization
migrate
ethnic group

Key People and Places

Louis Leakey
Egypt
Nubia

Today the dry sands of the Sahara cover most of North Africa. But until about 4,000 years ago, this large area held enough water to support many people and animals. Scientists think that Africa's first farmers lived there. Paintings on cliffs and cave walls tell their story.

But the history of people in Africa is even older. Several million years earlier, the continent's first people lived in East Africa. We know this because of the stones and bones they left behind. These East Africans were the very first people to live on the Earth.

Hunter-Gatherers

The earliest humans probably survived by gathering wild fruits, nuts, and roots. These hunter-gatherers also hunted animals for meat and clothing. They made tools out of wood, animal bones, and then stone. The first use of stone tools marks the beginning of a period scientists call the Stone Age.

These stone tools worked very well. The scientist Louis Leakey found some of the first evidence of early people in East Africa. He also taught himself to make and use their tools. Using a two-inch, 25,000-year-old stone knife, Leakey could skin and cut up a gazelle in just 20 minutes.

▼ This painting was found in Algeria. The horns on this woman's helmet show that the Sahara may once have supported animal life.

When hunter-gatherers settled down in one area and began farming, they faced longer, harder work days. Farmers spent many hours tilling the soil, planting seeds by hand, tending fields, harvesting crops, and caring for domesticated animals. They used only tools such as these, which they could make by hand. Farmers used axes (left) to clear the land. After butchering a cow, sheep, or goat, farmers used scrapers (top) to clean the hide, and cleavers (bottom) to cut the meat.
Critical Thinking Since farming is harder work than hunting and gathering, why would a hunter-gatherer want to become a farmer?

The Thirst Zone Africa's first farmers probably lived in Algeria, in North Africa. Thousands of years ago, more rain fell in this region. But today, much of North Africa is known as the "Thirst Zone." People need to drink about 2.5 quarts (2.4 l) of water per day. People also use water for washing and farming. All in all, each person needs at least 21 quarts (20 l) of water per day. In the Thirst Zone, only about five quarts (5 l) of water per person is available.

Farming and Herding

Between 10,000 and 6,000 years ago, hunter-gatherers began to farm and to herd animals. The first farmers probably planted wild grains such as wheat, barley, sorghum, and millet. At first, gatherers just protected the areas where these grains grew best. Then, they began to save some seed to plant for the next year's crop.

Later, people began to **domesticate** plants, or adapt them for their own use. They threw away seeds from weaker plants and saved seeds from stronger ones. People domesticated animals by breeding certain animals together.

Domesticating plants and animals meant people could plant their own crops. They did not have to travel to places where grains were already growing. As a result, they could settle in one place. Most people settled where the land was fertile, or productive. Some communities produced a food **surplus**, or more than they needed. Surpluses allowed some people in the community to do work other than farming.

Civilizations on the Nile

Over hundreds of thousands of years, some Stone Age groups became civilizations. A **civilization** is a society with cities, a government, and social classes. Social classes form when people do a variety of jobs. As a result, some people are rich, some are poor, and others are middle class. Civilizations also have architecture, writing, and art. One civilization arose on the Nile River about 5,000 years ago.

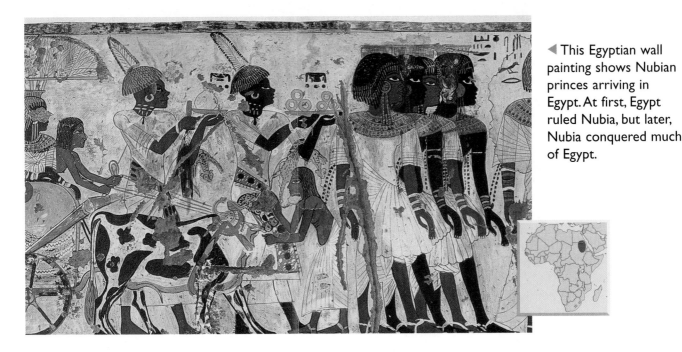

◄ This Egyptian wall painting shows Nubian princes arriving in Egypt. At first, Egypt ruled Nubia, but later, Nubia conquered much of Egypt.

Egypt   Each summer, the Nile River flooded its banks. It left a layer of fertile silt that was ideal for farming. People began farming along the banks of the Nile by around 4000 B.C. They settled in scattered villages. Over the centuries, these villages grew into the civilization of ancient Egypt.

Ancient Egypt was ruled by kings and queens called pharaohs (FAY rohz). The people believed the pharaohs to be gods as well as kings. When pharaohs died, they were buried in pyramids. People painted murals and picture-writings called hieroglyphics (hy ur oh GLIF iks) on the walls in the pyramids.

Egyptian civilization included more than just the pyramids. The Egyptians were advanced in paper-making, architecture, medicine, and mathematics.

Nubia   Starting in about 6000 B.C., several civilizations arose south of Egypt. This area was called Nubia. The final and greatest Nubian kingdom arose in the city of Meroë (MER oh ee) during the 500s B.C. It thrived until about the middle of the A.D. 300s. Meroë was probably the first place in Africa where iron was made.

The Bantu Migrations

By about 500 B.C., West Africans had learned to heat and shape iron. They used it to form parts of tools such as arrowheads, ax heads, and hoe blades. The strong iron tools made farming easier and created food surpluses. As a result, West Africa's population increased.

Around 2,000 years ago, a group of people who spoke Bantu (BAN too) languages began to **migrate,** or move, out of West Africa, perhaps looking for new land to farm. Over hundreds of years, these

READ ACTIVELY

Visualize What does a pyramid look like?

Routes of the Bantu Migrations

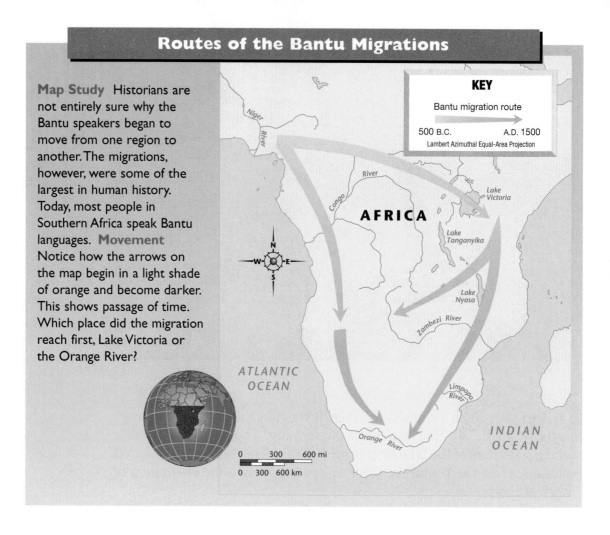

Map Study Historians are not entirely sure why the Bantu speakers began to move from one region to another. The migrations, however, were some of the largest in human history. Today, most people in Southern Africa speak Bantu languages. **Movement** Notice how the arrows on the map begin in a light shade of orange and become darker. This shows passage of time. Which place did the migration reach first, Lake Victoria or the Orange River?

KEY

Bantu migration route

500 B.C. → A.D. 1500

Lambert Azimuthal Equal-Area Projection

0   300   600 mi
0   300   600 km

Bantu-speakers settled in Central and Southern Africa. They introduced farming, herding, and iron tools to these regions. Today, people in this part of Africa belong to hundreds of **ethnic groups,** or groups that share languages, religions, family ties, and customs. But almost all of these ethnic groups speak Bantu languages.

SECTION 1 REVIEW

1. **Define** (a) hunter-gatherer, (b) domesticate, (c) surplus, (d) civilization, (e) migrate, (f) ethnic group.

2. **Identify** (a) Louis Leakey, (b) Egypt, (c) Nubia.

3. How did iron tools, farming, and herding spread to Southern Africa?

4. Name some achievements of ancient Egyptian and Nubian civilizations.

Critical Thinking

5. **Drawing Conclusions** How did early Africans adapt to their environment?

Activity

6. **Writing to Learn** Make a poster that illustrates, step-by-step, an important idea from this section. For example, you might show how scientists learn about early people or how ideas spread from one part of Africa to another.

Kingdoms and Empires

BEFORE YOU READ

Reach Into Your Background

What things do you own or have at home that were made in other countries? What things were made in the United States? Make a short list and share it with a classmate.

Questions to Explore

1. How did trade enrich Africa's kingdoms and city-states?

2. How did the religion of Islam spread to different parts of Africa?

Key Terms

Quran
pilgrimage
Swahili
city-state

Key People and Places

Mansa Musa
Aksum
Ghana
Mali
Songhai
Tombouctou
Kilwa
Zimbabwe

In the year A.D. 1, a Greek writer made a list of things you could buy in Adulis, East Africa. Adulis was the most important city in Aksum, a bustling trade center along the Red Sea. There, you could buy:

> "Cloth made in Egypt . . . many articles of flint glass . . . and brass, which is used for ornament and in cut pieces instead of coin; sheets of soft copper, used for cooking utensils and cut up for bracelets and anklets for the women; iron, which is made into spears used against the elephants and other wild beasts, and in their wars."

▼ These beads are from Zimbabwe, but thanks to the traders of Aksum, they could have journeyed all the way to Europe or India.

Aksum

Aksum was located in East Africa. If it still existed today, it would be in the countries of Ethiopia and Eritrea. Around 1000 B.C., African and Arab traders began settling along the west coast of the Red Sea. They were the ancestors of the people of Aksum. Over time, Aksum came to control trade in

Ask Questions What questions do you have about trade in ancient Africa?

the Red Sea. Aksum came to power after the Nubian kingdom of Meroë fell. By then, Aksum controlled a trade network that stretched from the Mediterranean Sea to India.

Ideas, as well as goods, traveled along trade routes. The Christian religion traveled to Aksum along these routes. In the mid-300s, many people in Aksum became Christian. Aksum became a center of the early Ethiopian Christian Church. But Aksum began to decline in the 600s. Then Arabs took control of much of the region's trade.

West African Kingdoms and Trade Routes

▶ **Map Study** Three kingdoms —Ghana, Mali, and Songhai— ruled West Africa for hundreds of years. Their rule was based on control of trade with North Africa. **Place** What West African kingdom controlled the largest area?

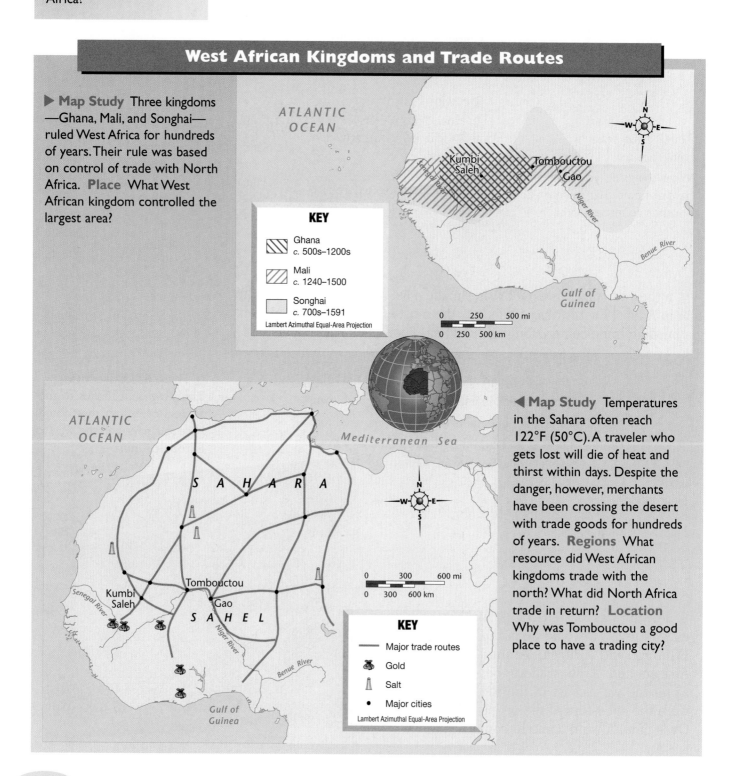

KEY

Ghana
c. 500s–1200s

Mali
c. 1240–1500

Songhai
c. 700s–1591

Lambert Azimuthal Equal-Area Projection

0   250   500 mi

0   250   500 km

KEY

— Major trade routes

🛍 Gold

⛊ Salt

• Major cities

Lambert Azimuthal Equal-Area Projection

◀ **Map Study** Temperatures in the Sahara often reach 122°F (50°C). A traveler who gets lost will die of heat and thirst within days. Despite the danger, however, merchants have been crossing the desert with trade goods for hundreds of years. **Regions** What resource did West African kingdoms trade with the north? What did North Africa trade in return? **Location** Why was Tombouctou a good place to have a trading city?

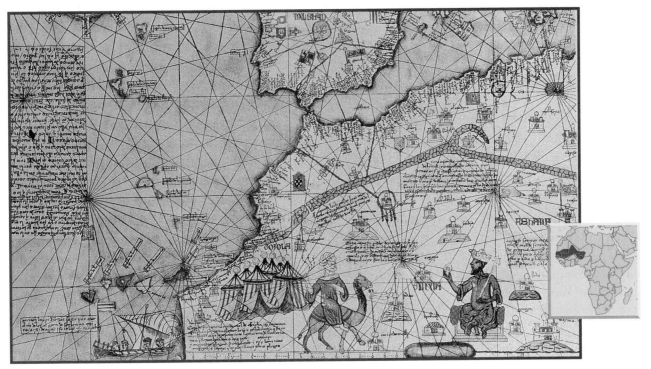

▲ Impressed with Mansa Musa's gold, Europeans included a picture of him on their maps of Africa. He appears in the lower right-hand corner of this map.

West African Kingdoms

As Aksum declined, great kingdoms arose on the other side of the continent, in West Africa. The power of these kingdoms was based on the trade of salt and gold. People need salt to survive, especially in hot areas like West Africa. The people of West Africa had no local sources of salt. However, they had plenty of gold. For the people of North Africa, the opposite was true. They had salt, but no gold.

A brisk trade between North Africa and West Africa quickly grew. Control of this trade brought power and riches to three West African kingdoms—Ghana (GAH nuh), Mali (MAH lee), and Songhai (SAWNG hy).

Ghana   Look at the map on the previous page. Note that the kingdom of Ghana was located between the Senegal and Niger rivers. From this location Ghana controlled trade across West Africa. Ghana's kings grew rich from the taxes they charged on the salt, gold, and other goods that flowed through their land. The flow of gold was so great that Arab writers called Ghana "land of gold." But in time, Ghana lost control of the trade routes. It gave way to a new power, the kingdom of Mali.

Mali and the Spread of Islam   The kingdom of Mali arose in the mid-1200s in the Upper Niger Valley. The word Mali means "where the king lives." Mali's powerful kings controlled both the gold mines of the south and the salt supplies of the north. In Mali, the king was called Mansa, which means "emperor."

Mali's most famous king, Mansa Musa, gained the throne about 1312. His 25-year reign brought peace and order to the kingdom. An Arab visitor to Mali found "safety throughout the land. The traveler here has no more reason to fear thieves than the man who stays at home."

READ ACTIVELY

Visualize Visualize the court of the king of Ghana. How would you know you were in the presence of wealth and power?

The Spread of Islam From Arabia, Islam began to spread west through Southwest Asia and North Africa in the 600s. But Islam also spread east—to central Asia, India, Pakistan, Bangladesh, and Indonesia. The Muslim community in the country of Indonesia is one of the largest in the world.

Mansa Musa based his laws on the **Quran** (koo RAHN), the holy book of the religion of Islam. Over the centuries, Muslim traders had spread their religion into many parts of Africa. Muslims are followers of Islam. Mansa Musa and many of his subjects were Muslims.

In 1324, Mansa Musa made a **pilgrimage**—a religious journey—to the Arabian city of Mecca. Muslims consider Mecca a holy place. Muhammad, the prophet who first preached Islam, was born there. Mansa Musa brought 60,000 people with him on his pilgrimage. Eighty camels each carried 300 pounds (136 kg) of gold. Along the way, Mansa Musa gave people gifts of gold.

Mansa Musa's pilgrimage brought about new trading ties with other Muslim states. It also displayed Mali's wealth. Hearing the reports, Europe's rulers grew interested in African gold.

Songhai After Mansa Musa's death around 1332, Mali declined. Mali was finally destroyed by an empire called Songhai. In time, Songhai became West Africa's most powerful kingdom. Songhai's rulers controlled important trade routes and wealthy trading cities.

The wealthiest trading city, Tombouctou (tohn book TOO), also was a great Muslim learning center. People said of Tombouctou:

> "Salt comes from the north, gold from the south, and silver from the city of white men. But the word of God and the treasures of wisdom are only to be found in Tombouctou."

Invaders from North Africa defeated Songhai in 1591. But Songhai people still live near the Niger River, and Islam remains important in the region.

East African Trade Routes

KEY

→ Trade routes

Lambert Azimuthal Equal-Area Projection

To Mediterranean

Cairo

Mecca

To India

Mogadishu

Malindi

Mombasa

Kilwa

INDIAN OCEAN

To East Asia

Great Zimbabwe   Sofala

0   500   1,000 mi
0   500   1,000 km

Map Study Traders visiting East African city-states could buy gold from Africa, cotton from India, and porcelain from China. **Location** How were the East African city-states ideally located to become centers of trade?

East African City-States

As in West Africa, trade helped East African cities to develop. Around the time that Aksum declined, trading cities arose along East Africa's coast. Traders from these cities used seasonal winds to sail northeast to India and China. They carried animal skins, ivory, and gold and other metals. When the winds changed direction, the traders sailed with them. They brought many goods, including cotton, silk, and porcelain.

Trade affected the culture of coastal East Africa. Some of the traders who visited the area were Muslims. Many of them settled and introduced Islam to East Africa. In time, a new language developed in the area. Called **Swahili** (swah HEE lee), it

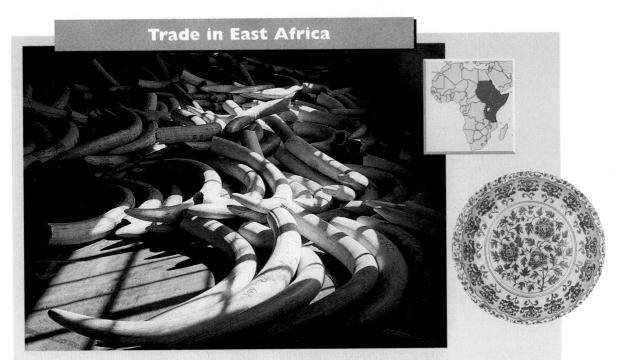

As early as A.D. 1100, traders in East Africa bought and sold goods from many parts of the world. Traders bought animal skins, gold, ivory, or elephant tusks (above left) from Africa, and sold them in India and China.

From India, traders brought back cloth, grain, oil, and sugar. From China, they brought back dishes and vases made of porcelain, a hard substance made by baking clay (above right).

was a Bantu language with some Arab words mixed in. Today, many East Africans still speak Swahili.

Some East African cities grew into powerful city-states. A **city-state** is a city that has its own government and often controls much of the surrounding land. Among the greatest of these city-states were Malindi (muh LIN dee), Mombasa (mahm BAH suh), and Kilwa (KIL wah). Look at the map on the previous page. How do you think the locations of these city-states helped them to become important trade centers?

Kilwa Ibn Batuta (IHB uhn ba TOO tah), a Muslim traveler from North Africa, visited Kilwa in 1331. He had seen great cities in China, India, and West Africa. But Batuta wrote that Kilwa was "one of the most beautiful and best-constructed towns in the world." In Kilwa, people lived in three- and four-story houses made of stone and sea coral.

Kilwa and other East African city-states grew rich from trade and taxes. Traders had to pay huge taxes on goods they brought into the city. "Any merchant who wished to enter the city paid for every five hundred pieces of cloth, no matter what the quality, one gold [piece] as entrance duty," reported one visitor. "After this, the king took two thirds of all the merchandise, leaving the trader one third."

In the early 1500s, Kilwa and the other city-states were conquered by the European country of Portugal. The Portuguese wanted to build their own trading empire.

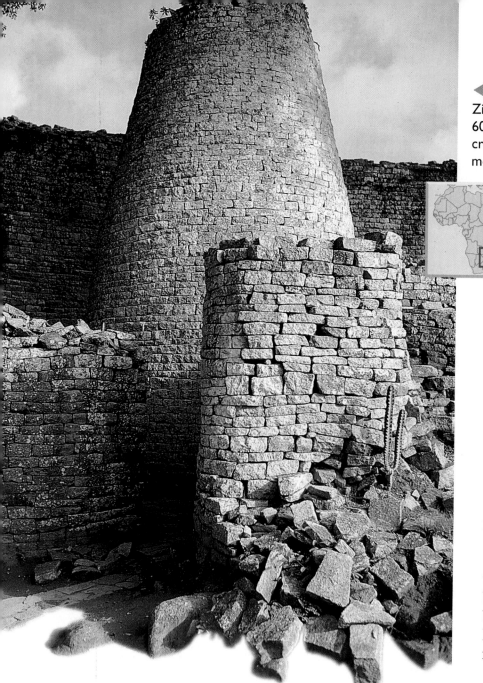

◄The walls of Great Zimbabwe are more than 600 years old. Builders created them without using mortar or cement.

Zimbabwe South and inland from the East African city-states lay another great trading civilization. Great Zimbabwe (zim BAH bway) was located near the bend of the Limpopo (lim POH poh) River in Southern Africa. Great Zimbabwe reached its peak about the year 1300. Today only ruins of it remain. But once, more than 200 gigantic stone buildings covered the area. (Great Zimbabwe means "stone dwelling.")

Upon seeing the ruins in the late 1800s, European explorers did not think that Africans had the skill to build them. They were wrong. The builders were the Shona, a group of Bantu speakers who had lived in the region since the 900s.

SECTION 2 REVIEW

1. **Define** (a) Quran, (b) pilgrimage, (c) Swahili, (d) city-state.

2. **Identify** (a) Mansa Musa, (b) Aksum, (c) Ghana, (d) Mali, (e) Songhai, (f) Tombouctou, (g) Kilwa, (h) Zimbabwe.

3. On what was the wealth and power of the city-states based?

4. How did Islam become a major religion in West and East Africa?

Critical Thinking

5. **Drawing Conclusions** How did Ghana, Mali, and Songhai become wealthy from gold and salt even though they did not mine either one?

Activity

6. **Writing to Learn** You are a traveler visiting one of the West African kingdoms or city-states. Write a short letter home about some of the things you see.

The Conquest of Africa

BEFORE YOU READ

Reach Into Your Background

What actions would you take to get something you really wanted? What would you do to hold on to something that was already yours?

Questions to Explore

1. Why did European contact with Africa increase?
2. What were the effects of European rule in Africa?

Key Terms
colonize

Key People and Places
Gorée
Cape of Good Hope
Olaudah Equiano

On the island of Gorée (gaw RAY), off the coast of the West African country of Senegal, stands a museum called the House of Slaves. It honors millions of Africans who were enslaved and shipped across the Atlantic Ocean. Many Africans passed through this building. Their last view of Africa was an opening called "The Door of No Return." Beyond it lay the ocean and the slave ships bound for the Americas.

Europeans on the Coast

The Atlantic slave trade began in the 1500s and continued through the late 1800s. But contact between Europeans and Africans began long before that. In North Africa, Europeans traded for gold from the empires of Ghana and Mali, and for salt from the Sahara. Why do you think Europeans' first contacts with Africans took place in North Africa?

After 1500, Europe's relationship with Africa changed. It had begun as trade between equals. But it turned into the enslavement and forced migration of millions of Africans. The African slave trade ended in the 1800s. Then Europeans wanted Africa's natural resources. By 1900, European countries had divided Africa among themselves.

▼ The Door of No Return in Senegal led to a pier, where slave ships were waiting to sail to the Americas.

LINKS
ACROSS THE WORLD

Europeans and the Americas Christopher Columbus sailed extensively along the coast of western Africa. He traveled several times to the Portuguese trading post in the Gold Coast. On these journeys, he sometimes found pieces of wood floating from the west. These signs helped to convince Columbus that there was land to the west. Such convictions increased his desire to take the journey westward.

In the 1400s, Portuguese explorers began exploring the coast of West Africa. They wanted to trade directly for West African gold and ivory, instead of dealing with North African merchants. They also wanted to trade with Asia.

Many inventions helped the Portuguese explore Africa's coast. The Portuguese used a lateen sail, a triangle-shaped sail designed in North Africa. The lateen sail allowed ships to sail against the wind as well as with it. And better instruments, such as the astrolabe (AS troh layb), helped sailors navigate at sea. With these improvements, Portuguese sailors became the first Europeans to travel south along Africa's coasts.

At first, both Africans and Europeans traded together as equals. Africans traded gold, cotton, ivory, skins, metal objects, and pepper. In return, Europeans traded copper, brass, and clothing. Europeans brought corn, cassava, and yams from the Americas. These plants became food crops in Africa. Some Africans also became Christians.

But soon this balance was upset. In 1498, three Portuguese ships rounded the tip of Southern Africa and sailed north along Africa's east coast. The wealth of the East African city-states amazed the Portuguese. More Portuguese ships followed—not to trade but to seize the riches of the city-states. Portugal controlled trade on East Africa's coast until well into the 1600s.

The Dutch, French, and English soon followed the Portuguese. They set up trading posts along Africa's coasts, where sailors could get supplies. The Dutch built a trading post on the Cape of Good Hope at Africa's southern tip. Soon, settlers arrived. They moved inland, building homes and farms.

▼ In 1482, the Portuguese built this fort, Elmina Castle, in Ghana to protect and supply its trade with West Africa.

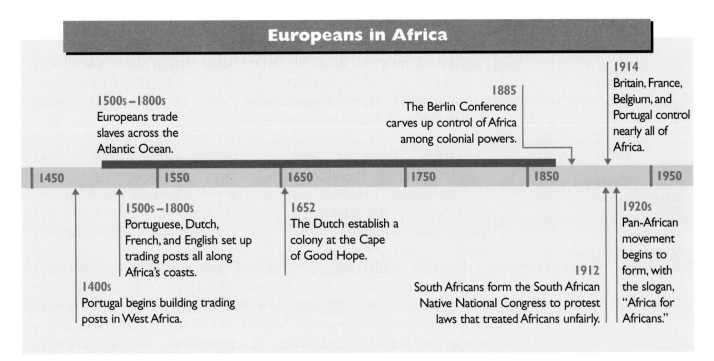

Europeans in Africa

1500s–1800s
Europeans trade slaves across the Atlantic Ocean.

1885
The Berlin Conference carves up control of Africa among colonial powers.

1914
Britain, France, Belgium, and Portugal control nearly all of Africa.

1450 | 1550 | 1650 | 1750 | 1850 | 1950

1500s–1800s
Portuguese, Dutch, French, and English set up trading posts all along Africa's coasts.

1652
The Dutch establish a colony at the Cape of Good Hope.

1920s
Pan-African movement begins to form, with the slogan, "Africa for Africans."

1400s
Portugal begins building trading posts in West Africa.

1912
South Africans form the South African Native National Congress to protest laws that treated Africans unfairly.

▲ Africans resisted European colonization, but, as this time line shows, Europe slowly took control of more and more of Africa. Why do you think it was possible for Europeans to colonize Africa?

As Europeans spread out, sometimes by force, their relations with Africans worsened. But the growing trade in enslaved Africans poisoned future contacts between Africans and Europeans the most.

The Atlantic Slave Trade

Before the 1500s, slavery was common in Africa. But slaves usually won their freedom after a few years. Some became important citizens among the people who had enslaved them. Slaves could even be bought out of slavery by their own people.

Then the European powers began to build colonies in North and South America. They practiced a new type of slavery there. The Europeans treated slaves like property, not like people. Freedom in the future was out of the question. The African slave trade did not end until the 1800s. By then, millions of Africans had been taken from their homelands, never to return.

The Demand for Slaves Spanish, Portuguese, and Dutch settlers in the Americas needed workers for their plantations and mines. At first they enslaved Native Americans. But many Native Americans became sick and died from diseases or brutal working conditions. Others ran away. To replace them, the Europeans started to import enslaved Africans.

The Europeans thought that Africans would make good slaves. Africa's climate was similar to that of the Americas. Africans were skilled farmers, miners, and metal workers. They also did not know the territory. It would be almost impossible for them to escape.

By the 1600s, Portuguese traders were trading goods for African slaves. Some African groups refused to join the trade. But other groups

Visualize Visualize the inside of a slave ship. What do you think it would have been like to cross the Atlantic in these conditions?

sold slaves captured during battles. In return, the Europeans gave the Africans cheap guns. By 1780, about 80,000 African slaves were being transported across the Atlantic each year. But even this did not satisfy the demand for slaves. Some African leaders began to kidnap people from neighboring areas to sell as slaves.

The Horror of Slavery   Captured Africans were branded with hot irons. In the slave ships, captives lay side by side on filthy shelves stacked from floor to ceiling. They got little food or water on the journey across the Atlantic. As many as 20 percent of the slaves died during each crossing. To make up for these losses, ships' captains packed in more people.

Olaudah Equiano (oh LOW duh ek wee AHN oh), described this horrible experience in a book he wrote about his life. In 1756, at about age 11, Equiano was captured and sold at a slave auction. He was sure he was going to die. He wrote, "when I looked around the ship and saw a large furnace of copper boiling and a multitude of black people of every description chained together . . . I no longer doubted of my fate."

Equiano proved luckier than most African slaves. In time, he was able to buy his freedom. For most slaves, freedom was little more than a distant dream.

The Cramped Journey Across the Atlantic

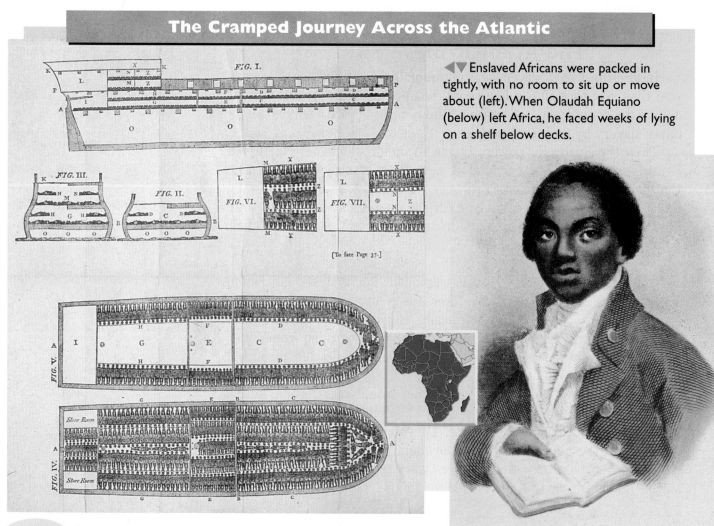

Enslaved Africans were packed in tightly, with no room to sit up or move about (left). When Olaudah Equiano (below) left Africa, he faced weeks of lying on a shelf below decks.

The Effects of Slavery on Africa Some Africans grew wealthy from the slave trade. The slave trade, however, was a disaster for West Africa. The region lost more than a large number of its population to slavery. It lost many of its youngest, healthiest, and most capable people. Robbed of their families and their skilled workers, many African societies were torn apart.

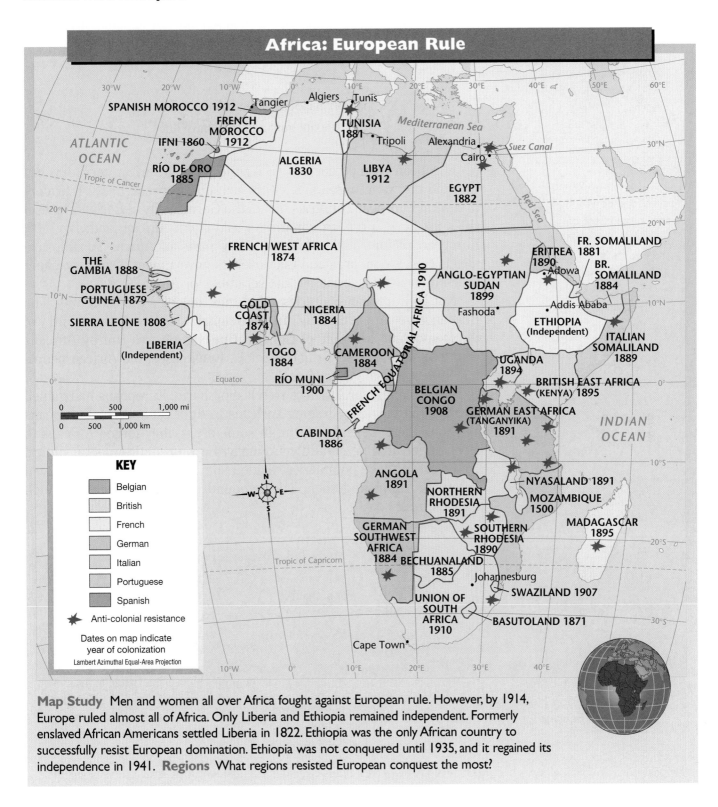

Africa: European Rule

KEY

- Belgian
- British
- French
- German
- Italian
- Portuguese
- Spanish
- ★ Anti-colonial resistance

Dates on map indicate year of colonization

Lambert Azimuthal Equal-Area Projection

Map Study Men and women all over Africa fought against European rule. However, by 1914, Europe ruled almost all of Africa. Only Liberia and Ethiopia remained independent. Formerly enslaved African Americans settled Liberia in 1822. Ethiopia was the only African country to successfully resist European domination. Ethiopia was not conquered until 1935, and it regained its independence in 1941. **Regions** What regions resisted European conquest the most?

Europeans Carve Up Africa

After the slave trade ended, Europeans then began to raid Africa's interior for resources. They wanted the resources to fuel the new factories that were springing up all across Europe. Europeans also saw Africa as a place to build empires.

Africans fiercely resisted European conquest. But their cheap guns proved no match for Europe's weapons. Europeans carried the Maxim gun, the first automatic machine gun. A British author wrote at the time:

> "Whatever happens we have got
> The Maxim-gun; and they have not."

Europeans competed with each other to gain African territory. But they did not want to go to war with each other over it. In 1884, leaders of several European countries met in the German city of Berlin. They set rules for how European countries could claim African land. By 1900, European nations had colonized many parts of Africa. To **colonize** means to settle an area and take over its government. One newspaper called this rush for territory "the scramble for Africa."

Not all European countries ruled their colonies the same way. The Belgian government directly ran the Belgian Congo (now the country of the Democratic Republic of Congo). But Nigeria was run by Africans who took orders from British officials. In all cases, the African people had little power in government.

The scramble for Africa caused lasting harm. Europeans had gained power in part by encouraging Africans to fight each other. Europeans also took the best land to farm. In some areas, they forced Africans to labor under terrible conditions. Finally, Europeans drew new political boundaries. These boundaries divided some ethnic groups and forced differing groups together. These boundaries were to cause much conflict in Africa.

Ask Questions What questions do you have about the effect of European colonization on the people of Africa?

SECTION 3 REVIEW

1. **Define** colonize.
2. **Identify** (a) Gorée, (b) Cape of Good Hope, (c) Olaudah Equiano.
3. How did relations between Africa and Europe change over time?
4. In what different ways did the Europeans govern their African colonies?

Critical Thinking
5. **Identifying Central Issues** How did the European conquest affect Africa?

Activity
6. **Writing to Learn** Write two brief editorials about the European conference in Berlin. Write one editorial from the point of view of an African. Write the other from the point of view of a European who attended the conference.

Independence and Its Challenges

BEFORE YOU READ

Reach Into Your Background

People have different ideas about what independence means. For some, it means having the freedom to make their own decisions. What does independence mean to you?

Questions to Explore

1. What techniques did African nations use to win independence from European powers?
2. What challenges did new African leaders face after independence?

Key Terms

nationalism
Pan-Africanism
boycott
democracy

Key People

Robert Mugabe
Léopold Sédar Senghor
Kwame Nkrumah

On April 18, 1980, the people of Rhodesia took to the streets. They had recently elected Robert Gabriel Mugabe (mu GAHB ee) as Prime Minister. It was the first free election in Rhodesia's history. People waited excitedly through the night. At midnight, the British flag came down for the last time. People cheered loudly. At that moment, the British colony of Rhodesia became the independent country of Zimbabwe.

The fight for independence had been hard and sometimes violent. Now, Prime Minister Mugabe asked all the people to work together. They would have to build a new nation. "The wrongs of the past must now stand forgiven and forgotten," said Mugabe. Zimbabwe was one of the last African countries to win independence. But the movement for freedom in Zimbabwe had begun many years before.

▼ Zimbabwe's flag went up for the first time when the country became independent of Great Britain.

The Growth of Nationalism

Many Africans dreamed of independence after Europe's scramble for Africa in the late 1800s. In 1897, Mankayi Sontanga (mun KY ee suhn TAHN guh) put this dream to music. His song, called "Bless, O Lord, Our Land of Africa," expressed the growing nationalism of Africans. **Nationalism** is a feeling of pride in one's homeland.

Education and Nationalism   Many African leaders worked to encourage pride in being African. The colonial powers had drawn political borders that brought together many ethnic groups. Some of these groups were old rivals. African leaders saw that to end colonial rule, they would have to build a spirit of togetherness.

Nationalism grew during the early 1900s. In 1912, Africans in South Africa formed a political party. Today this party is the African National Congress (ANC). Party members protested laws that limited the rights of black South Africans. Five years later, African lawyers in British West Africa formed the West African National Congress. This group also worked to gain rights for Africans, including the right to vote.

Pan-Africanism   In the 1920s, Africans formed a movement called **Pan-Africanism.** This movement stressed unity and cooperation among all Africans. Pan-African leaders tried to unify all Africans, whether they lived in Africa or not. Their slogan was "Africa for Africans." The movement won many supporters.

One of the greatest leaders of Pan-Africanism was Léopold Sédar Senghor (san GAWR) of Senegal. Senghor was a poet as well as a political leader. He encouraged Africans to look carefully at their traditions. They should be proud of their culture, he said. Senegal became independent in 1960, and Senghor became its first president.

LINKS ACROSS THE WORLD

The Right to Vote African Americans have also struggled to win the right to vote. By law, African American men received the right to vote in 1870. African American women received the right to vote at the same time as other American women, in 1920. But violence often prevented African Americans from exercising their right to vote. Change came about slowly as the result of a nonviolent social movement. Today, African Americans can exercise their right to vote in peace.

Pan-Africanism in the U.S.

W.E.B. Du Bois was one of the first leaders of the movement to gain equal rights for African Americans in the United States. Du Bois also was an early leader of the Pan-African movement. He worked with African leaders, such as Jomo Kenyatta and Kwame Nkrumah, to make plans for African countries to become independent.

These Ghanaians fought in the British army in 1942. Here, they are on their way to defend North Africa against the armies of Germany and Italy. Fifteen years later, they and other Ghanaians achieved independence for their own country. **Critical Thinking** During World War II, Allied armies fought to preserve democracy around the world. How do you think fighting in the war affected Africans' feelings about democracy and independence?

World War II

A major boost to African independence came unexpectedly in the 1930s and 1940s, out of the global conflict called World War II. A group called the Allies included Great Britain, France, and the United States. They fought the armies of Germany, Italy, and Japan, who were invading much of the world. German and Italian forces invaded North Africa.

Africa played a huge role in support of the Allies. The colonies supplied metals for guns and other equipment. Allied planes used their airfields to move supplies into Asia. African soldiers fought and died to help free Europe from conquest. About 80,000 soldiers from Tanganyika alone served in the British Army.

Africans came home victorious. Now, they wanted their own freedom. One soldier said, "We have been told what we fought for. That is 'freedom.' We want freedom, nothing but freedom."

Different Paths to Independence

The war not only inspired Africans to win their freedom. It also weakened colonial powers like Great Britain. Many people in Britain felt that they could no longer afford a colonial empire. The United States and the Soviet Union—Britain's allies during the war—began to speak out against colonialism.

READ ACTIVELY

Ask Questions What else would you like to know about how African nations became independent?

African Independence

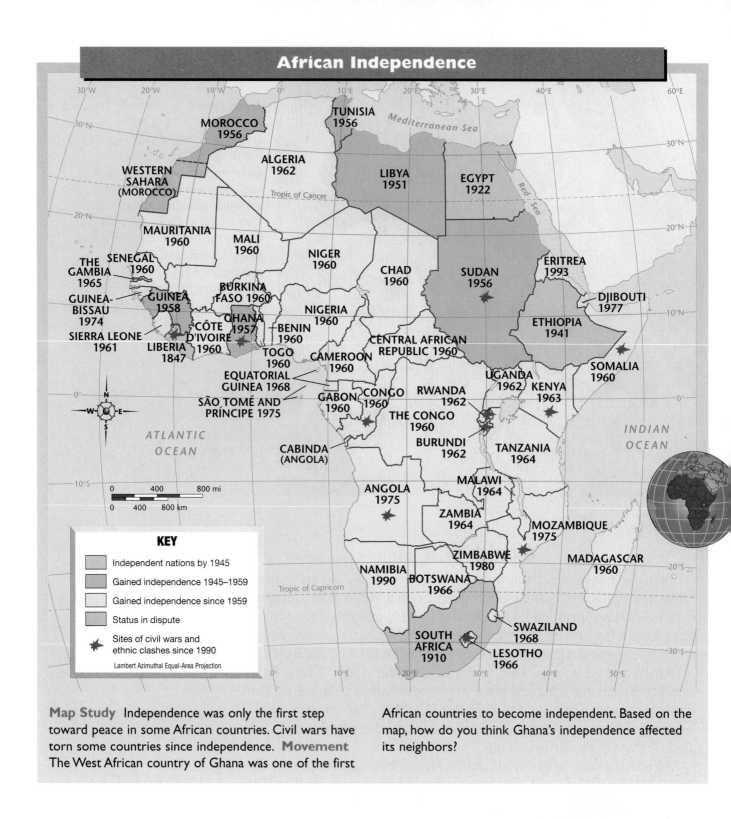

Map Study Independence was only the first step toward peace in some African countries. Civil wars have torn some countries since independence. **Movement** The West African country of Ghana was one of the first African countries to become independent. Based on the map, how do you think Ghana's independence affected its neighbors?

British leader Harold Macmillan realized that Britain would not be able to keep its African colonies. "The winds of change are blowing across Africa," he said. Soon, European countries began to give up their African colonies.

Some colonial powers let go willingly, while others fought to keep power. Ghana won its independence from Britain peacefully. But Algeria, a former French colony, had to fight for its freedom.

From Gold Coast to Ghana   In the British West African colony of the Gold Coast, Kwame Nkrumah organized protests against British rule in the early 1950s. These protests took the peaceful form of strikes and boycotts. In a **boycott,** people refuse to buy or use certain products or services. The British threw Nkrumah in jail for his actions. But the protests continued without him. In 1957, he achieved his goal: independence for the Gold Coast. The country took the new name of Ghana, after the great trading kingdom that lasted until the 1200s. It was a name that recalled Africa's earlier greatness. Released from prison, Nkrumah became Ghana's first president in 1960.

War in Algeria   The French people who had settled in Algeria thought of it as more than a colony. To them, it was part of France. Algerians disagreed. They were willing to fight for the right to govern themselves. A bloody war began in Algeria in 1954. The eight-year struggle cost the lives of 100,000 Algerians and 10,000 French. But by 1962, the Algerians had won.

The Challenges of Independence   Africa's new leaders had spent many years working for independence. But they had little experience actually governing a country. The colonial powers had rarely allowed Africans to share in government. And even after agreeing to independence, the colonial powers did little to prepare the new leaders. As a result, some new governments in Africa were not very stable.

In some African countries, military leaders took control of the government by force. Military governments are not always fair. The people often have few rights. Further, citizens may be jailed if they protest. But this form of government has held together some African countries that otherwise would have been torn apart by war.

Other African countries have a long history of democracy. In a **democracy,** citizens help to make governmental decisions. Some countries have made traditional ways a part of governing. For example, in Botswana, lively political debates take place in "freedom squares." These outdoor meetings are like the traditional *kgotla* (KUHT luh), in which people talk with their leaders.

▼ Children wave goodbye to the British governor shortly after Ghana became independent.

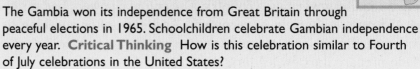

Gambians Celebrate Independence

The Gambia won its independence from Great Britain through peaceful elections in 1965. Schoolchildren celebrate Gambian independence every year. **Critical Thinking** How is this celebration similar to Fourth of July celebrations in the United States?

Connect The United States is a democratic country. How does democracy in the United States affect you?

Most African countries are less than 50 years old. In contrast, the stable, democratic country of the United States is over 200 years old. Many Africans feel that building stable countries will take time. One leader commented, "Let Africa be given the time to develop its own system of democracy."

SECTION 4 REVIEW

1. **Define** (a) nationalism, (b) Pan-Africanism, (c) boycott (d) democracy.

2. **Identify** (a) Robert Mugabe, (b) Léopold Sédar Senghor, (c) Kwame Nkrumah.

3. Compare Ghana's road to independence to that of Algeria.

4. In what ways did colonial rule cause problems for African countries after independence?

Critical Thinking

5. **Recognizing Cause and Effect** How did World War II boost the independence movement in Africa?

Activity

6. **Writing to Learn** Research one African country that won its independence after 1950. Write a headline and a short article for a newspaper that might have appeared on the day your country became independent. Compile all the articles from your class to create a bulletin board display about African independence.

Issues for Africa Today

BEFORE YOU READ

Reach Into Your Background
As you have grown, you have become more independent.

What challenges are you facing as you grow older? How have you met your challenges?

Questions to Explore
1. What challenges do African countries face today?
2. What actions may help Africans meet some of their challenges?

Key Terms
commercial farming
hybrid
literacy
life expectancy

Key Places
Niger
Senegal

In the past, nothing grew during the dry season in the Sahel. Farmers had to travel to cities to find work. Now, the West African country of Niger has a new irrigation program. This makes it possible for farmers to grow a second crop during the dry season. Farmer Adamou Sani (AH duh moo SAH nee) says that raising two crops a year means that he can stay on village land.

▼ Farmers in Niger use irrigation canals to bring water from the Niger River to their crops.

"Dry-season crops are such a normal practice now that everyone grows them. Before, each year after the harvest, I went to the city to look for work. But today, with the dry-season crops, I have work in the village. Truly it is a good thing."

Niger's irrigation program is one way Africans are improving their lives. Africans are also finding ways to meet economic, social, and environmental challenges.

Economic Issues

The colonial powers saw Africa as a source of raw materials and a market for their own manufactured goods. They did little to build factories in Africa. African countries still have little industry. Most economies are based on farming and mining.

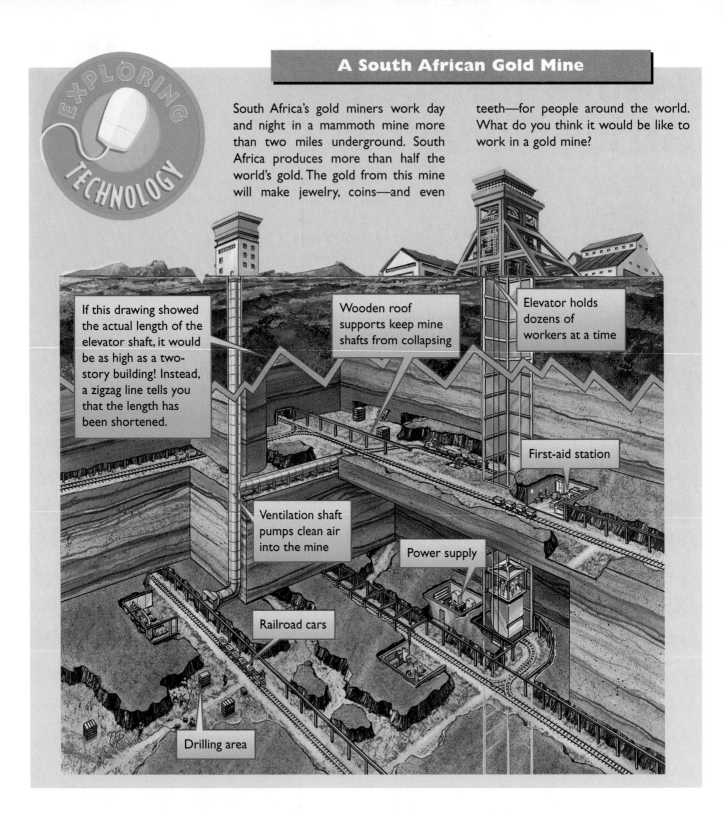

EXPLORING TECHNOLOGY

South Africa's gold miners work day and night in a mammoth mine more than two miles underground. South Africa produces more than half the world's gold. The gold from this mine will make jewelry, coins—and even teeth—for people around the world. What do you think it would be like to work in a gold mine?

If this drawing showed the actual length of the elevator shaft, it would be as high as a two-story building! Instead, a zigzag line tells you that the length has been shortened.

Wooden roof supports keep mine shafts from collapsing

Elevator holds dozens of workers at a time

First-aid station

Ventilation shaft pumps clean air into the mine

Power supply

Railroad cars

Drilling area

Farming and Mining Farming is the most important activity in Africa. About 75 percent of workers are farmers. And more than half of what Africa sells overseas are farm goods. Africans practice two kinds of farming—subsistence and commercial. With subsistence farming, farmers work small plots of land. They raise just as much food as their families need. **Commercial farming** is the large-scale production of cash crops such as coffee, cocoa, and bananas for sale.

Many African nations have rich mineral resources. They export minerals to other countries. Nigeria has oil and coal. Congo and Zambia have copper, while South Africa has gold. Look at the diagram on the previous page. How does South Africa produce its gold?

Economic Challenges About 75 percent of African countries have economies that are specialized—they depend on exporting one or two products. The Gambia depends on peanuts, while Zambia relies on the export of copper. As a result, African economies are sensitive to the rise and fall of world prices. A fall in prices hurts economies that depend on the sale of one crop or mineral.

African countries are now trying to depend less on one export. They are trying to diversify their economies. For example, Senegal became independent in 1960. At the time, it earned more than 80 percent of its money by exporting peanuts. Today, Senegal has other industries such as fishing, fish processing, and mining. Peanuts account for only 9 percent of the money Senegal makes from exports.

World Copper Prices

Year	Cents Per Pound (kg)
1990	123.16 (271.52)
1991	109.33 (241.03)
1992	107.42 (237.01)
1993	91.56 (208.86)
1994	111.05 (244.82)
1995	138.33 (304.97)
1996	109.04 (240.39)
1997	106.92 (235.72)
1998	78.64 (173.37)

Source: United States Geological Survey

Chart Study Congo and Zambia both rely on copper mining for most of their income. Copper is used to make coins, wire, tubes, and jewelry.
Critical Thinking Based on these prices, what challenges do you think might face a country that gets most of its income from selling copper?

African nations face another economic problem—how to feed a growing population. Many governments are trying to help farmers grow more. One method they use is to develop hybrid plants. A hybrid is made by combining different types of the same plant. In the early 1980s, farmers in Zimbabwe who grew hybrid corn doubled their harvests. Today, most of Zimbabwe's corn comes from hybrids.

Predict What problems do you think can arise when a nation depends on one crop or resource?

Social Issues

African nations also must provide social services to a growing population. In the areas of health care and education, many African nations are working to keep their traditions alive while adapting to the modern world.

Education African children must often add to their family's income by working on family farms or selling goods in the market. When girls and boys go to school, families sacrifice. But many Africans gladly make this sacrifice in order to improve their lives.

► How is this school in Zimbabwe similar to your school? How is it different?

In South Africa, parents often help to build new schools. Even so, the schools are often overcrowded. As a result, students take turns attending. The headmaster at one such school said that students "who couldn't cram into the desks knelt on the floor or stood on their toes so as not to miss a word the teacher was saying."

The number of people who can read and write varies from country to country. But in all countries, more people have learned to read since independence. When the Portuguese left Mozambique in 1975, only 10 percent of the people in Mozambique were literate. Literacy is the ability to read and write. Today about 40 percent of the people are literate. In Tanzania, progress has been even more dramatic. At the time of independence only 15 percent of Tanzania's people were literate. Today, about 68 percent of Tanzanians can read and write.

Health   Like literacy, life expectancy—how long an average person will live—differs from country to country. In Morocco, life expectancy is between 67 and 71 years. In Southern Africa, however, the average life expectancy is under 50 years. In the Southern African country of Botswana, it is only 40 years.

The main reason for low life expectancy in Africa is disease. Insects spread diseases such as malaria. Unclean drinking water and living conditions help spread other diseases. Viruses, or tiny germs, spread diseases like measles and AIDS. AIDS is caused by a virus, called HIV. This virus attacks healthy cells in people's bodies. People with AIDS get very sick, and often die.

Though AIDS exists around the world, it is the worst in Southern Africa. Many people who are poor cannot afford drugs that might help them. Many people have not had access to education, so they could not learn how to prevent the disease. In Southern Africa, millions of people have died from AIDS. Millions more are sick because of it. African governments are working with the World Health Organization and other groups. Together, they work to prevent and treat AIDS, and overcome other health problems.

ACROSS THE WORLD

Virtual Eritrea Eritrea is a country in East Africa along the Red Sea. It won independence from Ethiopia in 1993. Now, Eritreans are using Internet technology to help them meet the challenges of self-rule. They have formed Dehai, an on-line community. Dehai is an Internet newsgroup. About 500 Eritreans living in other countries use Dehai to discuss issues related to Eritrea's new constitution.

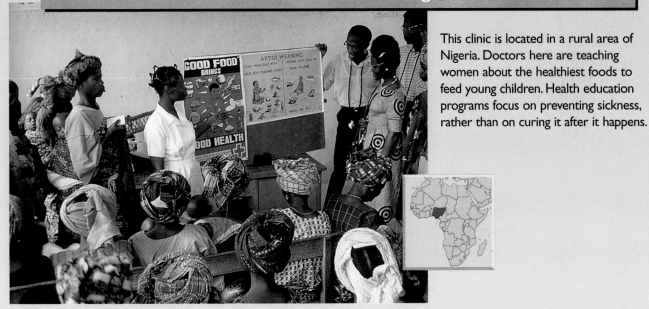

This clinic is located in a rural area of Nigeria. Doctors here are teaching women about the healthiest foods to feed young children. Health education programs focus on preventing sickness, rather than on curing it after it happens.

The Environment

Like the United States, Africa faces a number of environmental challenges. About two thirds of Africa is desert or dry land. And more and more of Africa is turning into desert. Forests are being cut down, which causes soil to wash away. This reduces the amount of land on which food can be grown. This, in turn, threatens many Africans with starvation.

But science can help feed Africans and save Africa's environment. Irrigation projects, hybrids, and vegetation that holds water in the ground have all increased crop harvests. To fight soil erosion, farmers in Nigeria now plant food crops such as yams in long rows. Between the rows they plant trees that hold the soil in place.

African nations still face many challenges. They are meeting them by using their resources, increasing education, and keeping traditions alive in a changing world.

READ ACTIVELY

Ask Questions What would you like to know about Africa's environment?

SECTION 5 REVIEW

1. **Define** (a) commercial farming, (b) hybrid, (c) literacy, (d) life expectancy.

2. **Identify** (a) Niger, (b) Senegal.

3. Why are African nations trying to diversify their economies?

4. List two challenges African countries face and describe the steps African countries are taking to meet these challenges.

Critical Thinking

5. **Drawing Conclusions** In what ways have Africans shown the high value they place on education?

Activity

6. **Writing to Learn** You are the economic adviser to the president of an African country. Write a brief report on some steps the president might take to improve the economy.

Recognizing Bias

When Latisha got to class, she looked at the chalkboard. Every day, Mr. Copeland began class by writing something on the board to discuss:

Life in West Africa is better than life in North Africa.

"Well, class? What do you think about that?" Mr. Copeland asked.

Latisha wondered how someone decided what made life better in one place than another. She raised her hand.

"That statement does not tell the whole story! Whose life are you talking about? And when?"

Mr. Copeland smiled. "Latisha, you've hit the nail on the head. The statement on the board does not tell the whole story—it may even be completely untrue. It shows you an example of *bias.*"

Get Ready

To be biased is to lean to a particular point of view. Sometimes, people who write about something only know one side of the story.

Other people leave out information on purpose to give their own viewpoint. Biased writing takes a side, even if at first it seems not to.

You need to be able to recognize bias in writing. It is the only way you can know whether you're getting a fair picture of a situation. When you read, you can look for certain clues that will point out a writer's bias.

Try It Out

To determine whether a writer is biased, do the following:

A. Look for opinions. Opinions are beliefs that cannot be proved. They are the opposite of facts, which can be proved. Biased writing often contains opinions disguised as facts. For example, the statement "Life in West Africa is better than life in North Africa" may sound like a fact, but it is an opinion.

B. Look for loaded words and phrases. Loaded words and phrases carry a hidden meaning. They give a positive or negative impression. Read this sentence: "The coastline of Nigeria is so beautiful it takes your breath away." The words "so beautiful it takes your breath away" are loaded. They give a very positive impression. However, this hidden meaning cannot be proved. It is not fact.

C. Look for what isn't there. Biased writers often leave out information that does not support their bias. For example, the writer might say "the Mali empire failed," but leave out the fact that before it declined, it succeeded for centuries.

◀ Everything you read was written by someone. You need to use your skills to sort out whether or not to believe what the writer says.

D. Think about the tone. Tone is the overall feeling of a piece of writing. It shows the writer's attitude toward the subject: "From burning desert to steamy tropics, the climates of Africa are unbearable." This sentence gives you the clear impression that the writer has negative feelings about the climates of Africa. Unbiased writing provides the facts and lets the reader form his or her own conclusions.

Apply the Skill

The selection in the box is a biased, one-paragraph description of the early African empire of Ghana. To spot the bias, follow steps A through D. Consider these questions: Are there any opinions disguised as facts in the selection? What words give a positive or negative impression of the West African kingdoms? What important facts about West African kingdoms does the writer fail to include? How would you describe the tone of the writing? Positive? Negative? After you have finished, describe the West African kingdoms in one paragraph without bias.

West African Kingdoms

Between the 3500s and the 1500s, West Africa was a terrible place to live. People couldn't even survive without salt. They were forced to trade their most precious gold just to get enough salt to stay alive. In the kingdom of Ghana, the kings forced people to pay money just to carry salt, gold, and other goods through the land. The Ghanaian kingdom became so weak that it fell to the crushing power of the kingdom of Mali.

Review and Activities

Reviewing Main Ideas

1. List some of the ways in which early Africans made a living.
2. What were Africa's earliest civilizations like?
3. List several effects of the Bantu migrations.
4. How did Africa's kingdoms and city-states become wealthy?
5. (a) How did the relationship of Europeans and Africans begin? (b) How did it change?
6. Explain two effects of the Atlantic slave trade on Africa.
7. What factors helped lead to independence for many African countries?
8. Describe two types of government used in African countries after independence.
9. How are Africans working to improve their economies?
10. How are Africans working to improve social conditions?

Reviewing Key Terms

Use each key term below in a sentence that shows the meaning of the term.

1. hunter-gatherer
2. surplus
3. civilization
4. migrate
5. ethnic group
6. Quran
7. city-state
8. colonize
9. nationalism
10. Pan-Africanism
11. democracy
12. commercial farming
13. literacy
14. life expectancy

Critical Thinking

1. **Recognizing Cause and Effect** Many of Africa's cities and countries are located along trade routes. How has trade affected Africa's history?
2. **Expressing Problems Clearly** The Atlantic slave trade lasted from the 1500s to the 1800s. Then the "scramble for Africa" began. How did the slave trade and the scramble for Africa affect traditional African cultures?

Graphic Organizer

Copy the web onto a sheet of paper. Then fill in the empty spaces to complete a web of African history.

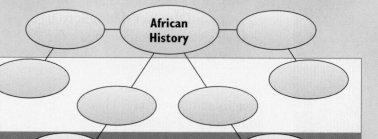

African History

Map Activity

Africa

For each place listed below, write the letter from the map that shows its location.

1. Senegal

2. Great Zimbabwe

3. Tombouctou

4. Cape of Good Hope

5. Kilwa

6. Kingdom of Mali

7. Nubia

8. Aksum

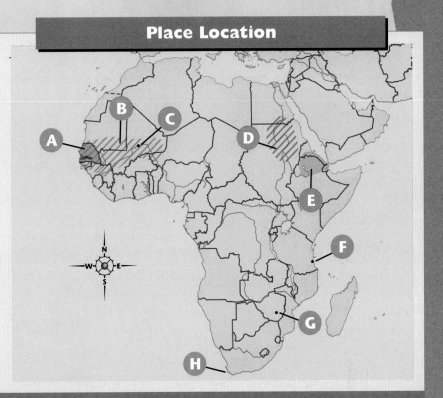

Place Location

Writing Activity

Writing a Speech

In the 1800s, many people in the United States spoke out against slavery. They were called abolitionists, because they wanted to abolish, or put an end to, slavery.

Pretend that you are an abolitionist living in the 1800s. Use what you have learned about the slave trade to write a speech that will help persuade people that slavery is wrong.

Take It to the NET

Activity Read more about the Swahili language and learn how to speak Swahili. For help in completing this activity, visit www.phschool.com.

Chapter 2 Self-Test To review what you have learned, take the Chapter 2 Self-Test and get instant feedback on your answers. Go to www.phschool.com to take the test.

Skills Review

Turn to the Skills Activity.
Review the steps for recognizing bias. (a) In your own words, explain the difference between biased and unbiased writing. (b) How can you determine whether a writer is biased?

How Am I Doing?

Answer these questions to check your progress.

1. Can I explain how early humans lived in Africa?

2. Can I identify the ancient civilizations of Africa and name their accomplishments?

3. Do I understand how European rule affected Africa?

4. Can I identify the challenges that African nations have faced since independence?

5. What information from this chapter can I include in my journal?

3

Cultures of Africa

PICTURE ACTIVITIES

An African market brings together a wide variety of people and goods. Here you can buy baskets, spices, or a lamb. You can get a haircut, listen to a storyteller, or watch acrobatic dancers perform. To help you begin to understand Africa's cultures, do the following activities.

Look for clues
From this picture, what can you tell about how these Africans live? How do they dress? What kinds of products do they make and sell?

Make a list of questions
Pick a person in the picture whose life you would like to know more about. Make a list of questions that you would ask this person if you could. As you read, see if some of your questions are answered.

The Cultures of North Africa

BEFORE YOU READ

Reach Into Your Background

Suppose you have been given the assignment of describing your way of life to students in North Africa. How would you answer the following questions:

What is a day in your life like? What is your school like? What is your home like? Think about your answers as you read this section.

Questions to Explore
1. What is culture?
2. How does Islam influence life in North Africa?
3. How has their Mediterranean location affected the cultures of North Africa?

Key Terms
culture
cultural diffusion

Key Places
Sahara
Mediterranean Sea

Thirteen-year-old Meena lives in the city of Marrakech (muh RAH kehsh) in Morocco, a country in North Africa. Every morning she works in a factory, weaving carpets. She learned to weave carpets from her mother, who learned the skill from her mother. Carpets play an important role in Moroccan life. They are an export. And in some Moroccan homes, they serve as more than just floor coverings. They are used as chairs, beds, and prayer mats. In the afternoon, Meena leaves the factory to attend school. Her day ends at sunset, when she hears the crier who calls out from the nearby mosque, a Muslim house of worship. Muslims are followers of the religion of Islam. When she hears the call, Meena recites this prayer in Arabic: "There is no God but God, and Muhammad is His prophet."

▼ Moroccan weavers decorate their carpets with intricate designs. Which of these carpets would you buy? What would you use it for?

What Is Culture?

Meena's way of life is different in some ways from yours. That is partly because her culture is different.

Building With Adobe
Adobe comes from an ancient Egyptian word. It refers to a brick made of earth and straw. Arabs brought adobe-making techniques to Spain. Later, the Spanish brought the use of adobe to what is now the southwestern United States. People in the Southwest still build adobe homes.

▼ Adobe bricks fall apart if they are often exposed to cold or wet weather. They can only be used in hot, dry climates. The picture below shows adobe houses in Morocco.

Culture is the way of life of a group of people who share similar beliefs and customs.

Culture has many elements. Culture includes food, clothing, homes, jobs, language, and so on. It also includes things that are not so easy to see, such as how people view their world and what their religion is. These ideas shape the way people behave. Meena, for example, takes time from her activities to pray several times a day.

Cultures in different places have common elements. In many rural villages in Morocco, for example, houses are made of thick adobe, a type of brick made from sun-dried clay. Thick adobe walls help keep out the heat. Across the globe, in Mexico, and in the southwestern United States, many people in rural areas also live in adobe houses.

The Influence of Islam

Religion is an important part of North African culture. Islam is the religion of most North Africans. More than 95 percent of North Africans practice Islam and are called Muslims.

Like Jews and Christians, Muslims believe in one God. Allah is the Arabic word for God. Muslims believe that Muhammad was God's final messenger. They also believe that the Old Testament prophets and Jesus were God's messengers. The main duties of a Muslim are outlined in the Five Pillars of Islam, shown in the chart on the next page.

The Five Pillars of Islam

Duty	Description
Declaration of Faith	Declaring belief in one God and in Muhammad as God's final messenger
Prayer	Reciting prayers five times a day: at dawn, at midday, in the afternoon, at sunset, and in the evening
Almsgiving	Giving a portion of one's wealth to the needy
Fasting	Not eating or drinking from sunrise to sunset during the ninth month in the Muslim year, Ramadan
Pilgrimage	Making the *hajj*, or pilgrimage to Mecca, at least once in a lifetime if able

Chart Study Actions speak louder than words, so one form of Muslim worship is to do things to please God, like helping other people. Muslims must also perform the Five Pillars of Islam. **Critical Thinking** Which of the Five Pillars do you think is illustrated by the photo on the right?

Five Pillars of Islam

The sacred book of Islam is the Quran. Besides teaching about God, the Quran provides a guide to life. Like the Bible, the Quran forbids lying, stealing, and murder. It also prohibits gambling, eating pork, and drinking alcohol.

The Islamic system of law is based on the Quran. Islamic law governs all aspects of life, including family life, business practices, banking, and government.

Islam Unifies the People of North Africa Islam and the Arabic language unify the different peoples of North Africa. These peoples are spread out over a large area that includes the following countries: Egypt, Libya, Tunisia, Algeria, and Morocco. People here have many different backgrounds and ways of life.

An ethnic group is a group of people who share language, religion, or cultural traditions. Most North Africans are Arabs. But the region has other ethnic groups, too. The largest of these is the Berbers who live mainly in Algeria and Morocco. Most Berbers speak Arabic as well as Berber. Some live in cities, but most live in small villages in rugged mountain areas. They make their living by herding and farming. The Tuareg (TWAH rehg) are a group of Berbers who live in the Sahara, the

When the Tuareg travel across the desert, they must bring with them everything they might need, including tents to provide shelter from the sun. North Africa's cities, however, are centers of trade. People who live there can buy things that they need. The city below is Tunis, in Tunisia.

Visualize What sights might you see if you were walking through an outdoor market in a North African city? How would these sights be different from what you might see inside a modern supermarket?

great desert that stretches across North Africa. The Tuareg herd camels, goats, and other livestock.

In parts of rural North Africa, some people live much as their parents and grandparents did. But traditional and modern ways of life mix in towns and large cities like Cairo (KY roh), Egypt, and Tunis, Tunisia. Like Meena, who weaves carpets, some city people work at traditional crafts. Others are architects, engineers, scientists, and bankers. Some sell baskets in outdoor markets. Others sell television sets in modern stores.

Arab and Berber, urban and rural, architect and herder—the peoples of North Africa live vastly different lives, yet almost all consider themselves fellow Muslims. Islam forms a common bond of culture among North Africans.

Cultural Change in North Africa

North Africa's mix of traditional and modern ways of life shows that culture does not stay the same forever. It changes all the time.

How Culture Spreads Cultural changes often occur when people travel. As they travel, people bring their customs and ideas with them. They also pick up new ideas and customs. In this way, customs and ideas spread from one place to another. The movement of customs and ideas is called **cultural diffusion.** The word *diffuse* means "to spread out."

A Mediterranean Outlook   One factor that has aided the diffusion of culture in North Africa is location. Find North Africa on the map below. North Africans have long viewed their region as a gateway to three continents: Africa, Europe, and Asia. Can you see why? This Mediterranean outlook dates back to early history.

Because of its location, North Africa has been a hub of trade. Throughout history, the people of North Africa have traded with people in Europe, Asia, and other parts of Africa. Thus, they have influenced, and been influenced by, cultures in all these places.

The mixing of cultures in North Africa did not occur only through trade. It also occurred through conquest. North Africa is home to one of the world's oldest civilizations—ancient Egypt. The ancient Egyptians developed trade links with ancient civilizations in both Europe and Southwest Asia. They both conquered and were conquered by other empires. These conquests helped bring about cultural diffusion.

READ ACTIVELY

Connect What cities in the United States are centers of trade?

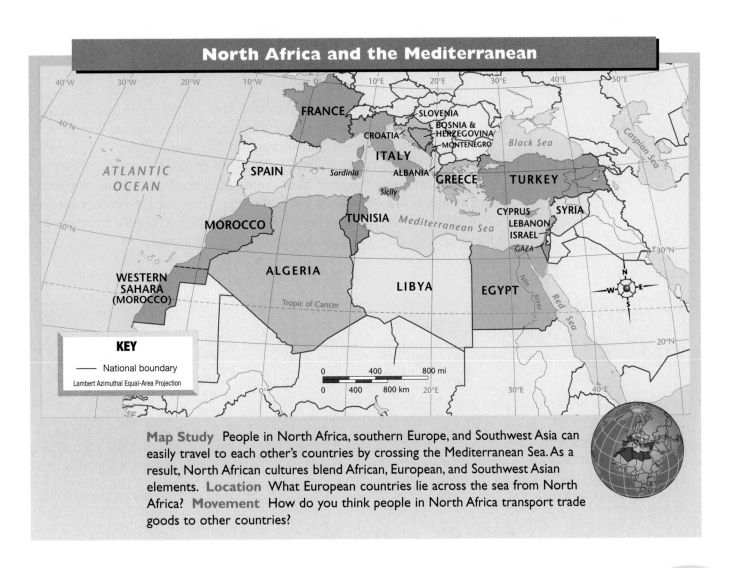

North Africa and the Mediterranean

KEY

—— National boundary

Lambert Azimuthal Equal-Area Projection

0   400   800 mi

0   400   800 km

Map Study People in North Africa, southern Europe, and Southwest Asia can easily travel to each other's countries by crossing the Mediterranean Sea. As a result, North African cultures blend African, European, and Southwest Asian elements. **Location** What European countries lie across the sea from North Africa? **Movement** How do you think people in North Africa transport trade goods to other countries?

▶ Muslims often build a large, empty space into the middle of their mosques. Why? In countries with more than one culture and religion, Muslims use mosques as community centers. The empty space can be used for many different kinds of activities, including education.

Preserving Muslim Culture   One of the more recent influences on North Africa is Western culture. Some Muslims are concerned that their countries are becoming too Western. More people are wearing Western clothes, buying Western products, seeing Western films, and adapting Western ideas. Some Muslims fear that this will lead to the loss of Muslim values and traditions. They want to preserve their way of life. All over Africa, people face the challenge of how to preserve the traditions they value as their countries modernize.

SECTION 1 REVIEW

1. **Define**   (a) culture, (b) cultural diffusion.

2. **Identify**   (a) Sahara, (b) Mediterranean Sea.

3. How does Islam affect everyday life in North Africa?

4. How has North Africa's location contributed to cultural diffusion?

Critical Thinking

5. **Making Comparisons** Which aspects of North African culture are similar to and which are different from your culture? Make a list of the similarities and differences.

Activity

6. **Writing to Learn**   What traditions in your culture do you think are worth preserving? Write an essay describing the customs you value most.

The Cultures of West Africa

Reach Into Your Background

How much do you know about different ethnic groups in the United States? Make a list of three or four groups. Jot down notes about each group's culture. Does the group speak a language other than English? What special customs or beliefs does the group have?

Questions to Explore

1. Why does West Africa have such a variety of cultures?
2. What effects do family ties have on West African culture?
3. How has urbanization affected the cultures of West Africa?

Key Terms

cultural diversity
kinship
nuclear family
extended family
lineage
clan
griot

In Mauritania, North Africa meets West Africa. Here, the Sahara merges into the savanna, or grasslands. Hamadi (hah MAH dee) is a teacher in a small village school in southern Mauritania. Although the country's official language is Arabic, Hamadi teaches French in the school. But at home, he speaks Poular, the language of the Halpoular, one of Mauritania's main ethnic groups.

▼ Children in Mauritania do not always have paper and pencils, but that doesn't stop them from learning. Instead, they use slates and chalk.

Cultural Diversity of West Africa

Being able to speak more than one language is useful in Africa, and especially in West Africa. Seventeen countries make up this region. West Africa also has hundreds of ethnic groups. Because of its many ethnic groups, West Africa is famous for its **cultural diversity**—it has a wide variety of cultures. Unlike the ethnic groups of North Africa, West Africans are not united by a single religion or a common language.

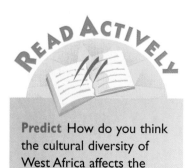

Predict How do you think the cultural diversity of West Africa affects the lives of its people?

West Africans Speak Many Languages Think about your community. Imagine that the people who live nearby speak a different language. How would you communicate with them? Suppose you wanted to shop in a store, eat in a restaurant, or attend a sports event in the next town. It might seem like visiting another country.

This situation is real for many West Africans. The hundreds of ethnic groups in West Africa speak different languages. Sometimes groups in neighboring villages speak different languages.

To communicate, most West Africans speak more than one language. Many speak four or five languages. They use these different languages when they travel or conduct business. This practice helps unify countries with many ethnic groups.

West Africans Have Many Ways of Making a Living
West Africa's ethnic groups differ in more than just the language they speak. Like North Africans, West Africans have many ways of making of a living. Most West Africans live in rural areas. A typical village consists of a group of homes surrounded by farmland. The village people grow food for themselves and cash crops to sell.

In the Sahara and the dry Sahel just south of the Sahara, many people herd cattle, goats, sheep, or camels. Along the coast, most West Africans make a living by fishing. Some West Africans live in large cities where they may work in hospitals, hotels, or office buildings.

A Market in Dakar, Senegal

At this open-air market in Dakar, Senegal, customers can buy many kinds of groceries, including fresh fish. Dakar is a wealthy port city on Senegal's Atlantic coast. Senegal has built up its fishing industry so much that fish are its most important export. **Critical Thinking** Besides the people who catch the fish, who benefits from Dakar's fishing industry?

Ways of making a living in West Africa vary from country to country. Most people in Mali (below left) make a living growing crops such as grains, corn, potatoes, yams, and cassava. But in some countries, such as Côte d'Ivoire, almost half the people live and work in cities. The University of Côte d'Ivoire (below right), in the largest city of Abidjan, employs hundreds of people.

Belonging to Groups

Like North Africans, West Africans see themselves as members of a number of groups. Just as you belong to a family, an ethnic group, and a country, so do West Africans.

The Strong Ties of Kinship One of the strongest bonds West Africans have is **kinship,** which refers to a family relationship. The first level of kinship is the **nuclear family,** which consists of parents and their children. The next level is the **extended family,** which includes other relatives besides parents and children. It may include grandparents, aunts, uncles, and cousins. Many West Africans live in extended families.

Extended families work together and take care of each other. Family members care for the elderly and those who are sick or less well-off. They make decisions together. And they watch over all the children in the village. This custom is reflected in the well-known African proverb, "It takes a village to raise a child." Neighbors always pitch in and help one another. Thus, kinship adds to a strong sense of community.

READ ACTIVELY

Connect How do people outside your immediate family help to raise you?

Larger Groups: Lineages and Clans In many rural areas, kinship reaches beyond extended families. A group of families may trace their descent back to a common ancestor. Such a group forms a lineage. Several lineages form a clan. The people in a clan all have roots back to an even earlier ancestor.

Tracing Lineage Different traditions also govern the way groups trace their lineage. Some groups are matrilineal. They trace their lineage through women ancestors. Property is passed on to children through the female side of a family. In a matrilineal society, if people marry outside the clan, the husband comes to live with the wife's clan. The result is that the village has a core of women who live there. The men they marry are newcomers, who move into the homes of the local women. Most groups, however, are patrilineal. They trace their descent through the male side of a family.

Changes in Family Life

Although traditional family ties remain strong in West Africa, family life is changing. More people are moving from rural villages to urban areas, or cities. This trend, called urbanization, is occurring throughout Africa and the world.

▼ In places like Tombouctou, Mali, where the climate is hot, some families in rural areas do many household chores outside.

Bus drivers must find their way carefully through the crowded streets of Lagos, Nigeria. Like people all over Africa, many of these people have come to Lagos to find work. **Critical Thinking** Why do you think it would be easier to find a job in a city than in a rural area?

Many young men come to West Africa's cities to find jobs. The women often stay in the rural homes. They raise the children and farm the land. The men come home from time to time to visit their families and to share what they have earned.

Keeping Traditions Alive

In West Africa today, people are adapting to change in various ways. But most West Africans still keep strong family ties. People still pass their history, values, and traditions on to the young.

One important way in which West African traditions are being preserved is through storytelling. Traditional West African stories are spoken rather than written. The stories teach children cultural values. A storyteller called a **griot** (GREE oh) passes this oral tradition from one generation to another. The oral tradition of West Africa tells the histories of ethnic groups and kinships. Stories of tricksters, animal fables, proverbs, riddles, and songs are also part of West Africa's oral tradition. This Yoruba proverb reflects the value placed on passing on traditions: "The young can't teach traditions to the old."

LINKS TO LANGUAGE ARTS

West African Folk Tales West Africa has a rich tradition of folk tales. One type of tale is the escape story, in which a clever person thinks of a way out of an impossible situation. One tale from Benin is about a cruel king who orders his people to build him a new palace. He tells them that they must start at the top and build down. The people despair. Then a wise old man invites the king to begin by setting the first stone in place. The people are saved.

When a griot tells a story, it can take all night or even several days. The audience does not mind, because the stories are usually scary, funny, or exciting. This griot, from Côte d'Ivoire, is telling these children a legend from their history. The children pay careful attention, because the griot acts out parts of the story as he goes along.

West African traditions have greatly influenced other cultures, especially American culture. About half of the enslaved Africans who were brought to the United States came from West Africa. They brought with them the only things they could: their ideas, stories, dances, music, and customs. The stories of Brer Rabbit as well as blues and jazz music have their roots in West Africa. Today, West African culture—the stories, music, dances, art, cooking, clothing—is more popular than ever. Griot guitarists and other musicians from West Africa have international followings. In recent years, three Nobel Prize winners for literature have been African. One of them, Wole Soyinka (WOH lay shaw YING kah), is from the West African country of Nigeria.

SECTION 2 REVIEW

1. **Define** (a) cultural diversity, (b) kinship, (c) nuclear family, (d) extended family, (e) lineage, (f) clan, (g) griot.

2. In what ways is West Africa culturally diverse?

3. Describe the importance of family ties to West Africans.

4. How has urbanization changed the lives of West Africans?

Critical Thinking

5. **Drawing Conclusions** How has the extended family helped to develop a sense of community among West Africans?

Activity

6. **Writing to Learn** Imagine that you live in a small village in an extended family in West Africa. Make a list of the advantages and disadvantages of your way of life.

The Cultures
of East Africa

Reach Into Your Background

Think about the language you speak. How many words can you identify that come from another language? What about the words *banjo, canyon,* or *succotash? Banjo* comes from an African language, possibly Kimbundu. *Canyon* comes from Spanish. *Succotash* comes from Narragansett, a Native American language. See if you can find other examples.

Questions to Explore

1. How has location affected the development of East African cultures?

2. What role does the Swahili language play in East African cultures?

3. How and why are ideas about land ownership changing in East Africa?

Key Terms
plantation

Key People and Places
East Africa
Julius Nyerere

Alemeseged Taddesse Mekonnen (ah LEM uh seh ged tah DAY say meh KOH nen) is an Ethiopian who works in a bakery in St. Louis, Missouri. Before coming to the United States, he lived with his extended family in Gonder, a city in northern Ethiopia. His father owned a large store there. Mekonnen speaks three languages: Amharic, Arabic, and English. At home, in Ethiopia, Amharic was his first language. Because he is Muslim, he learned Arabic to study the Quran. And he learned English in school, as other Ethiopians do.

Mekonnen misses life with his close-knit family in Ethiopia. "At home we ate every meal together. If anyone was missing, we waited until they came home," he says. Mekonnen hopes to return home someday. He lives in the United States, but his heart is in Ethiopia.

▼ Shown below is the city of Gonder, in northern Ethiopia. Ethiopia is one of the countries in East Africa.

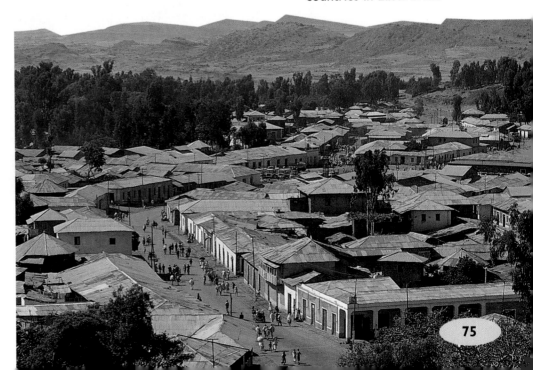

Living Along the Indian Ocean

Knowing three languages is not unusual for an East African, just as it is not for a West African. In Ethiopia alone, more than 70 different languages are spoken. Like West Africa, East Africa has many ethnic groups who speak different languages. The region has great cultural diversity.

East Africa's diversity is the result of its location. Many ethnic groups have migrated to East Africa from other regions of the continent. For example, about 2,000 years ago, Bantu-speaking peoples migrated to East Africa from West Africa. In addition, East Africa has a long coastline along the Indian Ocean. The ocean connects the people of East Africa to people living across the ocean to the east. These people include Arabs, Indians, and other Asians. The connection extends even to countries as far away as China and Malaysia.

This link dates back to early times. Arab traders began to settle in the coastal villages of East Africa nearly 2,000 years ago. They brought Arab culture into East Africa, where it mixed with various African cultures. This mixture produced the Swahili culture.

Lunch Time for a Kenyan Family

Shown above is a family from Kenya. Families in East Africa traditionally eat their meals together, using one bowl or plate. In the traditional style, they use their fingers rather than forks and spoons. **Critical Thinking** What foods do people in the United States share from one plate or bowl?

Kampala, Capital City of Uganda

Kampala is Uganda's largest city and leading trade center. It is a religious center as well. You can find Muslim mosques, Hindu temples, and Christian churches here.

Swahili Culture

The Swahili are Africans who have mixed African and Arab ancestry. They live along the east coast of Africa from Somalia to Mozambique. Their language is also called Swahili. It is a Bantu language, but it contains many Arabic words. The Swahili are just one of hundreds of ethnic groups in East Africa. But their language is widely used for business and communication among many ethnic groups throughout the region.

Swahili is the first language of about 49 million people worldwide. It also serves as the second language of millions of East Africans. Swahili is the official language of Kenya and Tanzania. In Tanzania, children are educated in Swahili through the primary grades. Later, they learn English as well. By promoting the use of Swahili, these nations are trying to preserve their African heritage.

A Mixture of Religions

Like languages, religious beliefs in East Africa reflect the cultural diversity of the region. Both Islam and Christianity have large followings in the region. Islam was introduced into East Africa by Arab traders. The Romans introduced Christianity into some of their North African territories. Later, it spread into Ethiopia. In the 1800s,

ACROSS THE WORLD

Kwanzaa Swahili culture and language have also come to the United States. Many African Americans celebrate Kwanzaa (KWAN zah), a holiday based on a traditional African harvest festival. The word *Kwanzaa* is related to the Swahili word for "first." Kwanzaa is based on a set of values that also have Swahili names. These include *umoja* (oo MOH juh), or unity; *kuumba* (koo OOM buh), or creativity; and *imani* (ee MAHN ee), or faith.

Europeans pushed into Africa and spread Christianity farther. In addition, traditional religions remain alive in East Africa and throughout the continent.

Changing Ideas About Land

In East Africa, as in the rest of Africa, most people live in rural areas, where they farm and tend livestock. The ways in which they view and work the land are part of the culture of East Africans.

Before Land Was Owned Before Europeans took over parts of Africa in the 1800s, individual Africans did not own land. People did not buy or sell land. The very idea of owning land did not exist. Families had the right to farm plots of land near the village, but the actual plots might vary in size and location over time.

Traditionally, extended families farmed the land to produce food for the whole group. Men cleared the land and broke up the soil. Women then planted the seed, tended the fields, and harvested the crops. Meanwhile, the men herded livestock or traded goods. This division of roles still exists in many parts of Africa today.

The Rise and Fall of Plantations The idea of privately owned land was introduced into many parts of Africa by European settlers. In parts of East Africa, the British set up plantations. A plantation is a large farm where cash crops are grown. When many African countries became independent, they broke up the old colonial plantations. They sold the land to individual Africans.

Some land in East Africa is still available to buy. But much of it is poor farmland in areas where few people live. In fertile areas like the Ethiopian Highlands and the Rift Valley,

land for farming is scarce. Many people live in these areas where the farmland is fertile. In densely populated countries, such as Rwanda and Burundi, conflicts have developed over land.

Where Is Home?

Traditionally, Africans feel a strong bond to the land where they grew up. Like the rest of Africa, East Africa is becoming increasingly urban. Yet even people who spend most of their time in a city do not call it home. If asked where home is, an East African will name the village of his or her family or clan. Most people consider their life in the city temporary. They expect to return to their villages at some time.

Tanzania's former president Julius Nyerere (nyuh RAIR ay) is one example. Nyerere continued to be involved in world affairs, but far from Dar es Salaam, the capital city of Tanzania. After he stepped down as

Connect How do you feel when you return home after being away for a long time?

◄ The coastal city of Mombasa, Kenya, began as a trading center in the 1200s. One of its chief exports was ivory. Today, metal arches shaped like elephant tusks memorialize Kenya's ivory trade. While cities like Mombasa can be beautiful and exciting, to most East Africans a city can never really be home.

president in 1985, Nyerere moved back to his home village. There, until his death in 1999, he grew corn and millet on his farm. He spent his mornings working in the fields. In an interview in 1996, Nyerere said: "In a sense I am a very rural person. I grew up here, and [working in] Dar es Salaam was a duty. I did my duty and after retiring in 1985, I came back here and said, 'Ah, it's good to be back.'"

Other East Africans feel the same. They do their duty by earning money in the city. But, their homes—and their hearts—are in their rural villages.

◀ On his family farm in Rwanda, this farmer grows potatoes, corn, beans, and cabbage. East Africans sometimes move away from their farms, but they almost always hope to return to them one day.

SECTION 3 REVIEW

1. **Define** plantation.

2. **Identify** (a) East Africa, (b) Julius Nyerere.

3. Describe some ways in which East Africa's location along the Indian Ocean has affected its cultures.

4. Why is Swahili spoken by so many people in East Africa?

5. Explain the changes in ideas about land ownership in East Africa.

Critical Thinking

6. **Making Comparisons** How did traditional East African ideas about land differ from the ideas of Europeans who took over parts of Africa?

Activity

7. **Writing to Learn** Write a description of the place that you consider home. Tell what it means to you and explain why.

The Cultures of Central and Southern Africa

Reach Into Your Background

Think of a goal you had to work hard to achieve at home or at school. Why was it important to you to achieve your goal? Think about the plan you made and the strategies you used to achieve your goal. What obstacles did you have to overcome? How did you feel when you finally succeeded?

Questions to Explore

1. How has the country of South Africa influenced the entire region of Southern Africa?
2. How did migrant labor give rise to a new group identity among the peoples of Southern Africa?
3. How does Central Africa reflect the cultural diversity of all of Africa?

Key Terms
migrant worker

Key Places
Republic of South Africa
Democratic Republic of Congo

The African National Congress (ANC), a political party in the Republic of South Africa, played a key role in gaining political and civil rights for all South Africans. Until 1991, Europeans in South Africa had denied equal rights to blacks, who make up a majority of the population. Three countries—Tanzania, Zambia, and Zimbabwe—adopted the ANC anthem for their national anthems. Here are the words to the ANC anthem:

> "Bless, O Lord, our land of Africa
> Lift its name and make its people free.
> Take the gifts we offer unto Thee
> Hear us, faithful sons.
> Hear us, faithful sons."

▼ These teenagers sang the ANC anthem for the opening of Parliament in Cape Town, South Africa.

The Pull of South Africa

South Africa is just one country in Southern Africa, but it has had, by far, the greatest impact on the region. Its political and economic influence has touched the lives of millions of people.

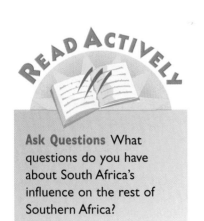
Political Influence of South Africa   Until the 1990s, a European minority ruled South Africa. In 1923, they separated South Africans into categories based on skin color. People of African descent were classified as black, people of European descent as white, and people of mixed ancestry as colored. Asians, who were mostly from India, formed the fourth category. Blacks, coloreds, and Asians could not vote and did not have other basic rights. For nearly 70 years, these groups struggled to gain their rights.

The struggle for basic rights created a sense of nationalism among black South Africans. White settlers, not blacks, had established the nation of South Africa. But as blacks struggled to gain political rights, they began to think of themselves as members of the nation. They wanted to take part as equal citizens in running the nation. The struggle for majority rule in South Africa lasted so long that it inspired similar movements in Namibia and what is now Zimbabwe.

A South African Gold Miner

This miner commutes to work by crawling through cramped tunnels until he reaches this room, where he does not have space to stand up. **Critical Thinking** What do you think a work day for this gold miner would be like?

Economic Influence of South Africa   South Africa is the richest and most industrialized country on the continent of Africa. It produces two fifths of the manufactured goods, half of the minerals, and one fifth of the agricultural products of the entire continent. Its economic power and needs have affected all of Southern Africa because its demand for labor has been so great. To provide a labor force for the mines, South African companies used workers from throughout Southern Africa.

To get jobs in South Africa, hundreds of thousands of workers migrated from nearby countries. Workers were allowed to stay in South Africa for only a short time. New workers were always needed. A large force of **migrant workers,** people who move from place to place to find work, was soon created.

In 1912, South African blacks organized the South African Native National Congress, which later became the African National Congress (ANC), to fight for equality. The ANC used boycotts, rallies, and work strikes to force the government to reform its laws. Many ANC members, including Nelson Mandela, were jailed for their actions. Mandela spent almost 30 years in jail. In the 1990s, South Africa ended its discriminatory laws and gave nonwhite South Africans the right to vote for the first time. Mandela became South Africa's president.

Migrant Workers Form a New Group Identity

Mine workers in South Africa were from many countries. They lived together in compounds, or fenced-in groups of homes. They were far from their families, clans, and ethnic groups. They worked long hours in dangerous conditions for low wages.

READ ACTIVELY

Predict How do you think South Africa's mines affected its culture?

A Person Is a Person Because of People   The migrant mine workers came to rely on one another. They began to think of themselves as a group—as workers. This kind of group identity was new for Southern Africans. It was not based on family or ethnic group. Group identity is very important in Africa. This is reflected in the African proverb "A person is a person because of people." It means that a person is who he or she is because of his or her relationships with other people. The migrant workers formed a new identity based on how they related to each other as workers.

Mine Workers Form a Union   In the 1980s, the mine workers in South Africa formed a union—the National Union of Mineworkers. This union was illegal at the time. But it played a leading role in the drive for equal rights. The union workers sometimes went on strike in support of their causes. Thus, the new identity of the mine workers led them to take group action.

Tradition and Change in Central Africa

Like people in Southern Africa and the rest of Africa, Central Africans have gone through many cultural changes in the 1900s. But many people in the region also follow old traditions. Like the rest of the continent, Central Africa displays great cultural diversity. The country of the Democratic Republic of Congo alone has about 200 ethnic groups.

One ethnic group in Congo is the Mbuti (em BOO tee), who live in the rain forests. The Mbuti are unique because they live much as their ancestors did. In forest camps of 10 to 25 families, they make their dome-shaped houses from branches and leaves. For food, they hunt wild animals and gather wild plants. The culture of the Mbuti is more than 3,000 years old.

In contrast, millions of people live in crowded shantytowns or cinder-block apartments in Kinshasa, the largest city in Congo. They walk or take buses or trucks to work in factories, offices, and hotels. Some people are Roman Catholics or Protestants. Others practice religions that blend Christian and traditional African beliefs. Still others are Muslims. On Saturday evenings, many people dance and listen to Congolese jazz in city dance halls.

Barkcloth Art The Mbuti of Congo use only renewable resources. For example, they make some of their cloth out of tree bark. Men pound the bark with mallets until it is almost as soft as velvet. Then women draw shapes and patterns on the cloth. Many art galleries in the United States and Europe collect Mbuti barkcloth drawings.

At Work in Cameroon

Cameroon is a country in northwest Central Africa. Most people in Cameroon live in rural areas and make a living by farming or by herding cattle. These men are building farm structures used in taking care of cattle.

A Modern City in an Old Location

Kinshasa is Congo's capital. People have lived here since the late 1400s, making a living by fishing or trading on the Congo River. Today, people still fish on the Congo River, and it remains an important source of transportation. However, Kinshasa is also a center of government and industry.

What one writer said about North Africa applies to Southern Africa as well. To define the real North African, he said, "you have to define which one you mean: the rich or the poor, the Berber women of the mountains or the college girls on motorbikes...." Old, new, and mixtures of the two live on in all regions of Africa.

SECTION 4 REVIEW

1. **Define** migrant worker.

2. **Identify** (a) Republic of South Africa, (b) Democratic Republic of Congo.

3. Describe the political and economic effects South Africa has had on the entire region of Southern Africa.

4. What was unusual about migrant workers in South Africa forming a group identity as workers?

5. In what ways are the cultures of Central Africa like those in other parts of Africa?

Critical Thinking

6. **Recognizing Cause and Effect** What positive and/or negative effects might South Africa's labor needs have had on the economies of nearby countries?

Activity

7. **Writing to Learn** Consider the life of a mine worker in a South African gold mine in the 1970s. Write the first verse of a song protesting miners' living and working conditions and wages.

SKILLS ACTIVITY

Assessing Your Understanding

Imagine you have a pen pal, a student your age from Africa. In one of her letters, she asks you this question: "What is your school like?" How would you answer?

You might describe it as a large school, or a small one. You could say whether it is in a rural area or in the heart of a big city. You could describe your school building, the classes you take, your teachers, your friends, and so on. This would be easy for you, because school is such a big part of your life. The classes you take, the people you see, and the books you read all seem normal to you.

But have you ever wondered what school is like for a person your age in Africa? You could ask your pen pal. Depending on where your pen pal lives, though, the answer would be different. A school in a big city in Egypt is very different from a school in rural Uganda. But every school in Africa has at least one thing in common with your school—students are there to learn. Like other students, if you want to study new things, you must learn to assess your understanding.

Get Ready

What does "assessing your understanding" mean? It means checking to see how well you understand something you are reading or studying. If you assess your understanding as you go along, you will know what areas you need to read or think more about to make sure you understand. You can concentrate on studying those things. This can help you to get better grades. For example, by assessing your understanding before a test, you can predict what grade you will get on the test. And you will know exactly what you need to study if you want to get a higher grade. It can help you get more out of your reading. If you realize something does not make sense to you, you can use some strategies such as rereading or making a graphic organizer to help you understand the information.

Try It Out

A good way of assessing your understanding is to play a simple game called "Do I Understand?" To play, choose one assignment you completed recently. Then ask yourself the questions on the checklist.

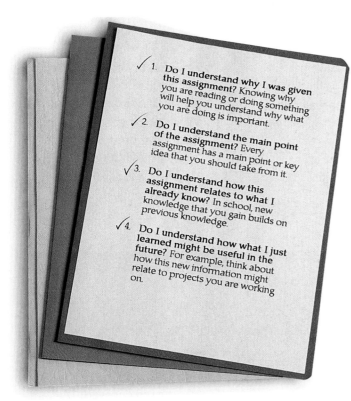

1. Do I understand why I was given this assignment? Knowing why you are reading or doing something will help you understand why what you are doing is important.

2. Do I understand the main point of the assignment? Every assignment has a main point or key idea that you should take from it.

3. Do I understand how this assignment relates to what I already know? In school, new knowledge that you gain builds on previous knowledge.

4. Do I understand how what I just learned might be useful in the future? For example, think about how this new information might relate to projects you are working on.

Apply the Skill

Practice assessing your understanding with the short reading assignment in the box, "An African School" by David Lamb.

1. Now, reread Question 1 in the list above. Why is it worthwhile to learn about a school in Kenya? What key ideas about the school does the writer try to communicate?

2. Reread Question 2. What do you think is the main point of "An African School"?

3. Reread Question 3. How does the writer's description fit with what you have already learned about Africa? Consider such things as languages, climate, and the condition of the school. Does anything in the reading assignment surprise you, or is it what you expected?

4. Look at Question 4. What are two ways that the knowledge you have just gained could help you in the future?

An African School

The Njumbi primary school [is] not far from the town of Karai in Kenya. . . . The headmaster, Michael Mathini, an energetic . . . man of thirty who rides a bicycle to work, greeted us at the door. He led us into his office and pointed with great pride to a wall graph showing that his students scored above the national average in the annual. . .examination.

The school has 620 students . . . and seventeen teachers who earned from $80 to $135 a month. . . . In the first-grade classroom across from Mathini's office, thirty or forty boys and girls were learning to count. . . They applauded . . . each time one of them gave the teacher the right answer. . . an ancient wooden radio sat on another teacher's desk and the dozen or so teenagers there strained through the heavy static to hear the creative writing lesson being broadcast in English from Nairobi.

Review and Activities

Reviewing Main Ideas

1. Describe how Islam has influenced the culture of North Africa.
2. What factor has greatly aided cultural diffusion in North Africa?
3. How is West Africa culturally diverse?
4. What role do family ties play in West African culture?
5. Explain how location has affected East African cultures.
6. How does the language of Swahili help unite the people of East Africa?
7. Why is the idea of privately owned land fairly new to East Africans?
8. How has South Africa affected the cultures of the entire region of Southern Africa?
9. What major effect did migrant labor have on the people of Southern Africa?
10. How is Central Africa like other parts of Africa?

Reviewing Key Terms

Use each key term below in a sentence that shows the meaning of the term.

1. culture
2. cultural diffusion
3. cultural diversity
4. kinship
5. nuclear family
6. extended family
7. lineage
8. clan
9. griot
10. plantation
11. migrant worker

Critical Thinking

1. **Identifying Central Issues** Explain why the proverb "A person is a person because of people" is particularly suited to African culture.
2. **Drawing Conclusions** What benefits and problems have come with modernization in Africa?

Graphic Organizer

Copy the chart onto a sheet of paper. Then complete the chart by describing one or more key features of the cultures of each region.

The Cultures of Africa				
Region	North Africa	West Africa	East Africa	Central and Southern Africa
Culture				

Map Activity

Africa

For each place listed below, write the letter from the map that shows its location.

1. Mediterranean Sea

2. North Africa

3. West Africa

4. East Africa

5. Central and Southern Africa

Writing Activity

Writing a Dialogue

An exchange student from an African country has come to stay at your home for six weeks. You and your family are sharing your first dinner with the visitor. Write a dialogue in which you ask your visitor about African culture. Use what you have learned in this chapter to write your visitor's answers.

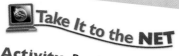

Take It to the NET

Activity Read an African fable and research the setting of the story. Use what you learn to write your own African fable. For help in completing this activity, visit www.phschool.com.

Chapter 3 Self-Test To review what you have learned, take the Chapter 3 Self-Test and get instant feedback on your answers. Go to www.phschool.com to take the test.

Skills Review

Turn to the Skills Activity. Review the steps for assessing your understanding. Then look at the Writing Activity on this page. Ask yourself questions to assess whether you understand the reason for this writing assignment.

How Am I Doing?

Answer these questions to check your progress.

1. Can I describe the cultural diversity of Africa?

2. Do I understand the role of kinship in African cultures?

3. Can I explain how urbanization has changed the way of life of many Africans?

4. What information from this chapter can I include in my journal?

The Language of Music

In the United States, you can hear music at parties, in concerts, on the radio, or even in supermarkets. It has many purposes. Music also has many roles in the cultures of African countries. Music may be used to send messages or to tell a story. It may organize work or celebrate a special occasion. In the United States, it is not uncommon to perform music by itself. People in African countries, however, rarely play music by itself. Most often, they combine music with dance, theater, words, games, or visual art.

Traditional African instruments include xylophones, lutes, harps, horns, flutes, clarinets, bells, and drums. Musicians can study for years to master their art, just as they do in the United States. In many African cultures, drums play an important role in traditional and modern music.

Purpose

In this activity, you will research traditional African drums and make your own drum. As you work on this activity, you will learn how Africans make and use drums.

Research African Drums

Traditionally, drums have been the most important instrument in African music. There are many types of drums, including the slit drum, the obodo, and the kettle drum. Use the information on this page to get you started. Then use encyclopedias, the Internet, and other resources to find out more about traditional African drums and how they differ. When you do research, look under subject headings such as African Arts, African Music, and Musical Instruments. You should also search under the names of specific drums.

Write down the names of several African drums. Then choose one drum to model your own after. Learn as much as you can about this kind of drum, including what materials it is made from, how it is played, how it is used, and where it is used.

Build Your Own Drum

Once you have chosen a traditional African drum as a model, you can build your own drum. You may want to use items such as buckets, cans, or cartons for the body of your drum. For the head of the drum, you might use cloth, plastic, or paper. Also consider the following questions:

- How will you attach the head of the drum to the body?
- Is one side of the drum open or are both sides covered?
- How will you strike your drum?

If possible, use materials that are similar to the materials the traditional drums are made from. Experiment with different methods to see which sounds best.

Play Your Drum

Figure out how you can use your drum in a way similar to the one you are modeling. For example, if the drum you are modeling was used to communicate messages across a long distance, think of a rhythmic code you can use to play a message to your classmates across the playground. If the drum was used as part of a drum group, you may want to write a short piece of music and play it with your classmates. If the drum accompanied a chant or song telling

the history of a community, write a song telling a story about something that has happened to you or someone you know.

Compare Drums

After you have built your drum and practiced with it, write a paragraph comparing your drum to its African model. You may want to present your work to the class and perform a piece of music.

ANALYSIS AND CONCLUSION

Write a summary that describes how you built and used your drum. Be sure to answer the following questions in the summary.

1. How is your drum similar to and different from the African drum you used as a model?

2. What factors affect the way your drum sounds?

3. How did you adapt the original uses of the model drum?

Exploring North Africa

KEY

— National boundary

⊛ National capital

• Other city

Lambert Azimuthal Equal-Area Projection

0 400 800 mi

0 400 800 km

MAP ACTIVITIES

Six countries make up the region of North Africa. Find them on the map above. To help you get to know this region, do the following activities.

Size up the region
Which country in the region looks the largest? Which country looks the smallest? What body of water lies on the region's northern boundary?

Consider the location
Find the major cities of North Africa shown on this map. How close are they to the Mediterranean Sea? How do you think that nearness to the sea might have affected North Africa's cultures?

Egypt

HEARING THE CALL OF ISLAM

SECTION

1

BEFORE YOU READ

Reach Into Your Background

You probably have a favorite holiday that you look forward to all year. Think about what you do during the holiday. What special foods do you eat? What different songs do you sing? Why do you and your family celebrate on that holiday?

Questions to Explore

1. How does religion affect Egypt's culture?

2. How has the role of Islam in Egypt changed in recent times?

Key Terms
bazaar
fellaheen

Key Places
Cairo

At noon, the restaurants in Cairo stand empty. Egyptian teenagers try not to think about pita bread or sweet dates. Only certain people, such as the very young or those who are sick, eat regular meals. Is there a food shortage in Egypt? No, it's the Muslim holiday of Ramadan (ram uh DAHN). Muslims are followers of the religion of Islam. For a month, Muslims fast from dawn to dusk. A fast is a period when people go without food. During Ramadan, Muslims eat only when the sun is down.

But Muslims do more than fast during Ramadan. They also think of those who are less fortunate than themselves. And they try not to get angry when things go wrong.

Islam in Egypt

Egypt is located in North Africa, where many of the world's Muslims live. Egypt is across the Red Sea from Saudi Arabia, where the messenger of Islam, Muhammad, was born. Islam spread from Saudi Arabia across North Africa. Today, the countries in this area have populations that are mostly Muslim. Islam is the major religion in Egypt. In fact, Islam is the country's official religion.

▼ More people live in Cairo than in any other city in Africa. Most of the people who live here are Muslim Arabs.

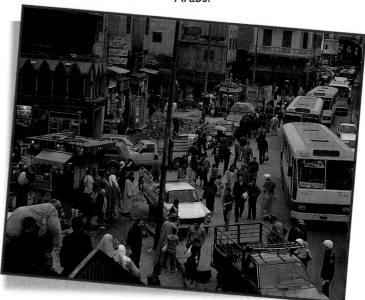

COUNTRY · PROFILE

A crowded street in Cairo

Culture The map and charts present information about the people of Egypt and where they live. **Map and Chart Study** (a) How does Egypt's geography affect where people live? (b) Use the information in the map and charts to write a brief paragraph about the people of Egypt.

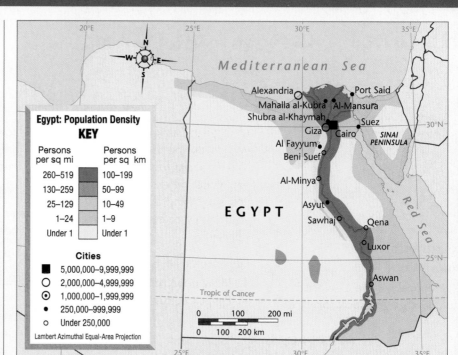

Egypt: Population Density
KEY

Persons per sq mi	Persons per sq km
260–519	100–199
130–259	50–99
25–129	10–49
1–24	1–9
Under 1	Under 1

Cities
- ■ 5,000,000–9,999,999
- ○ 2,000,000–4,999,999
- ◉ 1,000,000–1,999,999
- • 250,000–999,999
- ○ Under 250,000

Lambert Azimuthal Equal-Area Projection

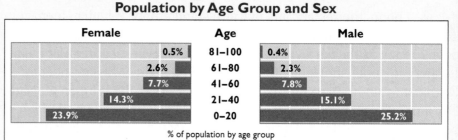

Population by Age Group and Sex

Female	Age	Male
0.5%	81–100	0.4%
2.6%	61–80	2.3%
7.7%	41–60	7.8%
14.3%	21–40	15.1%
23.9%	0–20	25.2%

% of population by age group

Urban and Rural Population

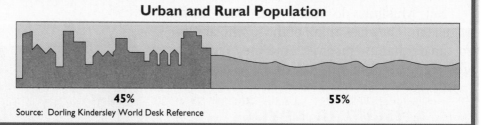

45%   55%

Source: Dorling Kindersley World Desk Reference

Take It to the NET
Data Update For the most recent data on Egypt, visit **www.phschool.com**.

Teachings and Practices The Quran is the sacred book of the Muslims. It contains the basic teachings of Islam. Muslims believe that the Quran contains the words of God, which were revealed to Muhammad during the month of Ramadan. Muslims also believe that the Jewish Torah and the Christian Bible are the word of God.

Recordings of the Quran have become very popular in Egypt. As Ahmed Abdel Rahman (AH med AHB del RAHK mahn), a record store manager in Cairo, says, "You can get bored by a song after a few days. But no one gets bored listening to the Quran." During the day, many Egyptians listen to the recordings on audiotapes or on the government radio station.

Islam's Contribution to Science

Muslim scholars do not limit themselves to studying the Quran. From the 600s on, Muslims have studied art, literature, philosophy, math, astronomy, and medicine. Muslim mathematicians invented algebra, and Muslim astronomers accurately mapped the locations of the stars. A Muslim astronomer drew this illustration of a comet in the 1500s. **Critical Thinking** What practical purpose do you think Muslim scholars may have had for studying astronomy?

"I have two ears," says Saad Eddin Saleh (SAH ahd EH deen SAH leh), a carpenter in Cairo, "one for work, and one for listening to the Quran."

The Quran requires that Muslims pray five times a day. Many Egyptians pray in a mosque, a building used for Muslim worship. During prayer, Muslims face in the direction of Mecca, Saudi Arabia, where Islam's holiest shrine is located. A mosque may also offer religious training for schoolchildren. The young students who attend these schools learn to read and memorize the Quran.

An Islamic Renewal The Quran is one of the main sources of Sharia (sha REE ah), or Islamic law. The Sharia is also based on the words and deeds of Muhammad, and on comments written by Muslim scholars and lawmakers. Muslims in North Africa and Southwest Asia try to renew their faith by living each day according to Sharia.

Praying and fasting are two of the ways that Egyptian Muslims have brought their religion into their daily lives. But the Quran includes many teachings that govern day-to-day life. It stresses the importance of honesty, honor, and giving to others. It also requires Muslims to love and respect their families.

Most Muslims in Egypt agree that the laws of Egypt should be based on Islamic law. In 1978, Egypt's government studied its laws and discovered that most already were in agreement with Sharia. But in recent years, some Egyptians have said that all of Egypt's laws should match Islamic law. And this has led to disagreements among Egyptian Muslims.

READ ACTIVELY

Ask Questions What else would you like to know about the religion of Islam?

L·I·N·K·S

ACROSS TIME

King Tut's Clothes
Scientists are studying the clothes of Pharaoh Tutankhamen, the boy who became ruler of Egypt at the age of nine, in about 1333 B.C. They have learned that Egyptian clothing had no hooks or buttons. King Tut had to tuck, wrap, and tie his clothes on. Because of their clothing, ancient Egyptians had to take small steps and walk carefully.

▼ Some Egyptian women veil their faces, while others do not. Why do you think a woman would choose to veil her face? Why might she not?

Dressing Modestly   One part of the debate about Sharia has centered on how women should dress in public. Muhammad taught that men and women are equal in the eyes of God. And Islamic law requires that both men and women dress modestly in public. Men and women must wear loose-fitting clothing that covers most of the body. Sharia requires that women cover all parts of their body except their hands, face, and feet.

However, some Muslims believe that women should also veil their faces, except for the eyes. They believe that covering the face is an important way for women to show their Muslim faith. Many other Muslims, including some government leaders, disagree. In 1994, these leaders banned female public school students from veiling their faces. This upset many Egyptians who were not strongly religious. They feel that the kind of veil a woman wears should be a matter of individual choice.

Life in Egypt

People in Egypt's cities and villages alike practice Islam. However, except for the time they spend in prayer, people in the cities and the villages live very different lives.

City Life   Nearly half of all Egyptians live in cities. Cairo, the nation's capital and largest city, is home to about six million Egyptians. More people live in Cairo than in Los Angeles and Chicago combined. It is the largest city in Africa. Some

A Traffic Jam in Cairo

Some people think that Cairo is the loudest city in the world because of its honking horns and roar of car engines. More than 14 million people live in the city and surrounding urban areas, but even more drive or take buses and trains in from the suburbs during the day. At night the streets are empty, but it can be difficult to find even one open parking space.

parts of Cairo are more than 1,000 years old. Other parts of Cairo look just like a Western city. Most people live in apartment buildings with electric fans or air-conditioning. However, they often shop in traditional open-air markets called **bazaars.**

Many people move to the cities from rural areas. They hope to find jobs and better education. As a result, Cairo is very crowded. There are traffic jams and housing shortages. Some people live in tents that they have set up on rowboats on the Nile. Others live in homes they have built in the huge graveyards on the outskirts of Cairo. So many people live in the graveyards that they are considered suburbs of the city, and the government has provided the graveyards with electricity.

Rural Life Most of the people in Egypt's rural areas live in villages along the Nile River or the Suez Canal. In Egyptian villages, most of the people make their living by farming. Egypt's rural farmers are called *fellaheen* (fel uh HEEN). Most of the fellaheen do not own land. Land is scarce because the river banks are so narrow. Some fellaheen farm small, rented plots of land. Others work in the fields of rich landowners.

Many of the fellaheen live in homes built of mud bricks or stones. Most of these homes are small. They have one to three rooms and a courtyard that the family often shares with its animals. The roofs of village houses are flat. The fellaheen use their roofs as places to store food and firewood, spread dates out to dry, and dry wet clothes.

Connect How does urban life differ from rural life in the United States?

▲ With power from a water buffalo, a fellaheen woman runs a traditional machine that separates the seeds of grain from the plants.

Egypt's people differ from each other in many ways. Some live in cities, while others live in rural areas. Some people make a living by programming computers, while others farm using ancient techniques. Despite their differences, however, most Egyptians are unified by one thing—their faith in Islam. Egyptian Muslims hope that renewing their faith every day will help them to maintain traditional values and customs in a modern age.

SECTION 1 REVIEW

1. **Define** (a) bazaar, (b) fellaheen.

2. **Identify** Cairo.

3. Give two examples of how Islam affects everyday life in Egypt.

4. Compare the lives of city and village dwellers in Egypt.

Critical Thinking

5. **Identifying Central Issues** How have Egyptian Muslims tried to renew their faith?

Activity

6. **Writing to Learn** In a journal entry, describe how the clothes people wear and the music they listen to may reflect their beliefs. Use examples from your own experience as well as from this section.

Algeria

THE CASBAH AND THE COUNTRYSIDE

Reach Into Your Background

How do you adapt to the climate in your area? How do you change your schedule or your choice of clothing based on the weather?

Questions to Explore

1. What are some differences and similarities between the Berbers and the Arabs of Algeria?

2. How is life in Algerian cities different from life in the villages?

Key Terms

terrace
souq
casbah

Key People and Places

Sahara
Berber
Arab

Like people in many parts of the world, Algerians adapt to their climate by resting during the hottest hours of the day. Journalist William Langewiesche described part of his visit to Adrar, an oasis city in the Algerian Sahara, as follows:

▼ The Tuareg, a nomadic Berber group, normally relax under tents during the hottest hours of the day. This Tuareg man is brewing green tea.

"We . . . waited out the hot midday hours, drinking brown water from a plastic jug. The water was brown because Miloud had mixed in cade oil. The cade is an evergreen bush that grows in the Atlas Mountains. Saharan nomads use its oil to seal the inside of goatskin water bags. Miloud did not have a goatskin, but he came from a long line of desert travelers. He bought the oil in small bottles and added it to his water for flavor and good health. The mixture smelled of pine sap and tasted of clay. . . . But I would have drunk anything. I had been for a walk."

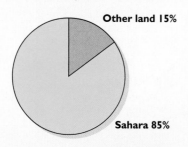
Algeria: Climate and Physical Features

Percent of Land Covered by the Sahara

Other land 15%

Sahara 85%

Source: Infoplease Internet Encyclopedia

Homes on the coast of Algeria

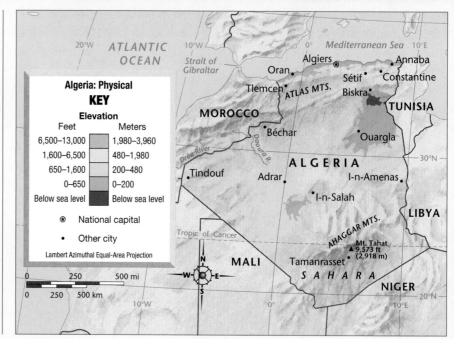

Algeria: Physical
KEY
Elevation

Feet	Meters
6,500–13,000	1,980–3,960
1,600–6,500	480–1,980
650–1,600	200–480
0–650	0–200
Below sea level	Below sea level

⊛ National capital

• Other city

Lambert Azimuthal Equal-Area Projection

0   250   500 mi
0   250   500 km

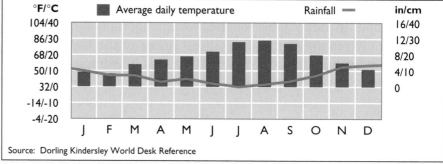

Weather Chart

°F/°C — Average daily temperature — Rainfall — in/cm

Source: Dorling Kindersley World Desk Reference

Geography The map above shows Algeria's elevation and physical features. The charts provide information on Algeria's climate and environment. **Map and Chart Study** (a) Why do you think most people in Algeria live in coastal areas? (b) In which three months does Algeria receive the most rainfall?

Take It to the NET
Data Update For the most recent data on Algeria, visit **www.phschool.com**.

READ ACTIVELY

Predict How do you think people in Algeria make a living?

Algeria's People

The temperature outside while Langewiesche was walking was 124°F (51°C). To survive in that heat, people must drink enough water to produce 2 to 4 gallons (8 to 16 l) of sweat a day. Look at the map in the Country Profile. The Sahara covers all of Algeria south of the Atlas Mountains. Water is in short supply in this area. For this reason, fewer than three percent of Algeria's people live here. But because of their resourcefulness, Berber and Arab nomads have survived in the Sahara for hundreds of years.

The Berbers   The Berbers and the Arabs are Algeria's two main ethnic groups. The Berbers have lived in North Africa since at least 3000 B.C. No one knows exactly where they came from, but many historians think they migrated from Southwest Asia. They settled in the Atlas Mountains and on plains near Algeria's coast. More than 90 percent of Algerians still live near the coast, where the weather is milder than in the Sahara.

Some Berbers live in Algeria's cities. Most, however, live in villages in rural areas. Many Berbers continue to follow traditional ways of life. Berber households form an extended family, which includes more relatives than just a mother, a father, and their children. Each Berber house has an open courtyard in the back. The windows in the house face the courtyard, not the street. Each married couple in a family has its own home, opening onto the family courtyard. In this way, grandparents, parents, sons, daughters, and cousins can all live close together.

Family is so important to the Berbers that their village governments are based on it. The head of each family is a member of the village assembly, which makes laws for the village.

Most families in Berber villages make a living by farming and herding. They get up as soon as it is light. In the middle of the day, when the sun is hottest, people rest for several hours. Then they work until dark. Farmers use wooden plows drawn by camels. They grow wheat and barley and raise livestock. In the mountains, the Berbers build **terraces,** or platforms cut into the mountainside, for their crops. The terraces increase the amount of farmland and stop the soil from washing away when it rains.

LINKS TO MUSIC

The Professional Poet
Many Berber villages have a professional poet. The poet is always a woman who improvises songs in one of the Berber languages. A chorus of women accompany the poet with their voices and with small drums.

A Desert Lifestyle

These men live in the Sahara's Atakar Mountains. Even in the mountains, the sun is so hot that people must wear clothes that cover most of their skin. **Critical Thinking** How do the clothes these men are wearing help them adapt to living in the desert?

Arabs in Algeria The Berber way of life changed in the A.D. 600s, when Arabs spread across North Africa. The Arabs conquered North Africa gradually, over hundreds of years. Peace in the region came about when most Berbers accepted the religion of Islam.

Arab traditions are like Berber traditions in many ways. For example, both Muslim Arabs and non-Muslim Berbers traditionally live with extended families. However, Arabs and Berbers do differ.

Muslim Arabs created a central government in Algeria that is based on Islam. The Berber tradition is for each village to govern itself. But Berbers adapted to Arab rule by keeping their own governments along with the new one.

Another difference between the Berbers and the Arabs was that most Arabs were nomads. They usually camped near a well or stream in the summer and herded animals across the desert during the rest of the year. As a result of Arab influence, many Berbers of the hills and plains changed from a farming to a nomadic lifestyle. Sometimes there were conflicts between farmers and nomads. More often, however, they achieved peaceful settlement. Usually, the farmers would let the nomads' herds graze on their land in exchange for livestock and goods. The farmers also sold grains to the nomads. Most Berbers today are farmers, but some Berber nomads still migrate across the Sahara.

An Algerian Market

Traditionally, Algerians bought goods in open-air markets. Shopkeepers in Algeria today still put some of their goods outside their stores, so that Algerians can continue to enjoy shopping in the open air. This shop is in the town of El Dued.

Berbers and Arabs Today

Berbers and Arabs have mixed over the centuries. Today, it is hard to recognize a Berber or an Arab based on language or religion. Berbers and Arabs alike are Muslim. Most Berbers speak Berber and Arabic. Because France ruled Algeria for part of its history, many Berbers and Arabs also speak French.

Most Berbers and many Arabs in Algeria live in rural areas. Some are farmers, while others are nomads. In some rural areas, the Berber way of life has hardly been touched by Arab ways. Berbers in these areas speak Berber languages, and some do not speak Arabic at all. Many have combined Islam with traditional African religions.

READ ACTIVELY

Visualize Visualize yourself walking through a village in rural Algeria. What would you see? What might you see along a city street?

◀▲ Algiers, the capital of Algeria, has a modern section of high-rise buildings, shown at the left. The old section of the city (above) is called the Casbah. What clue shows that the Casbah was not built in the 1900s?

Life in the Cities   Berbers and Arabs who live in Algeria's cities have the most in common with each other. More than half of Algeria's people live in cities, and most speak Arabic. Mosques and open-air marketplaces called *souqs* (sooks) fill the cities. Older parts of the cities are called *casbahs* (KAHZ bahz). The houses and stores here are close to each other on narrow, winding streets. Newer parts of the cities look like cities in Europe and the United States. They have tall buildings and wide streets.

The Berbers and the Arabs of Algeria have had many conflicts in the past. However, there have also been long periods during which they learned from each other peacefully. Algeria's future will continue to mix Berber and Arab, old and new.

SECTION 2 REVIEW

1. **Define** (a) terrace, (b) souq, (c) casbah.

2. **Identify** (a) Sahara, (b) Berber, (c) Arab.

3. How did the Berber way of life change when Arabs came to North Africa?

4. How are Arabs and Berbers similar today?

Critical Thinking

5. **Drawing Conclusions** What differences might have caused conflicts between Berbers and Arabs? How did Berbers and Arabs sometimes overcome their differences?

Activity

6. **Writing to Learn** Suppose that you were a member of a Berber village assembly at the time that the Arabs first came to North Africa. Write a speech in which you discuss the possible impact of this change on your community.

SKILLS ACTIVITY

Using Regional Maps

Have you ever seen anyone try to drive around town with a map of the whole world?

It would never work. A world map is useful for looking at the world as a whole. You can easily see the shapes and locations of the continents and oceans. They do not show you street names, however. Because they cover such a large area, world maps lack the detail to show much about a specific part of the world.

That is why we have regional maps. You already know that a region is an area of the Earth that shares some common characteristics. A regional map is a map of a region. Regional maps are probably the most common type of map. Road maps and bus maps are regional maps. So are the weather maps you see on the news. Throughout your life, you will see regional maps in newspapers and magazines, in textbooks and on television. It pays to know how to use them.

Get Ready

Regional maps focus on one part of the world, showing it in greater detail. Because of this detail, you can learn a lot about the region that is shown on the map. Since regions can be defined by many different characteristics—landforms, economies, political boundaries, and so on—there are many different types of

regional maps. But if you learn how to read one type of regional map, you can use your skills to help you read others.

Try It Out

Follow these steps to read the map in column two on the next page.

A. Identify the region. What region is shown on the map? What defines the region?

B. Use the map key to learn about the region. What basic information is shown on the map? What do the solid lines represent? What do the single dots represent?

C. Use the regional map as a tool. What landforms can be found on either side of the Nile River valley? Where are most cities in the Nile River valley located?

D. Extend your learning. Why might the Nile River be important to people in Egypt? How is the Nile related to the location of Egyptian cities?

Apply the Skill

The map below is a regional map of North Africa. Work independently to apply the four basic regional map reading skills to this map.

1 Identify the region. What region is shown on the map? What defines the region?

2 Use the map key to learn about the region. What basic information is shown on the map? What physical features are identified on this map?

3 Use the regional map as a tool. How many countries are in North Africa? Which countries are they? Do you see any bodies of water in North Africa?

4 Extend your learning. Why would this map be useful in learning about the ways of life of this region? How might it help you understand the history of the region? What do you think might have been very important to people of this region?

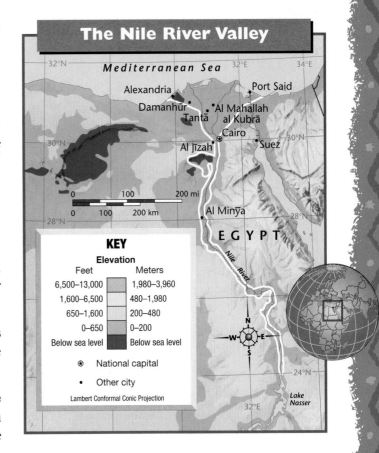

The Nile River Valley

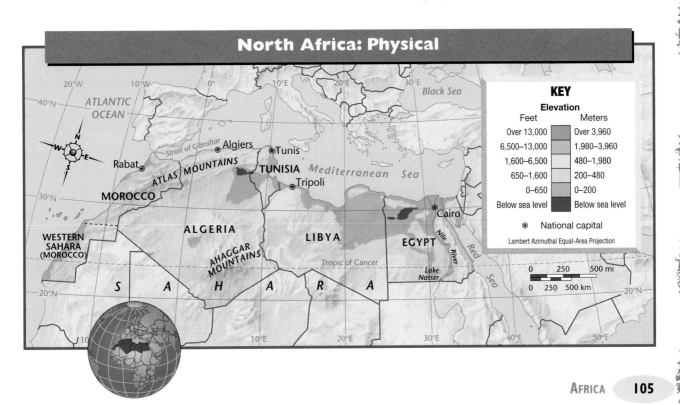

North Africa: Physical

Review and Activities

Reviewing Main Ideas

1. Why do most Muslims study and memorize parts of the Quran?

2. How do Egyptians show their faith in Islam in their daily lives?

3. How does life in Egypt's cities differ from life in Egypt's rural areas?

4. Explain what Berbers and Arabs in Algeria have in common and what sets them apart.

5. How does Algeria's geography affect the people who live there?

6. How do Algeria's cities blend the old and the new?

Reviewing Key Terms

Decide whether each statement is true or false. If it is true, write "true." If it is false, change the underlined term to make the statement true.

1. A traditional Egyptian open-air market is called a <u>casbah</u>.

2. Egypt's rural farmers are called <u>fellaheen</u>.

3. <u>Souqs</u> are platforms cut into the side of a mountain.

4. In Algeria, an open-air market may be called a <u>nomad</u>.

5. The old section of Algiers is called the <u>Sharia</u>.

Critical Thinking

1. **Recognizing Cause and Effect** Why do you think that the Berbers who lived in isolated areas maintained their language and traditions after Arabs came to Algeria?

2. **Drawing Conclusions** How do you think religion affects the way people in Egypt and Algeria feel about their communities?

Graphic Organizer

Copy the web onto a sheet of paper and then complete it. Narrow your focus each time you move to a new level on the web. Fill in the web with as many people and ideas as you can.

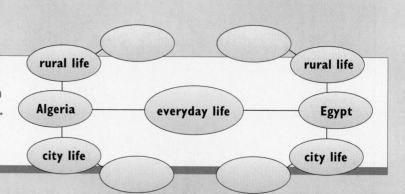

Map Activity

North Africa
For each place listed below, write the letter from the map that shows its location.

1. Cairo

2. Algeria

3. Mediterranean Sea

4. Egypt

5. Sahara

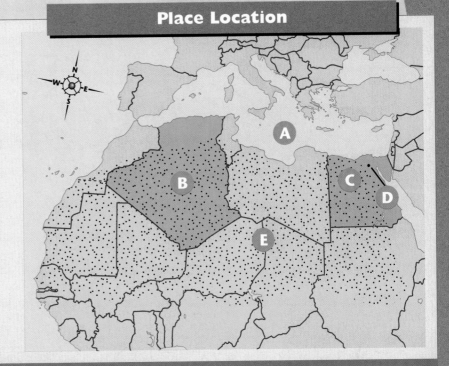

Writing Activity

Writing a Poem
The Berber languages are rarely written down. Most Berber history is preserved by professional poets. Pretend that you are a professional poet living in the 600s, when Arabs first came to North Africa. Write a poem explaining some of the differences and similarities between Arabs and Berbers.

Take It to the NET

Activity Learn more about Algeria and write a report on what you find most interesting. For help in completing this activity, visit **www.phschool.com.**

Chapter 4 Self-Test To review what you have learned, take the Chapter 4 Self-Test and get instant feedback on your answers. Go to **www.phschool.com** to take the test.

Skills Review

Turn to the Skills Activity.

Review the steps for using regional maps. Then answer the following questions: (a) How can you use the map key to help you learn about a region? (b) How can you use a regional map as a tool?

How Am I Doing?

Answer these questions to check your progress.

1. Do I understand how Islam has influenced life in both Egypt and Algeria?

2. Can I identify some historic events that have shaped the modern cultures of North Africa?

3. Do I understand how cultures in North Africa compare to other African cultures I have studied?

4. What information from this chapter can I include in my journal?

CHAPTER 5

Exploring West Africa

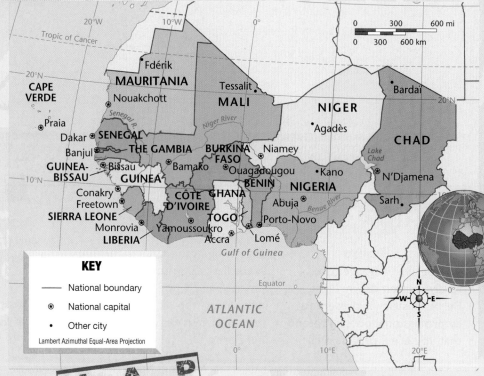

KEY

— National boundary

⊛ National capital

• Other city

Lambert Azimuthal Equal-Area Projection

MAP ACTIVITIES

Seventeen countries make up the region of West Africa. To help you get to know this region, do the following activities.

Consider the location

What ocean do many of West Africa's countries border? What capitals of West African countries are close to rivers and lakes? What cities are far from rivers and lakes?

Think about the cities

Where are many of West Africa's cities? What factors might explain the locations of West African cities?

Consider the climate

Nearness to the Equator is one factor that can influence a country's climate. Where does most of West Africa lie in relation to the Equator and the Tropic of Cancer? Based on West Africa's location, what do you think its climate might be like?

Nigeria

ONE COUNTRY, MANY IDENTITIES

Reach Into Your Background

Think about the ways in which you use language in daily life.

How would you communicate with people who do not speak your language?

Questions to Explore

1. What are Nigeria's main ethnic groups?
2. How are Nigeria's main ethnic groups similar to and different from each other?

Key Terms

multiethnic
census

Key Places

Lagos
Abuja
Kano

The language of England is English. The language of Spain is Spanish. The language of Greece is Greek. But the language of Nigeria is not Nigerian. In fact, there is no such language as Nigerian. Nigerians speak about 400 languages!

The languages of Nigeria match its ethnic groups. Nigeria's three most widely spoken languages are Hausa, Yoruba, and Igbo. There are places called Hausaland, Yorubaland, and Igboland. Most people in Hausaland are Hausa and speak Hausa. Most people in Yorubaland are Yoruba and speak Yoruba. And most people in Igboland are Igbo and speak Igbo. But these places are not countries. In fact, Hausaland and Yorubaland both lie partly in Nigeria and partly in other countries.

Nigeria's History

Why are there so many ethnic groups and languages within one country? Before Europeans arrived, what is now Nigeria was ruled by many ethnic groups, including the Hausa, the Yoruba, and the Igbo. But when Europeans drew Nigeria's borders, they did not think about ethnic groups. Look at the map in the Country Profile. You can see that Nigeria's borders do not match the borders of any one ethnic group.

Nigeria contains so many ethnic groups in part because it is so big. Nigeria is about as big as the states of California, Arizona, and New Mexico combined. More people live in Nigeria than in any other country in Africa. Its population is nearly twice that of Ethiopia, the second most populous country in Africa. And Nigeria is **multiethnic,** which means that many ethnic groups live within its borders.

Nigeria: Population and Ethnic Groups

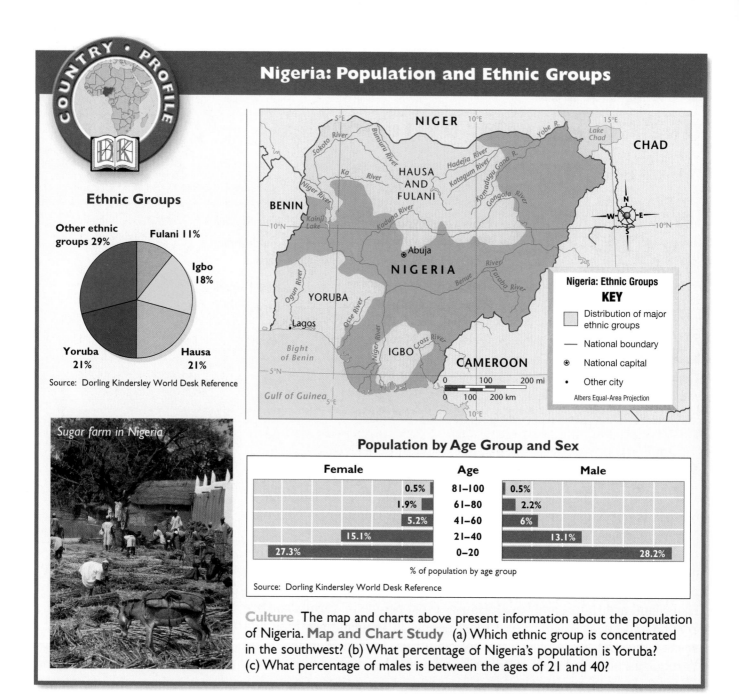

Ethnic Groups

Other ethnic groups 29%
Fulani 11%
Igbo 18%
Yoruba 21%
Hausa 21%

Source: Dorling Kindersley World Desk Reference

Sugar farm in Nigeria

Nigeria: Ethnic Groups
KEY
- Distribution of major ethnic groups
- National boundary
- ⊛ National capital
- • Other city

Albers Equal-Area Projection

Population by Age Group and Sex

Female	Age	Male
0.5%	81–100	0.5%
1.9%	61–80	2.2%
5.2%	41–60	6%
15.1%	21–40	13.1%
27.3%	0–20	28.2%

% of population by age group

Source: Dorling Kindersley World Desk Reference

Culture The map and charts above present information about the population of Nigeria. **Map and Chart Study** (a) Which ethnic group is concentrated in the southwest? (b) What percentage of Nigeria's population is Yoruba? (c) What percentage of males is between the ages of 21 and 40?

Take It to the NET
Data Update For the most recent data on Nigeria, visit www.phschool.com.

The Colonial Legacy The Hausa, the Fulani (FOO lah nee), the Yoruba, and the Igbo were each governing their own regions when Europeans arrived. In the late 1400s, Portugal began to buy slaves in West Africa. Later, Great Britain, the Netherlands, and other countries entered the slave trade.

By 1914, Great Britain had taken over the government of Nigeria. The borders of the British colony of Nigeria included part of Hausaland, part of Yorubaland, and Igboland.

Nigeria became independent in 1960. Ethnic groups that had always lived separately then worked together to create one nation. To help unify the country, in 1991 the government moved the nation's capital from Lagos, in the south, to Abuja (ah BOO jah). The new capital is located in the central portion of the country, where several ethnic groups live.

Unifying the large number of ethnic groups in Nigeria was not easy. Only a few years after the country became independent, fighting broke out among some groups. A military group took control of the government in 1967. This began a long period in which various military groups ruled. Many of Nigeria's people struggled to create a democratic government free of military rule. Finally, on May 29, 1999, military leaders gave up their power to a new democracy controlled by the people.

Three Different Ways of Life

Making Abuja the capital helped bring Nigeria together, because it meant that the capital would be close to more than one ethnic group. The Hausa, the Fulani, the Igbo, and the Yoruba each live in different regions. Most Hausa and Fulani live in the north. The Igbo live mainly in the southeast, and the Yoruba in the southwest. Many smaller ethnic groups live in central Nigeria and throughout the country.

The Hausa and Fulani: Traders of the North Both the Hausa and the Fulani built city-states in northern Nigeria. The Fulani conquered Hausaland in the early 1800s. Many Hausa and Fulani have intermarried since that time. The Hausa and the Fulani make up about 32 percent of Nigeria's people. Together, they are called the Hausa-Fulani. Most Hausa and Fulani are Muslims.

LINKS TO LANGUAGE ARTS

Pidgin How do people talk to each other when they speak different languages? One way is to create a language that includes a little of each language. This kind of language is called pidgin. Nigerian pidgin mixes English words with the grammar of Nigerian languages. Enslaved Africans and their captors may have been the first people in Africa to use pidgin.

Central Mosque in Kano, Nigeria

The Central Mosque in the city of Kano attracts many visitors. This is particularly true on Fridays, when people gather there for services led by a prayer leader called an imam (ih MAHM).

Calabash Carver in Kurmi Market

A carver decorates a calabash, or empty gourd, at his stall in Kano's Kurmi Market. A plain calabash makes a light and inexpensive bowl. A highly decorated calabash may, in time, become very valuable. At the Kurmi Market, you can buy crafts from not only Nigeria, but also many other African countries.

For hundreds of years, the Hausa-Fulani have made an important part of their living by trading. Hausa-Fulani traders dealt in goods from as far away as Spain, Italy, and Egypt. The Hausa-Fulani built cities at the crossroads of trade routes. Each of these cities had its own ruler, was enclosed by walls, and had a central market. Kano, the oldest city in West Africa, is a Hausa city. Kano has been a center of trade for over 1,000 years. The Kurmi Market in Kano is one of the largest trading centers in Africa. People from around the world visit its thousands of stalls. These stalls sell everything from fabrics and dyes to electric appliances.

READ ACTIVELY

Ask Questions What would you like to know about the differences among the Hausa-Fulani, the Yoruba, and the Igbo?

The Yoruba: Farmers Near the Coast The Yoruba are Nigeria's second largest ethnic group. About 20 percent of Nigeria's people are Yoruba. By about A.D. 1100, the Yoruba had built several city-states. Many Yoruba still live in the city-state they built more than 500 years ago, Lagos. In the 1800s, Lagos was a center for the European slave trade. Many Yoruba were sold into slavery and sent to the Americas. But today, Lagos is a more peaceful center of trade. Its streets are lined with hundreds of small shops that sell many kinds of goods.

Most Yoruba are farmers. They live with their families in large compounds. Each compound has several houses grouped around a big yard. A Yoruba community is made up of many such compounds.

The Igbo: A Tradition of Democracy The Igbo have traditionally lived as rural farmers in the southeast. They have not built any large cities like Kano or Lagos. Instead, they live in farming villages. The people in each village work closely together. Unlike the Hausa-Fulani and the Yoruba, the Igbo rule themselves with a democratic council of elders. Instead of one or two leaders making decisions for an entire village, members of the council work together to solve problems.

The southeast was the first area of Nigeria to be affected by the arrival of Europeans. During colonial times, the Igbo were often educated by Christian missionaries. Many people in the south converted, or changed their religion, to Christianity. During British rule, some Igbo attended European or American universities and became teachers, doctors, and lawyers. Today, many Igbo have left rural villages and work in Nigeria's towns and cities.

Tensions sometimes arise between the Igbo and the other two major groups. In 1967, the Igbo tried to leave Nigeria to start their own country. For two and a half years the country was torn by war. In the end, Nigeria stayed united, and people tried to put the war behind them.

Counting Heads   It is hard to know exactly how many people belong to each ethnic group. Nigeria has tried to count its people. A count of all the people in a country is called a **census.** In Nigeria,

▼▲ Cities like Lagos (below) are not new to Nigeria. The skyscraper below is very modern, but the Yoruba built Lagos in the 1400s. The Yoruba traditionally trade in cities and farm (above) in rural areas.

▶ Kano's airport was closed for three days during Nigeria's 1991 census. No one could fly in or out of the country.

whenever a census is taken, it causes debate. This is because the largest ethnic group will have the most power in Nigeria's government.

In 1991, Nigeria conducted an unusual census. On November 26, the country was cut off from the outside world. No one could enter or leave the country for three days. And no one in Nigeria was allowed to move from one place to another between 7 A.M. and 7 P.M. Hundreds of thousands of census takers went from house to house, making a count of the people. The census showed that over 88 million people live in Nigeria, and that the Hausa-Fulani are the country's largest ethnic group. This gives them more political power than other groups.

Over the years, many Nigerians have challenged the census results. In 1963 and 1973, for example, some ethnic groups charged that other ethnic groups had reported too large a number of people. Nigerians hope that by taking accurate censuses, they will be able to hold the many ethnic groups together.

SECTION 1 REVIEW

1. **Define** (a) multiethnic, (b) census.
2. **Identify** (a) Lagos, (b) Abuja, (c) Kano.

3. What are the three largest ethnic groups in Nigeria, and where does each group live?
4. Why might taking a census create tension in Nigeria?

Critical Thinking
5. **Cause and Effect** How did the arrival of Europeans in Nigeria affect the ethnic groups that live in the region?

Activity
6. **Writing to Learn** Currently, Nigeria does not have one national language. Based on what you have learned about this country, do you think a national language might be useful? Why or why not? Write a paragraph explaining your opinion.

Ghana
FIRST IN INDEPENDENCE

Reach Into Your Background

Think about a turning point in your own life, such as moving to a new community or begin-

ning a new school. What was different after that turning point? What remained the same?

Questions to Explore

1. What changes did Kwame Nkrumah bring to Ghana?
2. How has life in Ghana changed since independence?

Key Terms
sovereignty
coup

Key People
Kwame Nkrumah
Jerry Rawlings

In 1935, Kwame Nkrumah, a 26-year-old student, sailed from Ghana to the United States. At that time, Ghana was called the Gold Coast. It had been ruled by Great Britain for over 60 years. Nkrumah's visit to the United States was a turning point in his life. He was well aware that the people of his country did not have true freedom or equality. When Nkrumah saw the Statue of Liberty for the first time, it made him determined to bring freedom not only to his country, but to the whole continent. As he looked at the statue, he thought, "I shall never rest until I have carried your message to Africa."

Moving Toward Independence

In 1947, Nkrumah returned to the Gold Coast. The Gold Coast was named for its gold, which is one of the country's most important natural resources. The Country Profile on the next page shows the country's other important resources. But while the Gold Coast had many resources, most of its people were poor. Nkrumah believed that the people should benefit from the wealth of their own country. He began traveling all over the country. He convinced the people to demand independence from Great Britain.

▼ Kwame Nkrumah, the first leader of independent Ghana, showed his respect for African traditions by wearing traditional clothing.

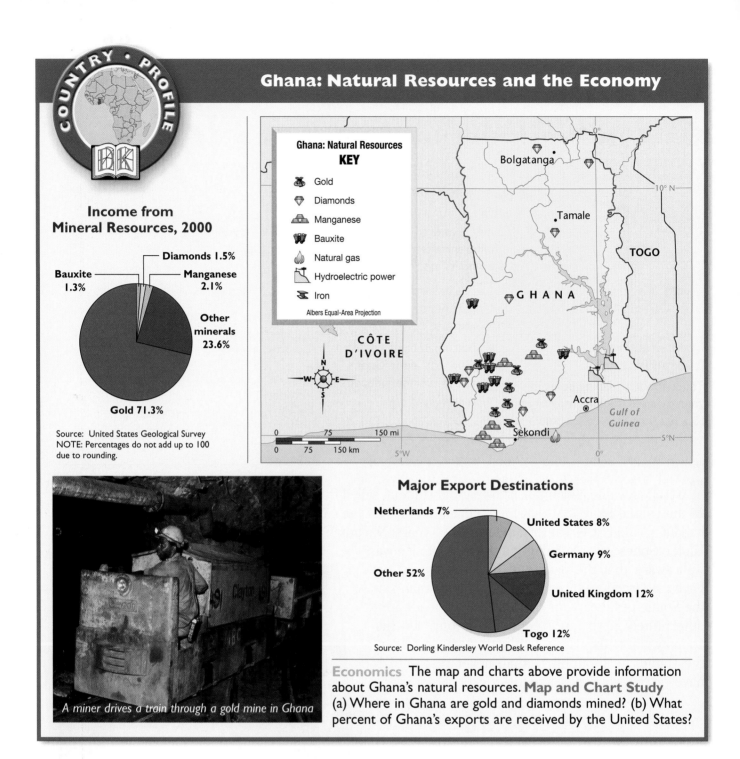

Income from Mineral Resources, 2000

Diamonds 1.5%
Bauxite 1.3%
Manganese 2.1%
Other minerals 23.6%
Gold 71.3%

Source: United States Geological Survey
NOTE: Percentages do not add up to 100 due to rounding.

Ghana: Natural Resources
KEY

- Gold
- Diamonds
- Manganese
- Bauxite
- Natural gas
- Hydroelectric power
- Iron

Albers Equal-Area Projection

Bolgatanga
Tamale
TOGO
GHANA
CÔTE D'IVOIRE
Accra
Gulf of Guinea
Sekondi

0   75   150 mi
0   75   150 km

Major Export Destinations

Netherlands 7%
United States 8%
Germany 9%
United Kingdom 12%
Togo 12%
Other 52%

Source: Dorling Kindersley World Desk Reference

A miner drives a train through a gold mine in Ghana

Economics The map and charts above provide information about Ghana's natural resources. **Map and Chart Study** (a) Where in Ghana are gold and diamonds mined? (b) What percent of Ghana's exports are received by the United States?

Take It to the NET
Data Update For the most recent data on Ghana, visit www.phschool.com.

Traditional Government in Ghana During the 1900s, Africans who were ruled by European countries pushed to become independent. But the European countries did not want to give up their colonies. Some Europeans claimed that the colonies were not ready to rule themselves. Kwame Nkrumah answered this with a question.

> "Wasn't the African who is now unprepared to govern himself governing himself before the advent [arrival] of Europeans?"

The Akan are the largest ethnic group in Ghana. When the Akan give power to a new leader, they also give a warning:

> "Tell him that
> We do not wish greediness
> We do not wish that he should curse us
> We do not wish that his ears should be hard of hearing
> We do not wish that he should call people fools
> We do not wish that he should act on his own initiative
> We do not wish that it should ever be said 'I have no time.
> I have no time.'
> We do not wish personal abuse
> We do not wish personal violence."

If the leader does not rule fairly, the people can give power to a new ruler. In this way, the Akan are democratic. The people have control over who rules them.

While the Europeans were trading in gold and slaves on the coast, some Akan groups formed the Asante kingdom. This kingdom became very rich from trade. It controlled parts of the northern savanna and the coastal south. The Asante used all their power to try to stop the Europeans from taking over West Africa.

The Influence of Colonialism   In 1874, Great Britain made the Gold Coast a colony. But it let the leaders of various ethnic groups continue to rule their people. Even today, there are at least 75 ethnic groups in Ghana, and their leaders are powerful people.

To Be a Leader The Asante did not submit to colonial rule without a fight. In 1900, Asante Queen Yaa Asantewa led a war against the British. Although the British were armed with modern rifles and machine guns, it took them more than three months to defeat the queen and her troops. Because of Yaa Asantewa's rebellion, the British began to treat the Asante more respectfully. In her memory, Asante children still sing a song about "Yaa Asantewa, the warrior woman who carries a gun and a sword of state into battle."

All That Glitters Is Gold

The leader of the Asante is called Asantehente. His power is symbolized by the Golden Stool, which sits in a place of honor on a chair beside him. If a leader does something wrong, the people may take the stool away. The Golden Stool is made of wood and decorated with real gold. **Critical Thinking** What does this picture tell you about the economic status of the Asante?

Since colonization, many Ghanaian women purchase machine-made cotton fabrics, instead of traditional kente cloth, for everyday dresses and head scarves.

The British were most interested in controlling the economy of the Gold Coast. They encouraged farmers to grow cocoa. Then, the British sent the cocoa to factories in Britain, where it was made into chocolate. The British also exported timber and gold. As these raw materials left the country, goods from other countries were shipped in. This led to a problem that was typical of much of colonial Africa. People grew fewer food crops because growing cash crops like cocoa brought in more money. Food, therefore, had to be imported. People also spent more time on farming and less on traditional crafts. The British sold food and factory-made goods to the people of the Gold Coast. Soon, they began to depend on these imports.

The British also built schools in the Gold Coast. Foreign missionaries ran the schools. Christianity began to replace traditional religions. By the time Ghana became independent in 1957, many new ideas and lifestyles had come to traditional communities. Many people blended the new ways and the old African ways. Kwame Nkrumah, for example, was a Christian. But he also believed in parts of the traditional African religion. Nkrumah's respect for old and new ways helped him govern when Ghana became independent.

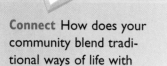

READ ACTIVELY

Connect How does your community blend traditional ways of life with modern ways?

Independence

In 1957, some 22 years after making his pledge to the Statue of Liberty, Nkrumah gave a moving speech to his people. Great Britain, he said, had finally agreed to grant them **sovereignty** (SAHV run tee), or political independence. Cheering, the people carried Nkrumah through the streets. Crowds sang victory songs to celebrate a dream come true.

Nkrumah became the leader of the new country. Later, he became the president. The government changed the country's name from the Gold Coast to Ghana, after an African kingdom that had ruled the region hundreds of years ago. Ghana was the first African colony south of the Sahara to become independent.

Since independence, Ghana has worked to balance new technology with traditional culture. Modern health care, electricity, transportation, and education are things that most Ghanaians want. Sometimes, however, these changes happened too quickly.

Nkrumah's Government Is Overthrown Nine years after being carried through the streets as a hero, Nkrumah was thrown out of office by a military **coup** (koo), or takeover. Army officers led the coup. Most Ghanaian citizens did not protest. In fact, many celebrated. People pulled down statues of Nkrumah.

How did this hero become an enemy? Nkrumah had big plans for Ghana. He borrowed huge amounts of money to make those plans happen fast. He spent millions of dollars to build a conference center. He spent millions more to build a super-highway. In addition, he made a deal with an American company to build a dam on the Volta River. The dam was to provide electricity and irrigation for people in rural areas. But when world prices for cocoa, Ghana's chief export, fell, Ghana could not pay back its loans. Many people blamed Nkrumah for the country's economic problems.

Nkrumah's downfall did not end Ghana's problems. The country alternated between military and democratically elected governments. Few were successful. In the meantime, people began to think better of Nkrumah. Many felt that he had done his best to help the country. When he died in 1972, he was hailed as a national hero. Leaders around the world mourned his death.

Ghana's Economy and Culture Today In the 1980s, Ghana's president, Jerry Rawlings, tried to reform Ghana's politics and economy. Rawlings stressed the traditional African values of hard work and sacrifice. Ghanaians supported Rawlings, and as a result, Ghana's economy began to grow.

Ghana is still dependent on the sale of cocoa. Even so, the economy has grown so much that Ghana has been able to build better roads and irrigation systems. The government under new president John Kufuor, elected in 2000, plans to improve education and health care. People have formed groups so they can voice concerns about issues that affect their lives.

Ghana's culture, as well as its economy, has benefited from Rawlings's renewal of

Nkrumah Toppled

Pulled down by angry citizens, the headless statue of Kwame Nkrumah lies on the grounds of the central police station in Accra. Nkrumah was out of the country when he was overthrown, in February 1966. He never returned to Ghana, but lived in exile in the nearby country of Guinea.

Talking Drums The talking drums of West Africa are used to send messages. The "language" of the talking drums is characterized by high and low tones. A drummer can relay a message to another drummer up to 20 miles away! In West Africa, news reports on the radio are often preceded by the drum beats that mean news is coming.

traditional values. Ghana now has special centers that have been set up to keep the country's traditional culture alive. People who visit Ghana may bring new ideas, but they also learn from Ghana's rich traditional culture. Art from Ghana is valued around the world. Ghana's culture can also be seen in daily life. Most people in Ghana live in small villages. Traditional dancing can be found even in the most modern dance clubs. In all forms, traditional Ghanaian culture exists alongside new ideas.

▼ Ghanaian crafts are popular all over the world. Below right are stamped *adinkra* cloth and woven *kente* cloth. Below left are hand-crafted beeswax candles.

SECTION 2 REVIEW

1. Define (a) sovereignty, (b) coup.

2. Identify (a) Kwame Nkrumah, (b) Jerry Rawlings.

3. How did colonization affect Ghana's economy?

4. Why did Kwame Nkrumah believe that Ghana should be independent?

Critical Thinking

5. Recognizing Cause and Effect Kwame Nkrumah went from being a Ghanaian hero to an unpopular figure. What caused this change in people's attitudes?

Activity

6. Writing to Learn Write about one or two changes you would like to see in your country or community. What obstacles might be in the way of this change? How could those obstacles be overcome?

Mali

THE DESERT IS COMING

Reach Into Your Background
Think about how the environment you live in affects your daily life. How does the clothing you wear reflect the climate? Are there sports or other activities that take place in only certain seasons?

Questions to Explore
1. How does the environment in Mali affect the country's economy?
2. How are the challenges faced by Mali typical of the challenges faced by other countries in the Sahel?

Key Terms
desertification
drought
erode

Key Places
Tombouctou
Sahara
Sahel

Outside the Hotel Bouctou in Tombouctou, Mali, sand piles up against buildings. It coats the fur of camels. It gives a yellowish tint to everything in sight. Inside, manager Boubacar Toure (boo buh CAR too RAY) sits in a lobby that is covered with a fine layer of red sand. Only 4 of his hotel's 29 rooms are taken. He is waiting for the river to rise, hoping that it will bring customers.

But each year, the river rises a little later. "Ten years ago the first boat arrived on July 1," says Tombouctou politician Moulaye Haidara (moo LAH ee HY dah rah). "Five years ago it was July 15. Now, we're lucky it's here by early August. In another five years, who knows?"

▼ Tombouctou's narrow streets used to attract crowds of tourists and traders. Now the city is slowly being covered with sand.

Mali's Environment

Tombouctou wasn't always so empty. From the 1300s to the end of the 1500s, Tombouctou was an important trade center. Caravans from North Africa crossed the Sahara to trade goods at Tombouctou. The Sahara covers much of West Africa, and it is getting bigger. The Sahara covers about one third of Mali. Few people live in the Sahara, however. Some Malians live in the savanna, the one area of the country that gets enough rain for farming. Other Malians live in the Sahel, the partly dry lands south of the Sahara. Tombouctou is in the Sahel.

Mali: Vegetation and Climate

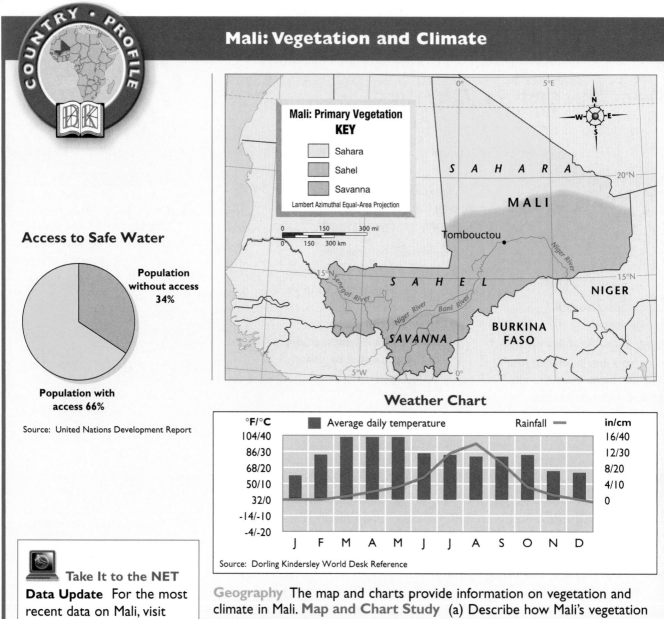

Mali: Primary Vegetation
KEY
- Sahara
- Sahel
- Savanna

Lambert Azimuthal Equal-Area Projection

0   150   300 mi
0   150   300 km

SAHARA

MALI   20°N

Tombouctou

SENEGAL River   15°N   SAHEL   15°N   NIGER

Niger River   Bani River

SAVANNA   BURKINA FASO

Access to Safe Water

Population without access 34%

Population with access 66%

Source: United Nations Development Report

Weather Chart

°F/°C	Average daily temperature	Rainfall —	in/cm
104/40			16/40
86/30			12/30
68/20			8/20
50/10			4/10
32/0			0
-14/-10			
-4/-20	J F M A M J J A S O N D		

Source: Dorling Kindersley World Desk Reference

Take It to the NET
Data Update For the most recent data on Mali, visit **www.phschool.com**.

Geography The map and charts provide information on vegetation and climate in Mali. **Map and Chart Study** (a) Describe how Mali's vegetation changes from north to south. (b) Why do you think such a large percentage of Mali's population is without access to safe water?

Life in the Sahel The Sahel is a zone between the desert and the savanna. Eleven African countries lie partly in the Sahel. The Sahel stretches through the middle of Mali. Look at the map in the Activity Atlas. What other countries are in the Sahel? The large, dry Sahel affects the economy of every country it touches. But people who live in the region have long used the resources of the Sahel to earn their living.

People have lived in the Sahel for thousands of years. For a long time, they did very well and even grew rich. The region's grasslands provide food for animal herds. And the Sahel's location between the Sahara and the savanna is important. People traveling south must pass through the Sahel before reaching the savanna. For this reason, Tombouctou became a wealthy center of learning and business.

Once European ships began trading along Africa's coast, trade through the Sahara decreased. Tombouctou and other trade cities declined. But life in Tombouctou still follows certain traditional patterns. As in past times, caravans still carry huge blocks of salt into Tombouctou. And women still bake bread in outdoor ovens in the traditional way.

The Desert Comes Closer Mali has little industry. Most people make their living by trading, farming, and herding. However, all of these kinds of work are being threatened by **desertification,** the change of fertile land into land that is too dry or damaged to support life. In Mali and other countries of the Sahel, the desert is spreading south. Even the wetter lands in southwest Mali are in danger.

The region facing the greatest threat is the Sahel. The people of the Sahel whose way of life is most affected by desertification may be the Tuareg (TWAR ehg). The Tuareg have lived in the desert and the Sahel for hundreds of years. Wrapped from head to toe in blue cloth, with only their eyes showing, the Tuareg gallop across the land on fast camels. They live a nomadic life, moving their herds of goats, sheep, and camels

Dogon Granary Doors
The Dogon live in a wetter part of Mali. They work as farmers. They use granaries to store grain. These granaries are made of twigs and mud but have very stylized wood doors. The Dogon believe the tree from which the wood came contains a spirit that protects the stored grain. Although the rain and sun often wear down the granaries, the Dogon transfer the symbolic door from one granary to another.

◄ Baking bread outside makes sense when average daily temperatures exceed 90°F (32°C). An oven inside would only heat your house up more.

south in the dry season and north in the wet season. Most Tuareg have never lived permanently in one place. The desertification of countries like Mali and Niger is threatening their way of life.

A Change in Lifestyle Major droughts in the 1970s and 1980s made life very difficult for the Tuareg. A **drought** is a time when there is little or no rain. Facing water and food shortages, some Tuareg settled on farms or in cities. Others built camps outside Tombouctou.

Ibrahim Ag Abdullah and his wife Fatimata are Tuareg. They live in a camp near Tombouctou. In the morning, Ibrahim Abdullah rides his camel into the city. Instead of tending his herds, Ibrahim Abdullah now sells camel rides to tourists. Fatimata Abdullah draws water from a well built by the government and grows vegetables. But the Abdullahs want to return to their nomadic life. "Each time I earn a little money, I buy a goat or a sheep. I save up so I can have enough animals to return to the desert," says Ibrahim Abdullah. But this way of life will only be possible if the Sahel's grasslands are maintained.

▼ This picture shows a Tuareg man dressed in traditional style. The Tuaregs' name for themselves means "free people." Clustered in small groups throughout the southwest Sahara, these nomads resist being controlled by any government. The Tuareg practice their own form of Islam, which keeps many elements of their original religion.

Preserving the Environment

Many people around the world are worried about the Sahel. The United Nations has created a committee to fight desertification. First people must understand why the fertile land changes into unusable desert.

Some environmentalists think that overgrazing can cause desertification. They say that grazing large herds of animals **erodes** the soil, or wears it away. That allows the desert to take over. When there are no roots to hold soil in place, the fierce winds of the Sahel blow it around. Yellow dust clouds fill the air. This loose soil is one reason that Tombouctou is slowly being covered in sand.

Other environmentalists say that grazing does not increase desertification. They think that grazing may actually help grasses grow once the area gets enough rain. These scientists think that long periods of

Desertification and the Economy

This is the West Africa Regional Bank in Bamako, Mali's capital and largest city. Desertification has hurt Mali's economy by making it harder for farmers to grow cash crops. Now Mali's government is trying to encourage people to start their own businesses, as well as encouraging existing businesses to come to Mali.

drought turn land into desert. Over the last 25 years, the Sahel has had much less rain than it did in the 70 years before. If these scientists are right, a few years of good rainfall could stop desertification. The Tuareg would not have to change their way of life.

Currently, Mali's government is studying the problem. Mali is working with the United Nations to educate people in rural areas about better ways to use land. The government is also irrigating and planting in some areas to create a greenbelt. In 2000, it set forth an action plan for tackling desertification.

SECTION 3 REVIEW

1. **Define** (a) desertification, (b) drought, (c) erode.

2. **Identify** (a) Tombouctou, (b) Sahara, (c) Sahel.

3. How does Mali's geography affect how people make a living?

4. How does desertification affect the people who live in the Sahel?

Critical Thinking

5. **Drawing Conclusions** Many Tuareg living around Tombouctou are now depending on the tourist trade for income. Based on what you have learned about Tombouctou, what will be some of the challenges of this new occupation?

Activity

6. **Writing to Learn** Overgrazing may contribute to the desertification of the Sahel. What common North American activities may present a threat to the environment? Do you think those activities should be discouraged? Why or why not?

Using Distribution Maps

Do you think in pictures? Most people do. They try to visualize what they read about. For example, if you read a story about a trip along the Niger River, you may imagine a wide river with dense forest along its banks. You may try to picture, in your own mind, what the writer saw. Thinking in pictures is a natural way to make sense of the world.

Geographers think in pictures, too. For them, of course, the pictures are often maps. There is an old saying: "A picture is worth a thousand words." This is especially true when the picture is a distribution map.

Get Ready

A distribution map is a map that shows how something is distributed. In other words, it shows where something is located. A "population distribution map" shows where people live. It is one of the most common distribution maps. A "resource distribution map" shows where resources are found. You can make a distribution map that shows how nearly anything is distributed. The location of ethnic groups, languages, vegetation, schools—and almost anything else you can think of—can all be indicated on distribution maps.

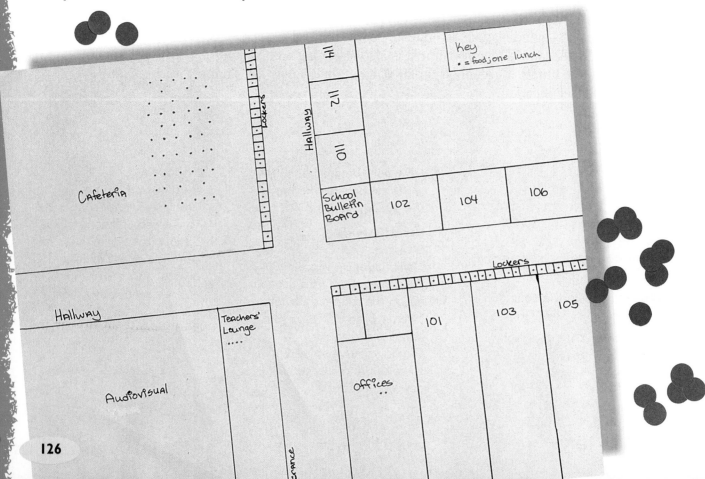

Try It Out

Imagine a map of your school. What would a "food distribution map" of your school look like? Chances are, it would indicate that food is located in the cafeteria, in student lunchboxes, and perhaps in the teacher's lounge.

How would this work exactly? To find out, make that map. Sketch a map, or floor plan, of your school. Make a map key that uses a symbol to indicate "food." One symbol on the map will indicate one food item, two symbols will represent two food items, and so on. Now mark the map with the symbols. When you're done, you'll probably have a map with many symbols in the cafeteria and some others scattered throughout the school.

Every distribution map tells you three basic things:

A. What is distributed Your map shows the distribution of food.

B. Where it is distributed By looking at the symbols, you can see where the food is located.

C. How many are distributed Because each symbol represents a certain number of food items, the map tells you approximately how many food items are located in each room in the school.

Apply the Skill

Now that you see how distribution maps are made and what three things they tell you, you can use what you have learned to read a real distribution map. Use the distribution map on the right to answer the following questions.

① **Determine what is distributed.** What resource does this map show the distribution of?

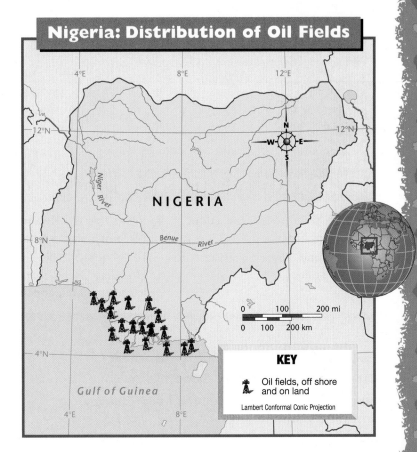

Nigeria: Distribution of Oil Fields

NIGERIA

Niger River

Benue River

Gulf of Guinea

0   100   200 mi
0   100   200 km

KEY

Oil fields, off shore and on land

Lambert Conformal Conic Projection

② **Determine where it is distributed.** How is the distribution indicated on the map? In what part or parts of Nigeria is this resource located?

③ **Determine how many are distributed.** How many symbols are shown on the map?

④ **Organize what you have learned.** Using the map as a guide, write a paragraph that explains the information on the map. After you have completed your paragraph, write another paragraph explaining whether or not you think the map is a more useful way of communicating this information than writing.

⑤ **Make a connection to the real world.** Explain why this map would be useful to each of the following people: the president of an oil company, an officer in the Nigerian armed forces, a member of the Nigerian government, a member of the government of neighboring Cameroon.

Review and Activities

Reviewing Main Ideas

1. Identify the three largest ethnic groups of Nigeria.
2. Explain how Nigeria's census affects politics.
3. What role did Kwame Nkrumah play in Ghana's move to independence?
4. How has Ghana changed since it became independent?
5. How has desertification affected the life of the Tuareg?
6. Describe two possible causes of desertification.

Reviewing Key Terms

Match the definitions in Column I with the key terms in Column II.

Column I
1. to wear away
2. composed of many ethnic groups
3. a group distinguished by race, language, religion, or cultural traditions
4. the change of fertile land into land that is too dry or damaged to support life
5. a long period of little or no rainfall
6. a systematic counting of the population
7. a sudden overthrow of a ruler or government
8. a country's freedom and power to decide on policies and actions

Column II
a. drought
b. erode
c. census
d. ethnic group
e. multiethnic
f. coup
g. desertification
h. sovereignty

Critical Thinking

1. **Making Comparisons** Compare Ghana's geography to that of Mali. How do you think each country's geography has affected its history?
2. **Recognizing Cause and Effect** How did the colonial histories of Nigeria and Ghana affect those countries after independence?

Graphic Organizer

Copy the chart onto a sheet of paper. Fill it in to show how Nigeria's Hausa-Fulani, Yoruba, and Igbo groups are similar and different.

	Hausa-Fulani	Yoruba	Igbo
Region of Nigeria			
Ways of Making a Living			

Map Activity

West Africa

For each place listed below, write the letter from the map that shows its location.

1. Nigeria

2. Ghana

3. Sahara

4. Tombouctou

5. Lagos

6. Abuja

7. Sahel

8. Mali

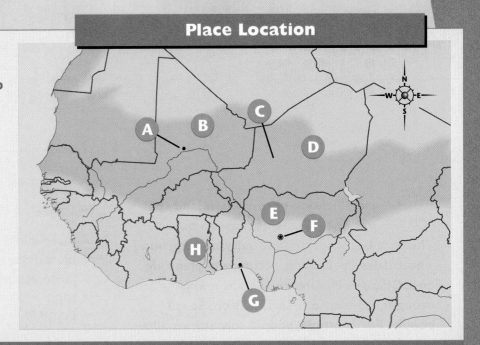

Writing Activity

Writing a News Report

Choose one of the recent events described in this chapter and write a news report about it. Remember to describe these five things for your readers: who, what, where, when, and why.

Take It to the NET

Activity Read about a girl's trip to Ghana, her parents' homeland. According to the author, how is life in Ghana different from life in the United States? For help in completing this activity, visit www.phschool.com.

Chapter 5 Self-Test To review what you have learned, take the Chapter 5 Self-Test and get instant feedback on your answers. Go to www.phschool.com to take the test.

Skills Review

Turn to the Skills Activity.

Review the three basic types of information a distribution map provides. Then answer the following questions: (a) What would a vegetation distribution map of Mali tell you? (b) What would a natural resources distribution map tell you about Ghana?

How Am I Doing?

Answer these questions to check your progress.

1. Can I describe the main geographic features of West Africa?

2. Do I understand how cultures in West Africa compare to other African cultures I've studied?

3. Can I identify some historic events that have shaped the modern cultures of West Africa?

4. What information from this chapter can I include in my journal?

Desertification

D esertification occurs when land that was once fertile becomes a desert. The land becomes dry and salty, underground water dries up, erosion occurs, and plant life dies. Changes in climate, such as a long drought, can cause desertification. So can people. For example, people sometimes allow animals to graze so much that most plants are killed.

Purpose

The Sahara is expanding into the edge of the savanna, or the Sahel. The desertification of the Sahel affects not only the environment, but also the people living there. In this activity, you will explore one cause of desertification.

Materials

- three-sided box
- blow-dryer
- piece of sod as wide as the box
- sand
- goggles

Procedure

STEP ONE

Set up your experiment. Place the box so that the open end is in front of you. Put on your goggles. Lay the sod in the box, with some space between the sod and the back of the box.

Pour the sand in a pile across the open end of the box, directly in front of the sod. Hold the blow-dryer at the open end of the box so that it will blow across the sand toward the sod.

STEP TWO

Create a windstorm over good land. Use the blow-dryer to create "wind." Lift handfuls of sand and let it sift through your fingers in front of the blow-dryer, so that the sand is blown across the grass. This represents the sandy winds that blow across the desert and over grassy lands. Do this for about one minute, holding the blow-dryer no higher than the top of the sod. Note how much sand gets caught in the grass.

STEP THREE

Begin the desertification process. Thin the vegetation by removing about half of the grass in the sod. This is similar to what happens when vegetation is grazed or dies from climate change. Use the blow-dryer and handfuls of sand to create another windstorm, again for one minute. How much sand is in the sod this time? How does the grass look?

STEP FOUR

Continue the desertification process. This time remove almost all of the grass in the sod. This represents more overgrazing and the death of vegetation. Make a final one-minute windstorm. How much sand is in the sod now? How does the sand affect the soil?

Observations

① What happened to the sand as it blew across the grass?

② What happened to the remaining grass and topsoil as the sand blew across the "overgrazed" sod?

③ Imagine you are a cattle herder who needs to feed your cattle. You know that if you let your animals graze, you might contribute to

desertification. But if your animals do not eat, they will die. What would you do? The agricultural officials in your region want to know your decision. Write them a letter explaining your decision.

ANALYSIS AND CONCLUSION

1. Why do you think that it is important to people living in the Sahel to slow desertification?

2. Pretend you are a journalist on a photo shoot. You see a farmer allowing animals to feed in an area where there is little vegetation. You know the farmer has no other place to let the animals graze. You take a photograph. Write an article to accompany your photograph.

The Distant Talking Drum

POEMS FROM NIGERIA
BY ISAAC OLALEYE

BEFORE YOU READ

Reach Into Your Background

Have you lived in your hometown all your life, or have you moved from place to place? How do you think it would feel to live somewhere far from where you grew up?

Writers who have moved far away from their homes often write about the place where they grew up. Many writers feel that writing helps them deal with their feelings of homesickness. Some writers respond to other changes in their lives, or to the loss of a friend or family member, in the same way.

Isaac Olaleye, the author of these poems, grew up in Nigeria and lived there for many years. He moved to England and lived there for several years. Now he lives in the United States.

Questions to Explore

1. What can you learn from these poems about the ways that many Nigerians make a living?
2. What can these poems teach you about some features of Nigerian culture?

READ ACTIVELY

Visualize How can people make light using palm oil?

gourd *n.:* a fruit with a hard skin, such as a melon or a pumpkin

radiant *adj.:* bright

My Village

Èrín is the name
Of my African village.
Laughter is what Èrín means
In the Yoruba language.

In streams,
Women and children
Still collect water in gourds
    and clay pots,
Which they balance on their
    heads.

Electric light has not shone in
    my village.
With ruby-red palm oil
Poured into a clay vessel
We see at night.

My village of Èrín is peaceful,
Like a hidden world.
It's ringed by radiant green
And surrounded by five
    streams.

Like a stream,
The love
For my village
Flows.

Village Weavers

Men and women
Weave cloth
From yarns
Dyed in herbs
In colors of green, blue,
　　black, and red.

Thick and heavy cloth
They weave.
Cloth thick for the sun,
Tough for the field,
And fancy for feasts.

In alleys,
Or under the shadow of
　　trees,
From morning to evening
Their hands and feet
Are busy weaving.

They work happily,
Singing and laughing,
So their mouths
Also keep busy.

READ ACTIVELY

Connect Do you like to keep your mouth busy talking when your hands are busy working? Why or why not?

◀ This Nigerian man is weaving in a workshop.

EXPLORING YOUR READING

Look Back
1. How do the people of the village use the cloth that the weavers weave?

Think It Over
2. Do you think the people in the poems live in rural or urban Nigeria? Why?

3. Why do you think that the author describes Èrín as peaceful?

4. How do you think the people in the village spend most of their time? Why?

Go Beyond
5. No electricity means no televisions, no light bulbs, and no air conditioning. How would your life be different without electricity? How would your life be the same? For example, you would not watch television, but you would still play with your friends. Think of other examples.

Ideas for Writing: Hometown Poem
6. If you were going to write a book of poems about your hometown, what topics would you write about? Make a list. Then choose one topic from your list and write a poem. Use Olaleye's poems as a model.

6

Exploring East Africa

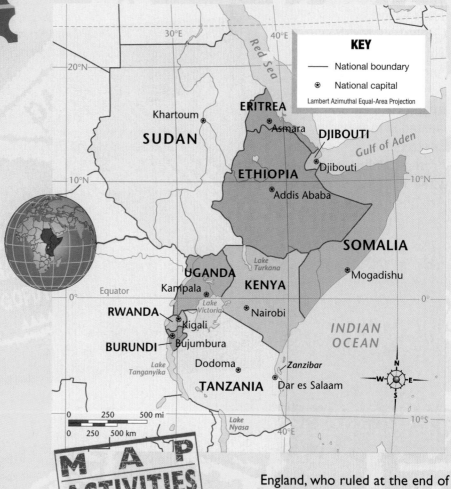

KEY
— National boundary
⊛ National capital
Lambert Azimuthal Equal-Area Projection

MAP ACTIVITIES

The borders of many East African countries were set by the Europeans who started colonies there. Borders often follow rivers and mountains. To get to know this region, do the following activities.

Rename a lake

Find Lake Victoria on the map. It was named after Queen Victoria of England, who ruled at the end of the 1800s. At that time, Tanganyika and Kenya were ruled by Great Britain. (Tanganyika later became part of the country of Tanzania.) Use features on the map to help you rename the lake.

Consider location

The countries of East Africa are located between the Red Sea, the Gulf of Aden, and the Indian Ocean. How do you think East Africa's location might have affected its history and cultures?

Ethiopia
CHURCHES AND MOSQUES

BEFORE YOU READ

Reach Into Your Background

Think about the subjects you study in school. Why is it important for you to be able to read and write? Why is it important for you to learn history and math? What might your life be like if you could not go to school? What kind of jobs could you do if you did not go to school?

Questions to Explore

1. What religions can be found in Ethiopia?

2. Why did Christianity in Ethiopia develop in a unique way?

Key Terms
monastery

Key Places
Lalibela
Addis Ababa

As a young boy, Iyasus Moa (ee YAH soos MOH uh) went to school and learned to read and write. But he dreamed of studying music and painting. He also wanted to learn another language, so Iyasus traveled to Tigray (TEE gray), in northern Ethiopia. He walked a distance that today would take three days to drive. Did he plan to enter a university in Tigray? No. The year was A.D. 1220, and there were no universities in Ethiopia. Iyasus entered a Christian **monastery**. This is a place where priests live, work, and study. A priest who lives in a monastery is called a monk.

Iyasus studied hard for many years. He became a monk. He also became a famous teacher and artist. His students built monasteries and schools all over the country.

Religions of Ethiopia

Iyasus Moa lived in Ethiopia, a country in East Africa. He studied Geez (gee EZ), one of the world's oldest languages. Geez is an ancient form of the language spoken by the Amhara, one of Ethiopia's larger ethnic groups. The Amhara were writing their language by A.D. 400. Ethiopia and

▼ The Debre Bizen monastery sits about 8,000 feet (2,438 m) up in the mountains of Eritrea, which was part of Ethiopia until 1993.

135

Ethiopia: Population and Ethnic Groups

Ethnic Groups

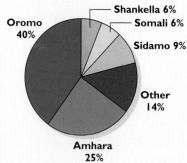

Oromo 40%
Shankella 6%
Somali 6%
Sidamo 9%
Other 14%
Amhara 25%

Source: Dorling Kindersley World Desk Reference

Ethiopia: Population Density
KEY

Persons per sq mi	Persons per sq km
160–685	62–265
78–159	20–61
15–77	6–19
Under 15	Under 6

Cities
- ○ 2,000,000–4,999,999
- ◉ 1,000,000–1,999,999
- ● 250,000–999,999
- ○ Under 250,000

Lambert Conformal Conic Projection

0   200   400 mi
0   200   400 km

SUDAN ERITREA Red Sea YEMEN Gulf of Aden DJIBOUTI
Adwa Mekele Gonder Bahir Dar Dese Dire Dawa Addis Ababa Harer Bedele Nazret Jima
15°N 10°N 5°N
25°E 30°E 35°E 40°E 45°E
UGANDA KENYA SOMALIA INDIAN OCEAN

Population by Age Group and Sex

Female		Age	Male	
	close to 0%	81–100	close to 0%	
	2.4%	61–80	2.3%	
	6.4%	41–60	5.9%	
	11.8%	21–40	11.6%	
29.2%		0–20		30.4%

% of population by age group

Source: Dorling Kindersley World Desk Reference

Take It to the NET
Data Update For the most recent data on Ethiopia, visit **www.phschool.com**.

Culture The map and charts provide information about the people of Ethiopia. **Map and Chart Study** (a) Which regions of Ethiopia are the least populated? (b) What is the largest ethnic group in Ethiopia? (c) Which age group makes up the largest percentage of the male population?

Church History The Egyptian Coptic Church was one of the first to leave the rest of the Christian Church. Later, the Christian Church divided even more. Today, there are many denominations, or types, of Christian churches.

Egypt are the only African countries that have a written history dating back to ancient times. Much of Ethiopia's history was preserved by monks like Iyasus, who copied books by hand.

The religion Iyasus studied was also very old. It had spread to Ethiopia along trade routes. Ethiopia was a center of trade. Look at the physical map of Africa in the Activity Atlas. Find the Nile River and the Red Sea. The main source of the Nile River is in Ethiopia's highlands. Ethiopia used to include the countries that today are Eritrea, Djibouti, and Somalia. These countries border the Red Sea. As people traded goods along the Nile River and the Red Sea, they also learned about each other's religions.

Ethiopian Christianity Alexandria, a city in Egypt, was one of the first centers of Christianity. Over time, Christians in Alexandria came to differ with Christians in Rome and Constantinople. In A.D. 451,

Egyptian Christians separated from the rest of the Christian Church. They formed the Coptic Christian Church. Coptic Christianity slowly spread from Egypt to Ethiopia.

Ethiopian Christians were isolated from Christians in other parts of the world. Ethiopia's mountains made it hard for people in the interior to travel to other areas. Some people traveled along the Nile River and the Red Sea. With the spread of Islam, however, these travel routes were cut off to Ethiopian Christians.

Islam   In the 600s, Arabs began to spread across North Africa. They brought their religion, Islam, with them. Muslim Arabs did not take over Ethiopia, but they moved into the areas around it. Over time, Arab traders built cities along trade routes. Eventually, Muslim Arabs came to control trade in the entire region. And, in time, some Ethiopians adopted the Muslim faith.

Christians and Muslims   As Muslim Arabs took control of Ethiopia's coastal regions, Ethiopian Christians began moving inland. Finally, Christian Ethiopia was surrounded by Muslim-controlled areas. As a result, Christians in Ethiopia had little contact with Christians elsewhere. The Ethiopian Christian Church developed into a unique form of Christianity. The Ethiopian Church still uses its own traditions and literary language, Geez.

Throughout Ethiopia's history, Christians and Muslims have sometimes fought over religious issues. They were at war with each other in the 1500s. But, for the most part, Christians and Muslims have lived together peacefully in Ethiopia. Today, about 35 percent of Ethiopians are Christians, and some 45 percent are Muslims. The rest practice traditional African religions.

READ ACTIVELY

Ask Questions What questions do you have about the spread of Islam to Ethiopia?

▼ Ethiopian Christians and Muslims both have histories that are rich in literature and education. The page at left is from the Quran and the page at right is from a hand-painted Christian document.

EXPLORING TECHNOLOGY

Most churches are built from the bottom up. In the 1100s, however, Ethiopians carved 11 churches from the top down. Workers carved the roof first. They worked their way from the top of the church to the bottom. They always left enough rock in place so that they could stand on it and still reach the area, inside or outside, that they were carving. How might carving a church starting at the top be easier than starting at the bottom? How might it be harder?

Because the churches at Lalibela were underground, Ethiopian Christians were able to hide them from invaders by piling earth on the roofs.

Workers carved the roof, windows, and floors of each church on a slight incline, to allow the heavy summer rains to run off.

Each church is connected to other churches by underground passages carved out of rock.

Workers used hand tools to carve each church out of solid underground rock. Some churches took 150 years to complete.

Contrasting Ways of Life

Most Ethiopians, regardless of their religious background, live in rural areas. What is life like for rural Ethiopians? A look at the town of Lalibela (lah lih BEL uh) provides some clues.

Lalibela Lalibela was the capital of Christian Ethiopia for about 300 years. Rural Ethiopia also has many towns with Muslim shrines and tombs.

Services such as electricity and running water are rare in rural Ethiopia. No one in Lalibela has electricity and there are more donkeys than cars. The people who live around Lalibela make a living by farming. In some areas, people make a living by herding cattle or fishing. Some families specialize in jobs such as woodworking and beekeeping.

Addis Ababa Some 200 miles (322 km) south of Lalibela lies Ethiopia's capital city, Addis Ababa (ad uh SAB uh buh). It has all the conveniences of city life—running water, electricity, and modern hospitals. The city also has a more traditional, rural side. In some areas, houses are made not of concrete and stone, but of wood and dried mud. And some families still wash their clothes in the river, leaving them to dry on the riverbanks.

Addis Ababa's mix of modern and traditional ways of living illustrates the outlook of many Ethiopians. While expressing great pride in their past, they look toward the future with confidence.

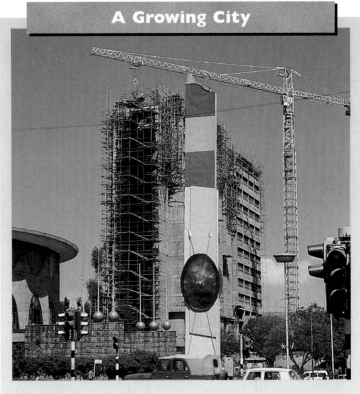

A Growing City

The population of Addis Ababa is growing. New buildings are always being constructed. This one lies near the center of the city.

READ ACTIVELY

Connect How is your community a mix of old and new?

SECTION 1 REVIEW

1. **Define** monastery.
2. **Identify** (a) Lalibela, (b) Addis Ababa.
3. How did Ethiopia's geography affect its role in the ancient world?
4. Why did Christian beliefs in Ethiopia differ from those of Christians in the rest of the world?

Critical Thinking
5. **Making Comparisons** How is life in Ethiopia's rural areas different from life in Addis Ababa? How is life similar in both areas?

Activity
6. **Writing to Learn** Write a paragraph encouraging travelers to visit the historic churches of Ethiopia. In your paragraph, explain how the Ethiopian Christian Church has been affected by the country's history.

Tanzania

WHEN PEOPLE COOPERATE

BEFORE YOU READ

Reach Into Your Background

Think about how you feel when things are about to change. Are you excited or nervous? Are you a little unsure about what the future might hold?

Questions to Explore

1. How is Tanzania's government changing?

2. What challenges have these changes produced?

Key Terms

lingua franca
foreign debt
multiparty system

Key People and Places

Dar es Salaam
Julius Nyerere
Zanzibar

▼ In October 1995, happy citizens rallied in Tanzania's capital, Dar es Salaam, as the country prepared to hold its first multiparty general elections.

In October 1995, the capital of Tanzania, Dar es Salaam, looked ready for a celebration. Flags hung from almost every building. Crowds of people chanted and sang in the streets. Why all this joy? Was it a special holiday? Had a Tanzanian sports team won a championship? Neither. An election was about to start. It would be the first election in over 30 years to include more than one political party. Finally, voters would have a real choice among candidates with differing views.

Tanzanians felt joyful, but they did not know what the future might hold. Their feelings were rooted in Tanzania's history.

Tanzania's History

Look at the map of Tanzania in the Country Profile. You can see that Tanzania lies on the Indian Ocean. Its location has made this area a center for trade. The people on the coast of East Africa traded with the ancient Greeks, Romans, Arabs, and Persians.

In the last 2,000 years, this part of East Africa has been ruled mostly by Arabs, who settled here, and by the Germans and the British, who did not. The British named the area Tanganyika. Tanganyika became independent in 1961. In 1964, it joined with the island of Zanzibar to form the nation of Tanzania.

Tanzania: Population and Ethnic Groups

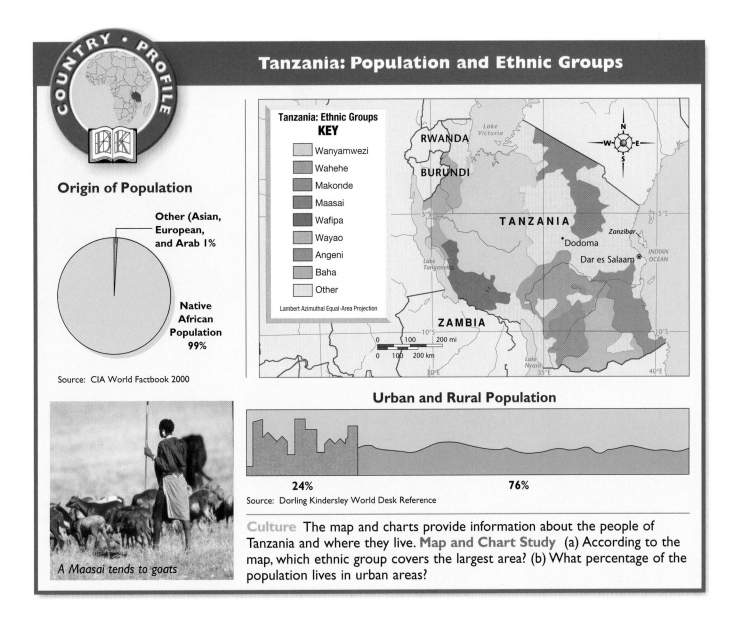

Origin of Population

Other (Asian, European, and Arab 1%)

Native African Population 99%

Source: CIA World Factbook 2000

Tanzania: Ethnic Groups
KEY
- Wanyamwezi
- Wahehe
- Makonde
- Maasai
- Wafipa
- Wayao
- Angeni
- Baha
- Other

Lambert Azimuthal Equal-Area Projection

RWANDA
BURUNDI
Lake Victoria
TANZANIA
Zanzibar
Dodoma
Dar es Salaam
INDIAN OCEAN
Lake Tanganyika
ZAMBIA
Lake Nyasa

0   100   200 mi
0   100   200 km

5°S   15°S   10°S   10°S
30°E   35°E   40°E

A Maasai tends to goats

Urban and Rural Population

24%   76%

Source: Dorling Kindersley World Desk Reference

Culture The map and charts provide information about the people of Tanzania and where they live. **Map and Chart Study** (a) According to the map, which ethnic group covers the largest area? (b) What percentage of the population lives in urban areas?

Nyerere's Changes

When Tanzania became independent, most of its people were poor. Few were literate. Literacy is the ability to read and write. Tanzania's new president was Julius Nyerere. According to Nyerere, the new republic had serious problems:

> We had 12 medical doctors in a population of 9 million. About 45 percent of children of school-going age were going to school, and 85 percent of the population was illiterate.

Nyerere also worried about keeping the peace among Tanzania's 120 ethnic groups. In many African nations, ethnic groups fought each other after independence. Nyerere wanted to make sure that would not happen in Tanzania.

Take It to the NET
Data Update For the most recent data on Tanzania, visit **www.phschool.com**.

Julius Nyerere—Tanzania's First Leader

After Julius Nyerere became Tanzania's first president, he also became famous for living simply. He drove a tiny compact car and would accept only a small salary. After he stepped down as president, he lived in a simple home on his family farm.

To bring about this goal, Nyerere adopted unusual social policies. While some of these policies met with approval both at home and abroad, others were sharply criticized. Even today, debate continues over Nyerere's legacy in Tanzania.

Swahili To help all the ethnic groups feel like part of one country, Nyerere made Swahili the national language. Swahili is an old Bantu language that contains many Arabic words. It is probably Africa's most widely spoken language, with as many as 50 million speakers. In the many countries of East Africa, Swahili is a *lingua franca.* This means that East Africans can use it to talk to each other if they speak different languages at home.

Nyerere's decision to adopt Swahili as Tanzania's national language had an important result. It made it less likely that the government would be controlled by just one ethnic group.

The One-Party System Nyerere also feared that political parties in Tanzania would be based on ethnic groups. Then, to win an election, a candidate from one party might promote hatred toward an ethnic group whose members belonged to another party. This had happened in other newly independent African nations.

To avoid ethnic conflict, Nyerere pushed to have only one political party. Voters still got to choose among several candidates. But all the candidates were members of the same party. Critics complained that having just one party encouraged corruption in government.

Economic Changes   Next, Nyerere turned to the economy. He told Tanzanians that independence meant *uhuru na kazi* (oo HOO roo nah KAH zee)—"freedom and work." This was his way of saying that only hard work could end poverty. Nyerere said that Tanzania should be self-reliant and not depend on other nations.

One part of self-reliance was *ujamaa* (oo JAH mah), which is Swahili for "togetherness" or "being a family." Tanzania's economy is based on farming. Nyerere called for all farmers to live in ujamaa villages, where they could work together and share resources. He knew that it would be easier for the government to provide clean water, education, and other services if people lived in organized villages. At first, some farmers volunteered to move to the ujamaa. Then Nyerere's government began to use force, and sometimes violence, to get others to move.

A Mixed Legacy   Tanzania had experienced great change by the time Nyerere stepped down as president. The country had a national language, and had avoided ethnic conflict. Education and literacy had improved greatly. Nyerere was proud of his success. He commented:

> ❝When I stepped down, 91 percent of the adult population was literate, 100 percent of the children of schoolgoing age were going to school, not just for four years, but for seven years. We did not have enough

An Ujamaa Village

The ujamaa villages were supposed to boost farm production. Communities could then sell their surplus produce. Some people, like the women hoeing corn above, were glad to take part in ujamaa. Many other Tanzanians, however, resisted leaving the small family farms where their ancestors were buried. In the long run, Tanzania ended the ujamaa program.

engineers, but we had thousands of engineers trained by ourselves. We did not have enough doctors, but we had many more than twelve, we had thousands trained by ourselves. That is what we were able to do ourselves in a short period of independence."

However, Tanzania was still one of the poorest countries in the world. The economy had suffered, and the ujamaa program had failed. Many farm families had refused to move to the new villages. Crop production had fallen throughout the nation.

Nyerere retired in 1985 and a new president was elected. Nyerere continued to work with leaders of other nations to study the challenges that face Africa. In 1996, he led an effort to stop a civil war in a nearby country, Burundi. Then Nyerere retired to the village where he had been born. He had never owned a fancy car or had a lot of money. But he had won respect for all the efforts he had made as the founding father of Tanzania. He died in 1999.

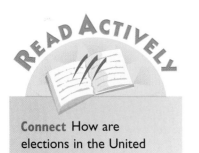

READ ACTIVELY

Connect How are elections in the United States like elections in Tanzania today?

Tanzania Today

After Nyerere left office, Tanzania's new leaders changed some of his unsuccessful programs. To begin with, they ended ujamaa. They also decided that farms should put more effort into producing cash crops to sell. They also asked foreign countries for more help. Tanzania

A Cash Crop That Smells Sweet

Tanzania's island of Zanzibar is the biggest producer of cloves in the world. People use cloves as a spice. A clove tree must grow for five years before it will begin to flower (right). When it does, farmers pick the buds by hand before the flowers open. They dry the cloves in the sun until they turn dark brown (below).

is still very poor. It has a huge foreign debt, or money owed to foreign countries. But the economy is improving.

Tanzania's new leaders also changed the election system. In 1992, the government started to allow new political parties to form. When a country has two or more political parties, it has a multiparty system. The first elections under the multiparty system were held in October 1995. Members of more than 10 parties ran for office. In the end, Nyerere's party won the most votes. But the election raised some issues that divided people. For example, one party suggested that the island of Zanzibar should no longer be part of Tanzania. This is exactly what Nyerere worried about.

As Tanzania's leaders face new challenges, they may keep in mind Nyerere's words: "There is a time for planting and a time for harvesting. I am afraid for us it is still a time for planting."

▲ New farming methods and seeds are helping some Tanzanian farmers to grow more than they could in the past. Changes like these are helping to improve Tanzania's economy.

SECTION 2 REVIEW

1. **Define** (a) lingua franca, (b) foreign debt, (c) multiparty system.

2. **Identify** (a) Dar es Salaam, (b) Julius Nyerere, (c) Zanzibar.

3. What changes did Julius Nyerere bring to Tanzania?

4. What challenges faced Tanzania in the 1990s?

Critical Thinking

5. **Identifying Central Issues** Why did Julius Nyerere want a one-party system? Do you think he was right? Why or why not?

Activity

6. **Writing to Learn** How does Nyerere's slogan, "uhuru na kazi," or freedom and work, apply to the kind of independence that comes from growing up? Write a paragraph explaining how you have experienced uhuru na kazi as you have grown older.

SKILLS ACTIVITY

Using Isolines to Show Elevation

"**W**hat on Earth is this?"

Alicia stared at the map. She could not imagine the purpose of the strange lines she was looking at.

"Those are isolines," her teacher, Ms. Washington, answered. "And they are not really on Earth. They are imaginary lines that people draw on maps. Think about the borders of countries. You can't see borders in the real world—there are no big, painted lines on the ground. Isolines are like that. They exist only on maps, to show information."

"Okay," Alicia said. "What do they show?"

"These isolines show elevation. By understanding isolines, you can make a flat map stand up! Let me show you how to figure them out."

Get Ready

Ms. Washington is right. Isolines do make flat maps stand up, in a way. How? Start with the word *isolines* itself. It comes from the Greek word *iso,* which means "equal," and the English word *lines.* Isolines outline equal parts of a map. When isolines are used to show elevation, they outline different parts of the map at the same elevation. Isolines that show elevation are also called contour lines because their pattern shows the contour, or shape, of the land. If you understand how to read isolines, you can see a two-dimensional map in three dimensions!

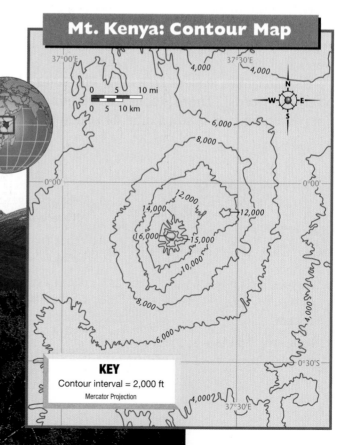

Mt. Kenya: Contour Map

KEY
Contour interval = 2,000 ft
Mercator Projection

Look at the opposite page. The picture on the left shows how a landform looks from the side. To the right, the landform is represented by isolines. Do you see how they match? Where the land is steeper, the isolines are closer together. Where the land is flatter, the isolines are farther apart.

Try It Out

You can learn to read isolines by playing a game. All you need are notecards, pens, and a partner.

A. Deal the cards. Deal six notecards to your partner and six to yourself.

B. Draw landforms. You and your partner should each draw a profile, or sideways view, of an imaginary landform on each of your cards.

C. Draw isolines. Now, on your remaining three cards, you and your partner should each draw isolines that represent different imaginary landforms, one per card. The isolines can be any shape you want.

D. Trade Cards. Work with your partner's cards. Draw a profile of the landform based on your partner's isolines, and isolines based on your partner's landforms. When you have finished, check each other's work.

Apply the Skill

The map on this page shows isolines of Ethiopia. Use the map to complete the steps that follow, and try to visualize the contour of the land of Ethiopia.

1 Remember that isolines connect places of equal elevation. The isolines on this map are labeled to show elevation. What is the lowest elevation in Ethiopia? What is the highest? What is the difference between each pair of isolines?

2 Use the isolines to get an idea of landscape. How would you describe the Ethiopian landscape—hilly, mountainous, flat? Where are the highest parts of the country? Which part of the country is the most rugged?

3 Use isolines to find the elevation near bodies of water. Look at the isolines around Lake Tana and Ethiopia's other bodies of water. Which is on higher land, Lake Tana or the rivers in the southeastern part of Ethiopia?

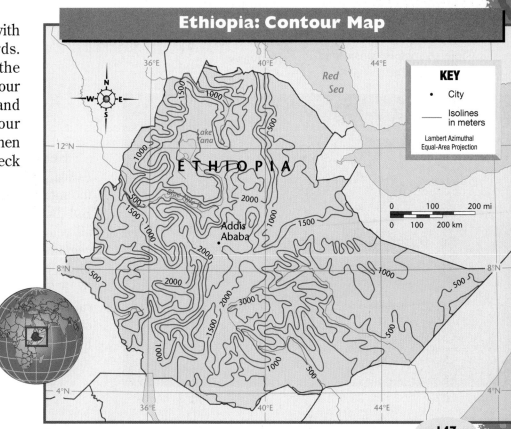

Ethiopia: Contour Map

KEY
- City
— Isolines in meters

Lambert Azimuthal Equal-Area Projection

SECTION 3

Kenya

SKYSCRAPERS IN THE SAVANNA

BEFORE YOU READ

Reach Into Your Background

How do you stay in touch with friends and family members after one of you moves? How do you cope with feeling homesick when you are away from home?

Questions to Explore

1. How do Kenyans who move to Nairobi from rural areas maintain ties to their homes and families?

2. Why do many more Kenyan men than women move from the country to the city?

Key Terms

harambee

Key People and Places

Jomo Kenyatta
Mount Kenya
Nairobi

▼ This series of buildings is called a shamba. It was built by members of Kenya's Kikuyu ethnic group. The whole shamba is considered the family home.

"Where is your shamba?" This is a question that two Kenyans usually ask each other when they first meet. A shamba is a small farm owned and run by a Kenyan family. Even Kenyans who live in the city think of the piece of land where they were born as home. They return to it throughout their lives. Land is very important to Kenyans.

Kenya's Geography and People

Kenya is a country in central East Africa. Mount Kenya, Kenya's highest mountain, lies just south of the Equator. But its twin peaks are covered with snow all year. Southwest of Mount Kenya is a region of highlands. This region has a high elevation. Its average temperature is 67°F (19°C). The area also gets plenty of rain, so the land is good for farming. Most of Kenya's people are farmers, and they live in shambas dotting the countryside in the highlands.

Kenya: People and the Environment

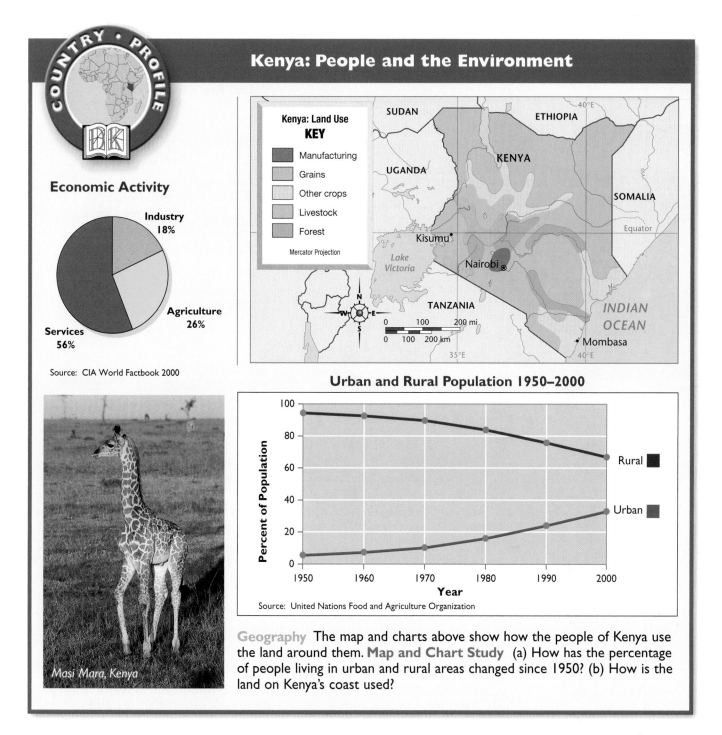

Economic Activity

Industry 18%
Agriculture 26%
Services 56%

Source: CIA World Factbook 2000

Kenya: Land Use KEY

- Manufacturing
- Grains
- Other crops
- Livestock
- Forest

Mercator Projection

Masi Mara, Kenya

Urban and Rural Population 1950–2000

Rural
Urban

Source: United Nations Food and Agriculture Organization

Geography The map and charts above show how the people of Kenya use the land around them. **Map and Chart Study** (a) How has the percentage of people living in urban and rural areas changed since 1950? (b) How is the land on Kenya's coast used?

The land near the coast is warmer than the highlands, but the area also has good farmland. Farther inland, plains stretch across Kenya. Here there is little rainfall. Because of this lack of rain, the plains support only bushes, small trees, and grasses. North of the plains lie deserts, where the temperature can sometimes climb as high as 135°F (57°C).

The Diversity of Kenya's People   Nearly all of Kenya's people are indigenous Africans. A few of Kenya's people are of European or Asian descent. Kenyans belong to more than 40 different ethnic groups. Each group has its own culture and language. Most Kenyans are Christian or Muslim.

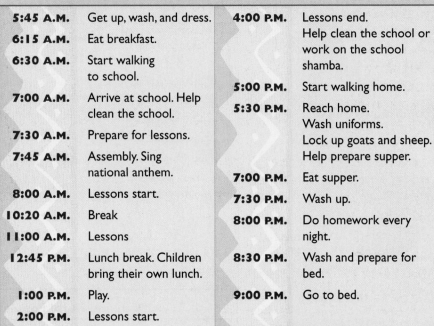

5:45 A.M.	Get up, wash, and dress.		**4:00 P.M.**	Lessons end. Help clean the school or work on the school shamba.
6:15 A.M.	Eat breakfast.			
6:30 A.M.	Start walking to school.		**5:00 P.M.**	Start walking home.
7:00 A.M.	Arrive at school. Help clean the school.		**5:30 P.M.**	Reach home. Wash uniforms. Lock up goats and sheep. Help prepare supper.
7:30 A.M.	Prepare for lessons.			
7:45 A.M.	Assembly. Sing national anthem.			
8:00 A.M.	Lessons start.		**7:00 P.M.**	Eat supper.
10:20 A.M.	Break		**7:30 P.M.**	Wash up.
11:00 A.M.	Lessons		**8:00 P.M.**	Do homework every night.
12:45 P.M.	Lunch break. Children bring their own lunch.		**8:30 P.M.**	Wash and prepare for bed.
1:00 P.M.	Play.		**9:00 P.M.**	Go to bed.
2:00 P.M.	Lessons start.			

Chart Study Like you, Kenyan children spend most of each day in school. **Critical Thinking** Compare your schedule with this one. How would your day be different if you lived in Kenya? How would it be similar?

LINKS
ACROSS THE WORLD

Running from Kenya to Boston Kenyan runners work together to train for athletic events—and it pays off. Kenyan runners won the Boston Marathon 10 times in a row, from 1991 to 2000. In 1995, they placed first, second, and third. One Kenyan, Cosmas Ndeti, won the race three times in a row, from 1993 to 1995. And Kenyan athletes have won numerous Olympic medals. No one is sure why Kenyan runners are so good at their sport, but some people think that training in Kenya's high elevations gives runners more endurance.

Despite the differences among Kenya's people, they have many things in common. As much as they value the land, Kenyans also value their families. Many families have six or more children. People also consider their cousins to be almost like brothers and sisters. An uncle may be called "my other father."

Harambee—Working Together After Kenya gained independence in 1963, the new president, Jomo Kenyatta (JOH moh ken YAH tuh), began a campaign he called *harambee* (hah RAHM bay). The word is Swahili for "let's pull together." One example of harambee is Kenyatta's approach to education. The government pays for some of a child's education, but not all of it. As a result, in many villages, the people have worked together to build and support schools.

Rural Kenya

The people who live in the rural areas of Kenya are farmers. Most of Kenya's farmers, like farmers all over Africa, are women. They grow fruits and vegetables to eat. They also herd livestock. Men also farm, but they usually raise cash crops, such as coffee and tea. Some women also grow cash crops.

Farming in the Highlands The Kikuyu (ki KOO yoo) are Kenya's largest ethnic group. Many Kikuyu live in shambas on the highlands near Mount Kenya. They build round homes with mud walls and thatched roofs. The Kikuyu grow food and cash crops such as coffee and sisal, which is used to make rope.

Children in a farming village have more responsibilities than most children in the United States. They may begin their day by carrying water from a stream to the village. They milk the cattle or goats and clean their homes before going to school. For fun, Kenyan boys play soccer, and the girls play dodgeball. Kenyan children also make toy cars, dolls, and other toys. Occasionally, someone will bring a truck with a generator, a film projector, and a screen to the village, and the people will enjoy a movie. To see what a typical day is like for a Kenyan child, look at the schedule on the previous page.

Moving to the City

The way of life of many Kenyans is changing. As the population increases, many men and some women are moving to the city to find work. Most women and children, however, stay in the rural areas. Women are the primary caretakers for children, and it is expensive for women with children to move from the country to the city. Many find it easier to support their families by farming.

A Nairobi Street Scene

Residents enjoy a stroll in downtown Nairobi, the largest city in East Africa. Nairobi is East Africa's most important business center. Many products are manufactured here. Tourists frequently come to Kenya to visit Nairobi National Park. In addition, much of East African banking and trade is centered in Nairobi. Because Nairobi is a thriving city, many Kenyans come here looking for jobs. **Critical Thinking** What in the picture looks familiar to you? What, if anything, looks unfamiliar?

Ask Questions What more would you like to know about what it's like to live in Nairobi?

Nairobi: Kenya's Capital City   Every day, people arrive in Nairobi (ny ROH bee) by train, bus, or *matatu* (muh TAH too)—a minibus. They are new residents of the city. Nairobi's population grew from one million in 1985 to three million in 1995, making it bigger than the city of Chicago in the United States. Many of Nairobi's newcomers walk to their jobs in the city from the outskirts of town. They may walk as far as 10 miles to work, because they cannot afford the few cents that it costs to take the bus.

When men move to Nairobi without their families, they often feel homesick for their loved ones in rural villages. Meanwhile, the women who are left behind in the villages must do twice as much work. Many people in Kenya have responded to this situation in the spirit of harambee—working together.

Women's Self-Help Groups   One of the best examples of harambee in rural Kenya are women's self-help groups. Women in rural areas all over Kenya have formed these groups to solve problems in their communities. The women grow cash crops in addition to the crops they grow for their families to eat. Then they sell the cash crops and save the money as a group. The women meet to decide what to do with the money they have saved.

Matatu Ride

Ian Kamau
Age 16
Kenya

Look carefully at the painting. Notice that, like the British, Kenyans have their steering wheels on the right side of vehicles. That's because Kenya used to be a colony of Great Britain. **Critical Thinking** This matatu is bound for Nairobi. Do you think the artist considers a visit to Nairobi a happy event? Why or why not?

In Mitero, a village in the mountains north of Nairobi, Kikuyu women's groups have built a nursery school and installed water pipes for the community. They also loan money to women who want to start small businesses. Sometimes they give money to women who need to buy such things as a cow or a water tank. They also save money individually and use it to educate their children.

However, it is not easy to grow cash crops, grow vegetables for the family, chop firewood, haul water, and take care of children all in one day. One woman commented, "My children were educated through the sweat of my brow."

Men in the City   Men who move to the city also work hard. Many are saving money to buy land in the countryside. Men in Nairobi who are from the same ethnic group often welcome each other, share rooms, and help each other.

Moses Mpoke (MOH zuz uhm POHK ay) is a Maasai. The Maasai of Kenya traditionally make a living farming and herding. Mpoke finished high school and now works in Nairobi. He has land in his home village. But the land is too dry for farming, and he could not move his livestock to find good grazing. He left the village to find work.

Now Mpoke is a filing clerk in the city. Mpoke lives outside the city, where he shares a room with two other Maasai. Their friendship makes his life in the city bearable. Like Mpoke, most newcomers to the city are made welcome by relatives or other members of their ethnic group.

Every weekend, Mpoke returns to his village to see his family and friends. Once, as Mpoke sat in his village home, a visitor asked him which was the real Moses Mpoke, the one in the city or the one in the village. He answered:

"This is the real Moses Mpoke, but the other is also me. In the week, I can live in the city and be comfortable. At weekends, I can live here and be comfortable. The city has not stopped me from being a Maasai.**"**

SECTION 3 REVIEW

1. **Define**   harambee.

2. **Identify**   (a) Jomo Kenyatta, (b) Mount Kenya, (c) Nairobi.

3. Describe the daily life of a child in a rural Kenyan village.

4. Why do so many Kenyan men move to Nairobi?

Critical Thinking

5. **Expressing Problems Clearly**   How are women in rural villages affected when men move to the city?

Activity

6. **Writing to Learn**   Describe an example of harambee in your community.

Review and Activities

Reviewing Main Ideas

1. What are the main religions in Ethiopia? How did they get there?

2. Compare life in Ethiopia's cities with life in its rural communities.

3. Did Nyerere's one-party system achieve its goals? Why or why not?

4. Explain the purpose of an ujamaa village.

5. How do men's and women's lives change when men move to Nairobi?

6. How are Kenyans in rural areas working together to improve their lives?

Reviewing Key Terms

Decide whether each statement is true or false. If it is true, write "true." If it is false, change the underlined term to make the statement true.

1. The Swahili word that means "let's pull together" is <u>shamba</u>.

2. Tanzania owes a huge <u>foreign debt</u> to other countries.

3. A building where priests live and work is a <u>multiparty system</u>.

4. People who speak different languages often communicate by speaking a <u>lingua franca</u>.

5. A country with two or more political parties has a <u>harambee</u>.

Critical Thinking

1. **Making Comparisons** What do you think would be the advantages of a one-party political system? What would be the advantages of a multiparty political system?

2. **Recognizing Cause and Effect** How did the spread of Islam cause Ethiopian Christians to become more isolated?

Graphic Organizer

Copy the web onto a sheet of paper. Then complete the web by filling in the empty circles with the ways that President Nyerere planned to help Tanzania to be self-reliant.

Self-reliance in Tanzania

Map Activity

East Africa
For each place listed below, write the letter from the map that shows its location.

1. Ethiopia

2. Nairobi

3. Tanzania

4. Dar es Salaam

5. Zanzibar

6. Kenya

7. Addis Ababa

8. Lalibela

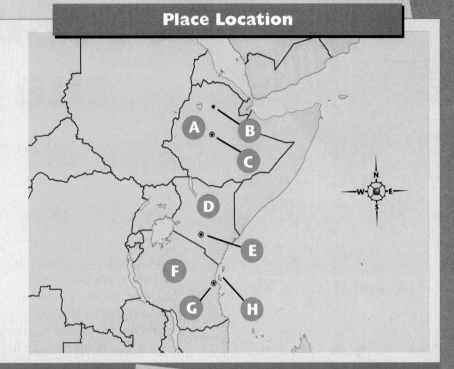

Place Location

Writing Activity

Writing a Newspaper Opinion Article
Think about your community. Is it growing or getting smaller? Hypothesize about why your community has developed in the way that it has. Is it developing in a way that benefits its citizens? What are some good things about the change in growth in your community? What are some bad things? Write a newspaper opinion article explaining your view.

Take It to the NET

Activity Explore Tanzania's culture, history, attractions, and more. Create a travel brochure including interesting facts about Tanzania and the country's most exciting attractions. For help in completing this activity, visit www.phschool.com.

Chapter 6 Self-Test To review what you have learned, take the Chapter 6 Self-Test and get instant feedback on your answers. Go to www.phschool.com to take the test.

Skills Review

Turn to the Skills Activity.
Review the steps for using isolines. Then complete the following: (a) Explain what information you can discover by using the isolines on a map. (b) How are isolines used on water maps?

How Am I Doing?

Answer these questions to check your progress.

1. Can I identify the main religions of Ethiopia?

2. Can I explain some of the ways Tanzania's government has changed in recent years?

3. Do I understand why men in Kenya are moving to the cities? Can I explain how their move affects people throughout the country?

4. What information from this chapter can I include in my journal?

A Promise to the Sun

BY TOLOLWA M. MOLLEL

BEFORE YOU READ

Reach Into Your Background
What does a promise mean to you? Have you ever made a promise that you later discovered you could not keep?

Promises are famous around the world for being easy to make but hard to keep. Making a promise is a serious matter, because a person who accepts a promise trusts that it will be kept. In most cultures, breaking a promise is the same as betraying a person's trust. This Maasai story from East Africa is about just such a broken promise.

Questions to Explore
1. What can you learn from this story about how people in East Africa make a living?
2. What does this story tell you about the values of the Maasai people?

maize *n.:* a type of corn
shrivel *v.:* to wrinkle as moisture is lost
wilt *v.:* to droop
withered *adj.:* shriveled and shrunken from drying out

Long ago, when the world was new, a severe drought hit the land of the birds. The savannah turned brown, and streams dried up. Maize plants died, and banana trees shriveled in the sun, their broad leaves wilting away. Even the nearby forest grew withered and pale.

The birds held a meeting and decided to send someone in search of rain. They drew lots to choose who would go on the journey. And they told the Bat, their distant cousin who was visiting, that she must draw, too. "You might not be a bird," they said, "but for now you're one of us."

Everyone took a lot, and as luck would have it, the task fell to the Bat.

Over the trees and the mountains flew the Bat, to the Moon. There she cried, "Earth has no rain, Earth has no food, Earth asks for rain!"

The Moon smiled. "I can't bring rain. My task is to wash and oil the night's face. But you can try the Stars."

On flew the Bat, until she found the Stars at play. "Away with you!" they snapped, angry at being interrupted. "If you want rain, go to the Clouds!"

The Clouds were asleep but awoke at the sound of the Bat

arriving. "We can bring rain," they yawned, "but the Winds must first blow us together, to hang over the Earth in one big lump."

At the approach of the Bat, the Winds howled to a stop.

"We'll blow the Clouds together," they said, "but not before the Sun has brought up steam to the sky."

As the Bat flew toward the Sun, a sudden scream shook the sky:

"Stop where you are, foolish Bat, before I burn off your little wings!"

The Bat shrank back in terror, and the Sun smothered its fire in rolls of clouds. Quickly the Bat said, "Earth has no rain, Earth has no food, Earth asks for rain!"

"I'll help you," replied the Sun, "in return for a favor. After the rain falls, choose for me the greenest patch on the forest top, and build me a nest there. Then no longer will I have to journey to the horizon at the end of each day but will rest for the night in the cool and quiet of the forest."

The Bat quickly replied, "I'm only a Bat and don't know how to build nests, but the birds will happily make you one. Nothing will be easier—there are so many of them. They will do it right after the harvest, I promise—all in a day!"

And down the sky's sunlit paths the Bat flew, excited to bring the good news to the birds.

The birds readily promised to build the nest.

"The very day after the harvest," said the Sparrow.

"All in a day," said the Owl.

"A beautiful nest it'll be," said the Canary.

"With all the colors of the rainbow," said the Peacock.

So the Sun burnt down upon the earth, steam rose, Winds blew, and Clouds gathered. Then rain fell. The savannah bloomed, and streams flowed. Green and thick and tall, the forest grew until it touched the sky. Crops flourished and ripened—maize, bananas, cassava, millet, and peanuts—and the birds harvested. The morning after the harvest, the Bat reminded the birds about

▲ "After the rain falls, choose for me the greenest patch on the forest top, and build me a nest there," the sun said.

horizon *n.:* the place where the Earth and the sky appear to meet

READ ACTIVELY

Predict Do you think the birds will ever build the nest for the sun?

the nest. Suddenly the birds were in no mood for work. All they cared about was the harvest celebrations, which were to start that night and last several days.

"I have to adorn myself," said the Peacock.

"I have to practice my flute," said the Canary.

"I have to heat up my drums," said the Owl.

"I have to help prepare the feast," said the Sparrow.

"Wait until after the celebrations," they said. "We'll do it then." But their hearts were not in it, and the Bat knew they would never build the nest.

What was she to do? A promise is a promise, she believed, yet she didn't know anything about making a nest. Even if she did, how could she, all on her own, hope to make one big enough for the sun?

The Sun set, and the Moon rose. The celebrations began. The drums throbbed, the flutes wailed, and the dancers pounded the earth with their feet.

Alone with her thoughts and tired, the Bat fell fast asleep.

She awoke in a panic. The Moon had vanished, the Stars faded. Soon the Sun would rise!

Slowly, the Sun peered out over the horizon in search of the nest.

Certain the Sun was looking for her, the Bat scrambled behind a banana leaf. The Sun moved up in the sky. One of its rays glared over the leaf. With a cry of fear, the Bat fled to the forest.

But even there, she was not long at peace. There was a gust of wind, and the forest opened for a moment overhead. The Bat looked up anxiously. Peeking down at her was the Sun.

She let out a shriek and flew away.

As she flew, a cave came into view below. She dived down and quickly darted in.

There, silent and out of reach, she hid from the glare of the Sun.

She hid from the shame of a broken promise, a shame the birds did not feel.

Outside, the celebrations went on. The Owl's drums roared furiously.

throb *v.*: to beat

shriek *v.*: to cry out with a sharp, shrill sound

▼ The Sun inched down toward the horizon.

The Canary's flute pierced the air. And the Sparrow cheered the Peacock's wild dancing.

The Sun inched down toward the horizon. It lingered over the forest and cast one more glance at the treetops, hoping for a miracle. Then, disappointed, it began to set. The birds carried on unconcerned, the sounds of their festivities reaching into the cave.

But the Bat did not stir from her hiding place that night. Nor the next day. For many days and nights she huddled in the cave. Then gradually she got up enough courage to venture out— but never in daylight! Only after sunset with Earth in the embrace of night.

Days and months and years went by, but the birds didn't build the nest. The Sun never gave up wishing, though. Every day as it set, it would linger to cast one last, hopeful glance at the forest top. Then, slowly, very slowly, it would sink away below the horizon.

Year after year the Sun continued to drag up steam, so the Winds would blow, the Clouds gather, and rain fall. It continues to do so today, hoping that the birds will one day keep their promise and build a nest among the treetops.

As for the Bat, . . . she made a home in the cave, and there she lives to this day. Whenever it rains, though, she listens eagerly. From the dark silence of her perch, the sound of the downpour, ripening the crops and renewing the forest, is to her a magical song she wishes she could be out dancing to.

And as she listens, the trees outside sway and bow toward the cave. It is their thank-you salute to the hero who helped turn the forests green and thick and tall as the sky.

READ ACTIVELY

Connect How do you feel if you break a promise?

venture *v.*: to move in the face of danger
embrace *v.*: to hug

EXPLORING YOUR READING

Look Back

1. What favor did the Sun ask of the Bat? Why didn't the Bat keep her promise?

Think It Over

2. What natural events are explained by this story?

3. Based on this story, how dependable do you think the Maasai people consider nature to be?

4. Why do you think that the birds did not feel as ashamed as the Bat?

Go Beyond

5. What lesson does this story teach about how all the different parts of the world relate to each other? What lesson does it teach about how the animals relate to each other?

Ideas for Writing: Short Story

6. Using this story as a model, write a story in which the Bat makes her peace with the Sun.

Exploring Central and Southern Africa

SECTION 1
Democratic Republic of Congo
RICH BUT POOR

SECTION 2
South Africa
THE END OF APARTHEID

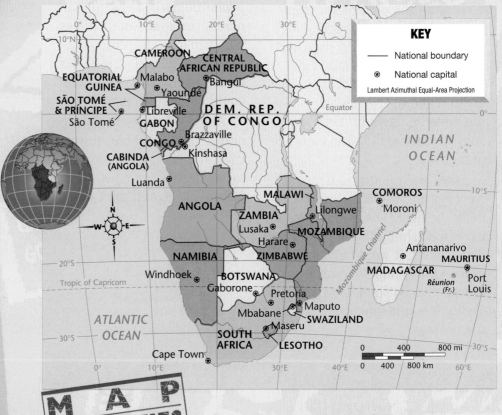

KEY
— National boundary
⊛ National capital
Lambert Azimuthal Equal-Area Projection

MAP ACTIVITIES

This map shows the nations that make up Central and Southern Africa. To help you get to know this region, do the following activities.

Consider the geography

How many countries can you count on this map? Which country is the biggest? The smallest? Which countries are near water? Which countries are landlocked, or surrounded by other countries?

Find the island countries

Look at the west coast of Central Africa. How many countries are completely surrounded by the Atlantic Ocean? Look at the east coast of Central and Southern Africa. How many countries are completely surrounded by the Indian Ocean?

Democratic Republic of Congo

RICH BUT POOR

BEFORE YOU READ

Reach Into Your Background

What resources do you think a country needs to provide a good life for its people? Make a list of these resources. Share your list with the rest of the class.

Questions to Explore

1. Why is mining important to Congo's economy?
2. What economic challenges has Congo faced since independence?

Key Terms
authoritarian
nationalize

Key People and Places
Katanga
King Leopold II
Mobutu Sese Seko

Copper mining in what today is the Democratic Republic of Congo began in ancient times. The demand for copper brought Europeans to the area in the early 1900s. In 1930, a mining company found copper in a place called Kolwezi (kohl WAY zee). The company built a mine and hired miners and a host of other workers. Soon a small city of workers' houses arose. Meanwhile, miners started to tunnel down into the Earth for the copper. They found it, too—right under their houses.

The Kolwezi area proved so rich in copper that, at first, miners found that they barely had to scratch the surface to find the mineral. After a time, however, the miners had to dig deeper. Soon, they had dug a huge pit. Miners are still digging for copper there today. The Kolwezi mine in southern Congo is one of the largest open-pit mines in Africa.

Congo's Physical Geography

Since the 1930s, Congo has become one of the world's main sources of copper. Congo also has supplies of many other resources, including gold, diamonds, copper, forests, water, and wildlife. Look at the map in the Country Profile and identify these resources. Congo's minerals and other resources have played an important role in the nation's history.

▼ In Congo, miners take copper out of the ground in layers, leaving an open pit behind.

Democratic Republic of Congo: Natural Resources

Sources of Electricity

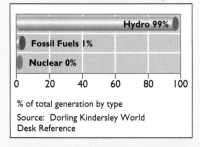

Hydro 99%

Fossil Fuels 1%

Nuclear 0%

0 20 40 60 80 100

% of total generation by type
Source: Dorling Kindersley World Desk Reference

Congo River

Take It to the NET
Data Update For the most recent data on the Democratic Republic of Congo, visit www.phschool.com.

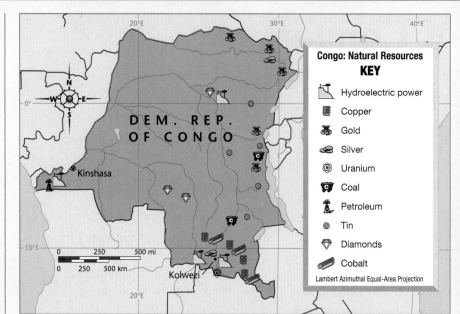

Congo: Natural Resources
KEY
- Hydroelectric power
- Copper
- Gold
- Silver
- Uranium
- Coal
- Petroleum
- Tin
- Diamonds
- Cobalt

Lambert Azimuthal Equal-Area Projection

Income from Mining, 1999

Sources	Millions of Dollars
Diamonds	
Petroleum	
Cobalt	
Copper	

$50 million

Source: United States Geological Survey

Economics The map and charts above show information about the natural resources of the Democratic Republic of Congo and how they help the country's people and economy. **Map and Chart Study** (a) Which resources are found in the southern region of the Democratic Republic of Congo? (b) In total, how much money did the Democratic Republic of Congo get from petroleum in 1999?

Connect How do people make a living on the grasslands of the United States?

Forests and Grasslands The Democratic Republic of Congo is located in west Central Africa. Equal in size to the United States east of the Mississippi River, it is Africa's third largest country. Congo has four major physical regions: The Congo Basin, the Northern Uplands, the Eastern Highlands, and the Southern Uplands.

The Congo Basin is covered by a dense rain forest. People who live in this region mostly farm for a living. Most Congolese live in the country's other regions. The Northern Uplands, along the country's northern border, are covered with savanna, or grasslands. The Eastern Highlands have grasslands and occasional thick forests. The Southern Uplands are high, flat plains of grasslands and wooded areas. In these regions, most people make a living by subsistence farming.

A Mineral-Rich Nation   While about two thirds of Congo's people work as farmers, mining produces most of the country's wealth. Congo has huge copper deposits in the southern province of Katanga (kuh TAHN guh). The country also has reserves of gold and other minerals. Congo produces more diamonds than any other country except Australia. And Congo has enough water power to run many hydroelectric plants. Congo has developed only a small part of its water power, mainly because the potential is so huge.

Natural Resources in Congo's History

Resources dominate the history of the Democratic Republic of Congo. By the 1400s, the kingdoms of Kongo, Luba, and Lunda ruled much of Central Africa. The power of these kingdoms was based on their knowledge of ironworking. The first Europeans who arrived in the area—the Portuguese in the 1480s—were not interested in iron. They came in search of gold.

Some 400 years later, during the scramble for Africa, King Leopold II of Belgium took control of the area, calling it the Congo Free State. Leopold ruled brutally, forcing Africans to harvest wild rubber without paying them. He grew wealthy while Africans suffered, starved, and died, probably by the millions. Later, Belgian government officials ruled less harshly. But they still were interested only in Congo's resources, especially its copper and diamonds.

During the 1950s, calls for independence echoed throughout Africa, including Congo. After a time of unrest, Congo won its independence in 1960.

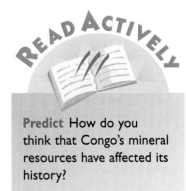

READ ACTIVELY

Predict How do you think that Congo's mineral resources have affected its history?

Agriculture in Eastern Congo

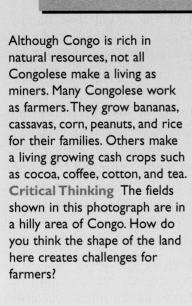

Although Congo is rich in natural resources, not all Congolese make a living as miners. Many Congolese work as farmers. They grow bananas, cassavas, corn, peanuts, and rice for their families. Others make a living growing cash crops such as cocoa, coffee, cotton, and tea. **Critical Thinking** The fields shown in this photograph are in a hilly area of Congo. How do you think the shape of the land here creates challenges for farmers?

Since Independence

LINKS ACROSS THE WORLD

Latin American Economies Like Congo, many Latin American countries used to depend on one resource. These countries have been working to diversify their economies. They are trying to earn more money by growing more types of cash crops. They are also working to build their own industries and mine their own resources without help from foreign countries.

Congo's first years as an independent country were difficult. Various groups fought each other for power. This worried the foreign companies that controlled Congo's mines. The unrest, they feared, might hurt their businesses. In 1965, these foreign companies helped a military leader, Mobutu Sese Seko (muh BOO too SAY say SAY koh), take power. With a strong ruler in control, they thought their businesses would thrive.

Mobutu tried to restore order in the country by setting up an **authoritarian** government. In this form of government, a single leader or small group of leaders has all the power. An authoritarian government is not democratic. Mobutu tried to cut some ties with the colonial past. First he renamed the country Zaire. Then he **nationalized,** or put under government control, industries that had been owned by foreign companies. Mobutu also borrowed money from foreign countries to start projects. Many were promoted by foreigners and were useless.

Mobutu's economic moves failed. Government officials who ran the nationalized companies often made poor managers. Others simply stole their companies' profits. Mobutu and his supporters added to the problem by keeping much of Zaire's wealth for themselves.

Then, in the mid-1970s, the world price of copper fell sharply. Suddenly, Zaire was earning less and less from the sale of its major export. It could not pay back the money it had borrowed, and the country's economy quickly collapsed.

Mobutu responded by cutting government spending. This hit the poor people of Zaire especially hard. Unemployment rose rapidly. When political groups formed to challenge Mobutu's policies, Mobutu cracked down. He threw many of his opponents into prison or had them killed.

Throughout the 1980s, Mobutu continued his harsh rule, and Zaire's economy continued to decline. Calls for reform came from inside and outside Zaire. In the early 1990s, Mobutu's grip on the country weakened. He made desperate promises—promises he wouldn't keep—to stay in power.

At Work in Kinshasa

At a truck assembly plant in Congo's capital city, Kinshasa, an employee works on a computer in an air-conditioned office. **Critical Thinking** What kind of work might he be doing? How does this office resemble one in the United States?

In 1996, a minor uprising began in a region of eastern Zaire some 800 miles from the capital, Kinshasa. A small ethnic group there clashed with Zairian troops. The neighboring countries of Uganda, Rwanda, Burundi, and Angola supported the small group. With their help the uprising turned into a rebellion against the Mobutu government. Zaire's army tried to put down the rebellion. Its soldiers, however, were poorly paid and poorly trained. Many of them surrendered or ran away to avoid fighting.

The rebel army gained popular support as it grew in strength. Within months, the rebels had taken control of much of eastern Zaire. Then they turned their sights on Kinshasa. By May 1997, the rebel army was closing in on the capital city. Alarmed, Mobutu fled the country for Morocco. He died there four months later.

The rebels took charge of the capital. Soon they controlled the whole country, which they renamed the Democratic Republic of Congo. They vowed to establish a new constitution and hold national elections. As months went by without the promised reforms, criticism erupted. Rival political groups demanded progress. By early 1998, popular support for the new government was fading.

In August 1998, another armed rebellion began. Uganda and Rwanda supported the new rebels. They seized land in eastern Congo and threatened to overthrow the government. Several other neighbors of Congo, including Angola, Namibia, and Zimbabwe, backed the government. The civil war continued month after month. Neither side was able to achieve victory.

In April 1999, the United Nations took steps to arrange a cease-fire in Congo. It called on both sides to end the fighting and urged Congo's neighbors to withdraw from the country. Still the war drags on. Meanwhile, the people of Congo continue to suffer. Most of them support neither the rebels nor the government. They simply want peace and a chance to rebuild Congo's shattered economy.

READ ACTIVELY

Predict Once peace returns to Congo, how will the Congolese people restore their country's economy?

SECTION 1 REVIEW

1. **Define** (a) authoritarian, (b) nationalize.

2. **Identify** (a) Katanga, (b) King Leopold II, (c) Mobutu Sese Seko.

3. (a) What are some of Congo's natural resources? (b) What role have they played in Congo's development as a nation?

4. (a) What economic changes did Mobutu Sese Seko make when he took power? (b) How successful were these changes?

Critical Thinking

5. **Drawing Conclusions** Why do you think Congolese people's wages and living conditions have declined since independence?

Activity

6. **Writing to Learn** Write a title and short description for a book about the history of Congo. Design a cover by deciding what images best represent Congo's history.

SKILLS ACTIVITY

Organizing Your Time

"Your reports are due Monday," the teacher said on Friday afternoon. To Claudia the teacher's words sounded more like this: "You will not have any fun this weekend. You will not have time to see your friends or play basketball. And if you're lucky, you will finish your report late Sunday night and come to school tired Monday morning."

"There goes the weekend," she muttered to Timothy, who sat at the next desk.

"Oh, I don't know," he responded. "I just need to fix up my final copy, and I'll be done."

"How come you're so far along?"

"Well, I started two weeks ago, when she assigned the reports." He paused. "You haven't started yet?"

"No," Claudia said. "But I guess I'd better get on it."

Has this ever happened to you? Or are you more like Timothy, who got an early start—and then a better grade and free time over the weekend for his efforts? The key is to organize your time.

Get Ready

Teachers know how long it takes for students to complete assignments. So they make sure to give you a reasonable amount of time. But they expect you to start assignments soon after they make them. This is the first rule of organizing your time—get started early.

But an early start does not guarantee success. You must also organize your time carefully.

Timetable for Report on Apartheid

	Steps	Amount of Time
Step 1		
Step 2		
Step 3		
Step 4		
Step 5		

Try It Out

First, set a goal. Then identify the steps you need to take to reach it. Put these steps in the form of a chart to make a plan.

A. Set your goal. Include it in the title of your chart. Suppose that your goal is to turn in a one-page report by Friday. The title of your chart might be "Timetable for Report on Congo's Natural Resources."

B. Identify the first step you will need to take to reach your goal. What do you need to find out about Congo's natural resources? How can you find the information?

C. Continue toward your goal. Write every single step in your chart. What will you need to do after you find books and magazine articles about your topic? List the steps you need to carry out to end up with your written report.

D. Estimate the time for each step. Look back over the steps you need to take. Think about the time you need to complete each one. Write the amount of time next to each step in the chart.

Apply the Skill

To see how your chart can help you organize your time, complete these steps.

1. **Identify the steps.** Suppose you must write a two-page paper on the history of apartheid in South Africa. Make a chart of the steps you will take to reach this goal.

2. **Use your chart to organize your time.** You have two weeks to complete this assignment. Estimate how long each step will take. A step might take a few minutes, a few hours, or several days. Next to each step, write how long you think it will take. Remember, *the total amount of time for this assignment cannot be more than two weeks.*

3. **Transfer this information to a calendar.** Copy each step in the chart onto the proper days on the calendar. If you follow the calendar, you will reach your goal.

South Africa

THE END OF APARTHEID

BEFORE YOU READ

Reach Into Your Background

Have you ever experienced being left out when you should have been included? Maybe you didn't get to do something you had planned, or you weren't chosen for a team. How did you deal with the experience of being unfairly left out?

Questions to Explore

1. How did the people of South Africa change their government and society?
2. How has life changed for the people of South Africa in the years since the end of apartheid?

Key Terms

apartheid
discriminate
homeland

Key People and Places

F. W. de Klerk
Nelson Mandela
Cape Town

▼ Many black South African children go to schools with real classrooms now, but on nice days they enjoy studying outside.

Nomfundo Mhlana, a young black woman, grew up on a white-owned farm. Both of her parents worked every day of the year, her father in the fields, her mother in the house. As a child, she wasn't allowed inside the white family's house, because she might get it dirty or steal something. The first time she went into the house, she was afraid the whites would chase her out.

Today, Mhlana says, "I do have hope that some whites are changing their minds. The whites on the farm now will come into our house and drink some tea with my mother. They also have a daughter who is nineteen, like me, and we are friends."

Life has changed for other South Africans, too. Just outside Johannesburg (joh HAN is burg) is a rural settlement called Orange Farm. Black South Africans escaping poor rural areas and crowded cities founded Orange Farm in 1989. At first, they lived in tents. Children attended school in what used to be chicken coops and horses' stables. Today, more than 900 Orange Farm children attend school in real buildings.

The changes experienced by Mhlana and other South Africans have been a long time coming. For many years, the Republic of South Africa was a divided country.

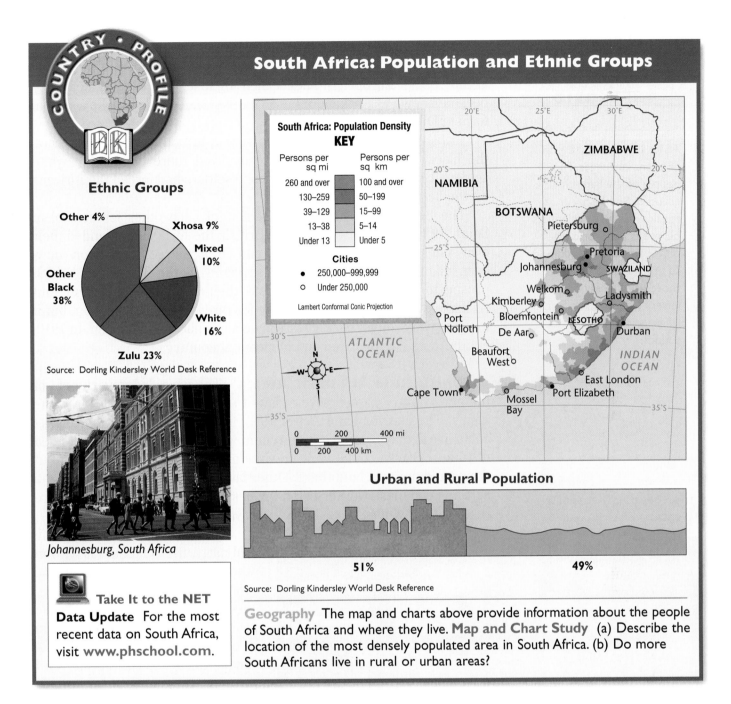

COUNTRY · PROFILE

Ethnic Groups

Other 4%
Xhosa 9%
Mixed 10%
Other Black 38%
White 16%
Zulu 23%

Source: Dorling Kindersley World Desk Reference

Johannesburg, South Africa

Take It to the NET
Data Update For the most recent data on South Africa, visit www.phschool.com.

South Africa: Population Density
KEY

Persons per sq mi	Persons per sq km
260 and over	100 and over
130–259	50–199
39–129	15–99
13–38	5–14
Under 13	Under 5

Cities
● 250,000–999,999
○ Under 250,000

Lambert Conformal Conic Projection

ZIMBABWE
NAMIBIA
BOTSWANA
Pietersburg
Pretoria
Johannesburg
SWAZILAND
Welkom
Kimberley
Ladysmith
Port Nolloth
Bloemfontein
LESOTHO
De Aar
Durban
ATLANTIC OCEAN
Beaufort West
INDIAN OCEAN
Cape Town
Mossel Bay
Port Elizabeth
East London

N
W E
S

0   200   400 mi
0   200   400 km

Urban and Rural Population

51%   49%

Source: Dorling Kindersley World Desk Reference

Geography The map and charts above provide information about the people of South Africa and where they live. **Map and Chart Study** (a) Describe the location of the most densely populated area in South Africa. (b) Do more South Africans live in rural or urban areas?

One Country, Two Worlds

South Africa lies at the southern tip of Africa. Look at the map in the Country Profile. Like the United States, South Africa has seacoasts on two oceans—the Atlantic Ocean and the Indian Ocean. The country of South Africa is larger than the states of Texas and California combined. It is one of the wealthiest African countries. Yet, until recently, white people controlled almost all its riches. Society was divided by law along racial and ethnic lines. How did such a system come to be?

Cultures Clash The ancestors of most of today's black South Africans arrived about 2,000 years ago during the Bantu migrations. White Europeans first arrived in South Africa about 400 years ago. In

READ ACTIVELY

Predict How do you think South Africa came to have laws that divided people by race?

LINKS ACROSS THE WORLD

The San Language South Africa is home to several different languages. The people of the San ethnic group of Southern Africa speak what many scientists believe is the world's oldest language. In addition to using sounds such as those used to say the letters T, S, or B, the San language also uses click sounds.

1652, Dutch settlers set up a colony at Cape Town on the southern tip of the continent. In time, these people began to think of themselves as not being European. They called themselves Boers. Later, they became known as Afrikaners (af rih KAHN erz). And they spoke a special form of Dutch called Afrikaans.

British and French settlers also settled in South Africa. For years, the black South Africans who already lived there battled the white settlers. But by the late 1800s, the white settlers had forced the Africans off the best land.

The British and Afrikaners also fought each other for control of South Africa. To get away from the British, the Afrikaners founded their own states, Transvaal (tranz VAHL) and Orange Free State. Soon, however, diamonds and gold were discovered in the Transvaal. British prospectors pushed Afrikaners off their farms. The British and Afrikaners fought over the territory for three years. Britain won, but it took the two groups several years to decide what would happen. In 1910, South Africa was declared an independent country.

White Rule in South Africa The white-led government of the new country passed several laws to keep land and wealth in white hands. The Natives Land Act of 1913, for example, stated that blacks could live in only 8 percent of the country. The rest of the land belonged to whites. Blacks could work in white areas—for very low wages. But they could not own land there. Other laws passed in the 1920s separated white and black workers. And the best jobs and the highest pay were reserved for whites.

▼ Under apartheid, blacks and whites were even forced to sit separately at sports events.

In 1948, the Afrikaners' political party, the National Party, won the election and took over the country. Afrikaner leaders added new laws to the system of white power. And they gave the system a new name—**apartheid** (uh PAHR tayt), which is an Afrikaans word meaning "separateness." Apartheid laws placed every South African into a category based on race. The laws also made it legal to discriminate on the basis of race. To **discriminate** means to treat people differently, and often unfairly, based on race, religion, or sex.

Apartheid separated South Africans into four groups—blacks, whites, coloreds, and Asians. Blacks included all Africans. Whites included people of European heritage.

Coloreds were people of mixed race. The term Asians usually meant people from India. Coloreds and Asians had a few rights. Blacks had practically no rights at all.

Apartheid forced thousands of South African blacks to move to 10 poor rural areas called **homelands.** These homelands had the driest and least fertile land. There, black South Africans lived in poverty.

Apartheid affected not only where blacks could live but every aspect of their lives. It denied them citizenship rights, including the right to vote. The system kept blacks and coloreds in low-paying jobs. It put them in poor schools. It barred blacks and coloreds from white restaurants, schools, and hospitals. Apartheid also strengthened the pass laws that required all blacks to stay in homelands unless they could prove they were useful to whites and could "pass" into white areas. In short, apartheid kept whites in control of the country.

First Multiracial Elections, 1994

Women in Johannesburg joyously displayed the identification papers that allowed them to vote in the historic election on April 26, 1994. Blacks had to wait in line for as long as eight hours to cast ballots for the first time in their lives. As a 93-year-old woman finally reached the polling booth, she said, "I am happy this day has come. I never thought it could happen here."

The Deadly Struggle Against Apartheid Many South Africans fought apartheid. During the 1950s and 1960s, blacks and some whites took to the streets in peaceful protest against it. The well-armed South African police met them with deadly force. Hundreds of men, women, and children were wounded or killed. Thousands more were thrown in jail. In the 1970s, black students and black workers protested against inequality. The government tried to end these protests with more force. But the demonstrations kept growing, even though thousands of blacks were killed. Many people were willing to risk everything for freedom.

Countries around the world joined the movement against apartheid. Many nations stopped trading with South Africa, or lending it money. Its athletes were banned from the Olympic Games and other international sports events.

In 1990, these struggles began to have an effect. Faced with a weakening economy and continuing protests, South Africa's president, F. W. de Klerk, pushed through laws that tore down apartheid.

CITIZEN HEROES

To Be a Leader The end of apartheid inspired Ivy Nonqayi to make a change. She made $80 a month tending the big house of a white town councilor, Peb Saunders. Nonqayi wanted jobs and housing for blacks, so in 1995 she took a brave step. She ran for her boss's seat—and easily ousted her. Despite her win, Nonqayi stayed on as Saunders' maid.

In April 1994, for the first time, South Africans of all colors peacefully elected a president. They chose Nelson Mandela, a black man who had spent 28 years in prison for fighting apartheid.

New Challenges

Under Nelson Mandela's government, legal discrimination on the basis of race finally ended. Blacks and some whites welcomed the changes. But many whites who had grown up with the privileges of apartheid were not as happy.

Despite new opportunities for millions of blacks, South Africa has remained a divided society. Blacks and whites usually live in different neighborhoods. Whites still control most of the country's biggest businesses and newspapers. Compared to blacks, whites have better-paying jobs and own more property.

Even though they still hold a lot of power, many whites do not like the recent changes in South Africa. Some oppose government plans to help blacks get jobs. One white woman, for example, wondered whether her white skin would be a drawback when she looked for a job. Other whites fear their children's education will suffer in schools attended by all races. Mandela's government had to find ways to reassure whites

Connect What do you think South Africans could learn from people who remember integration in the United States?

Children of the Orlando Children's Home
Ages 8-15
Soweto, South Africa

In 1989, the children of the Orlando Children's Home in Soweto painted this mural on the wall that surrounds their home. Apartheid had not yet ended. **Critical Thinking** This mural shows many ways of flying away from South Africa. However, it also shows people with parachutes jumping out of the airplanes. What feelings about South Africa do you think the children meant to express when they painted this mural?

Flying Away

while making certain that blacks had an equal chance for a good life. To meet its challenges, South Africa's government will need the help of all its citizens, regardless of race.

Building a New Nation

Nearly every day, television, radio, and newspapers report on the changes that have taken place in South Africa. Nomfundo Mhlana has been grateful for the changes. But she sees room for more change. She said, "Now that Mandela is president, I think our society is more equal, but I also think whites still have apartheid in their hearts." All South Africans are struggling to build the new South Africa.

David Bailes, a white South African, left the country in the early 1970s because he hated apartheid. Since then, he has been living in the United States. Today, Bailes is thinking about returning to South Africa to live. After a recent visit to Cape Town, he said:

> ❝There's still a lot of inequality there.... On the surface, things don't appear much different. But you know they are—you can feel it.... South Africa is becoming a brand new country. ❞

Nelson Mandela's government took steps to heal South Africa. It set up a Truth and Reconciliation Commission to examine the crimes of the apartheid era. In 1998, the commission issued its final report. The report condemned acts of murder and torture by both white and black South Africans. The commission also granted amnesty, or forgiveness, to some people who committed crimes. It withheld amnesty from others, which meant they could face trial.

In June 1999, South Africa held its second election open to all races. Mandela's political party stayed in power, and his deputy president replaced him as president. Mandela ended his political career, but his impact on the country continued. Thanks to his leadership, South Africans are working together to build a peaceful and prosperous nation.

▲ In 1993, South Africa's president, F. W. de Klerk, and Nelson Mandela— soon to be elected the first black president of South Africa—share a triumphant moment.

SECTION 2 REVIEW

1. **Define** (a) apartheid, (b) discriminate, (c) homeland.

2. **Identify** (a) F. W. de Klerk, (b) Nelson Mandela, (c) Cape Town.

3. How did apartheid affect South Africans?

4. What changes have taken place in South Africa since the collapse of apartheid?

Critical Thinking

5. **Expressing Problems Clearly** What challenges must the South African government meet in order to build a new nation based on equality for all?

Activity

6. **Writing to Learn** Write a letter to a friend, explaining your view of the changes in South Africa.

Review and Activities

Reviewing Main Ideas

1. (a) Describe Congo's four main geographic regions. (b) Which region brings in the most income?

2. How has mining affected the history of Congo?

3. What actions did Mobutu Sese Seko take after coming to power?

4. (a) How did the system of apartheid affect South Africans in their daily lifes? (b) How did South Africans struggle against apartheid?

5. (a) How is life in today's South Africa different than it was under apartheid? (b) How are people still divided by race?

6. What are some challenges faced by the new government of South Africa?

Reviewing Key Terms

Match the definitions in Column I with the key terms in Column II.

Column I

1. form of government in which a single leader or small group of leaders has all the power

2. a system of laws that legalized racial discrimination

3. rural areas in which black South Africans were forced to live

4. to treat people in a different way based on their race, religion, or sex

5. to put under government control

Column II

a. nationalize

b. authoritarian

c. discrimination

d. apartheid

e. homelands

Critical Thinking

1. **Making Comparisons** How did life in Congo stay the same after the rebels took power from Mobutu?

2. **Drawing Conclusions** South Africa's new government is trying to persuade its skilled white workers to remain in the country. Based on what you know about apartheid, why do you think much of South Africa's population lacks these skills?

Graphic Organizer

Copy the flowchart onto a sheet of paper. Then, fill in the empty boxes to show the impact of resources on Congo's history, from the first contacts with Europeans to the present.

Portuguese arrive looking for gold			

Map Activity

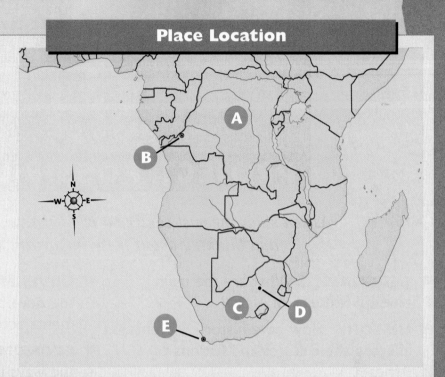

Place Location

Central and Southern Africa
For each place listed below, write the letter from the map that shows its location.

1. Cape Town

2. Johannesburg

3. Kinshasa

4. Democratic Republic of Congo

5. South Africa

Writing Activity

Writing Interview Questions
Choose either South Africa or Congo. Write a list of five interview questions you would ask someone who has been elected president of the country. Consider the challenges the new president faces. Then exchange questions with a partner. Pretend that you are the president. Write answers to your partner's questions.

Take It to the NET

Activity Explore Southern Africa's ancient civilizations and modern-day culture. For help in completing this activity, visit www.phschool.com.

Chapter 7 Self-Test To review what you have learned, take the Chapter 7 Self-Test and get instant feedback on your answers. Go to www.phschool.com to take the test.

Skills Review

Turn to the **Skills Activity.**

Review the steps for organizing your time. Then, in your own words, explain how a flowchart can help you to organize your time.

How Am I Doing?
Answer these questions to check your progress.

1. Can I explain the part that resources have played in Congo's history?

2. Do I understand the problems that have kept modern Congo a poor nation?

3. Can I describe how life has changed for black and white South Africans following the collapse of apartheid?

4. What information from this chapter can I include in my journal?

AFRICA
PROJECT POSSIBILITIES

As you study the vast continent of Africa, you will be reading and thinking about these important questions.

☛ **GEOGRAPHY** What are the main physical features of Africa?

☛ **HISTORY** How have historical events affected the cultures and nations of Africa?

☛ **CULTURE** How have Africa's cultures changed?

☛ **GOVERNMENT** What factors led to the development of different governments across Africa?

☛ **ECONOMICS** What factors influence the ways in which Africans make a living?

Show what you know by doing a project!

GEO CLEO

Project Menu

The chapters in this book have some answers to these questions. Now it's time for you to find your own answers by doing projects on your own or with a group. Here are some ways to make your own discoveries about Africa.

Africa on Stage Write a play about growing up in a country in Africa. Set the scene for your play in one of the African countries you have studied. Choose three or four characters. Next think about plot. What situation, serious or humorous, will the main character face? How will he or she react to the situation? How will the other characters affect the plot?

Write a script for your play that shows the lines each character will speak. Then present your play. Ask classmates to read aloud the parts of your characters. You may wish to videotape your live performance and show it to other classes or your family.

From Questions to Careers

AGRICULTURE

Farmers have always wanted to be able to produce more food. More and more, they face the newer problem of using up too much of the Earth's resources—good soil, land, or grazing material. In some places, people need to farm differently than before because of a changing climate. In Africa and all over the world, people are working on new and different ways of farming that will solve these problems.

Agricultural scientists and farmers work together to develop and try out different farming methods. It may take much time and patience to figure out whether a method works over one or several growing seasons. Engineers invent new machinery, fertilizer, and other products for farmers. Machinists and technicians help manufacture these products. Ecologists study the effects of farming on the surrounding environment.

Agricultural scientists, engineers, and ecologists all go to college. Farmers, technicians, and machinists may go to college or they may have training in specific skills for their jobs. Many farmers learn much of what they know through direct experience.

▲ This modern Nigerian farmer is using equipment suitable for his crops and his land.

Africa in Art The tradition of mask-making has special meaning in some African cultures. Look through books and magazines for information about different mask-making traditions in Africa. Research the kinds of masks people make, the ways of making them, and the meanings that they have. Prepare a mini-museum display with pictures or examples and detailed explanations of the masks and traditions you research.

You may want to try making a mask of your own. Use papier-mâché and your imagination.

Africa 2000 Hold an "All Africa" conference about life in Africa in the twenty-first century. Decide on several major topics for the conference, such as economic growth, agriculture, literature, and arts. Form committees to plan the conference. For example, a speakers' committee can find speakers to discuss the topics. Speakers can be students who have done research on these topics. A scheduling committee can plan the agenda for the conference. A publicity committee can make posters to let other students know about the conference. A food committee can make and serve African foods. A press committee can write news reports. Invite other classes to attend the conference.

Reference

TABLE OF CONTENTS

MAP AND GLOBE Handbook

This Map and Globe Handbook is designed to help you develop some of the skills you need to be a world explorer. These can help you whether you explore from the top of an elephant in India or from a computer at school.

You can use the information in this handbook to improve your map and globe skills. But the best way to sharpen your skills is to practice. The more you practice, the better you'll get.

GEO CLEO and GEO LEO

Table of Contents

Five Themes of Geography

Studying the geography of the entire world can be a huge task. You can make that task easier by using the five themes of geography: location, place, human-environment interaction, movement, and regions. The themes are tools you can use to organize information and to answer the where, why, and how of geography.

1 **Location** answers the question, "Where is it?" You can think of the location of a continent or a country as its address. You might give an absolute location such as "22 South Lake Street" or "40°N and 80°W." You might also use a relative address, telling where one place is by referring to another place. "Between school and the mall" and "eight miles east of Pleasant City" are examples of relative locations.

2 **Place** identifies the natural and human features that make one place different from every other place. You can identify a specific place by its landforms, climate, plants, animals, people, or cultures. You might even think of place as a geographic signature. Use the signature to help you understand the natural and human features that make one place different from every other place.

1. Location
Chicago, Illinois, occupies one location on the Earth. No other place has exactly the same absolute location.

2. Place
Ancient cultures in Egypt built distinctive pyramids. Use the theme of place to help you remember features that exist only in Egypt.

3 **Human-Environment Interaction** focuses on the relationship between people and the environment. As people live in an area, they often begin to make changes to it, usually to make their lives easier. For example, they might build a dam to control flooding during rainy seasons. Also, the environment can affect how people live, work, dress, travel, and communicate.

4 **Movement** answers the question "How do people, goods, and ideas move from place to place?" Remember that, often, what happens in one place can affect what happens in another. Use the theme of movement to help you trace the spread of goods, people, and ideas from one location to the next.

5 **Regions** is the last geographic theme. A region is a group of places that share common features. Geographers divide the world into many types of regions. For example, countries, states, and cities are political regions. The people in these places live under the same type of government. Other features can be used to define regions. Places that have the same climate belong to a particular climate region. Places that share the same culture belong to a cultural region. The same place can be found in more than one region. The state of Hawaii is in the political region of the United States. Because it has a tropical climate, Hawaii is also part of a tropical climate region.

PRACTICE YOUR WORLD EXPLORER SKILLS

1 What is the absolute location of your school? What is one way to describe its relative location?

2 What might be a "geographic signature" of the town or city you live in?

3 Give an example of human-environment interaction where you live.

4 Name at least one thing that comes into your town or city and one that goes out. How is each moved? Where does it come from? Where does it go?

5 What are several regions you think your town or city belongs in?

3. Human-Environment Interaction
Peruvians have changed steep mountain slopes into terraces suitable for farming. Think how this environment looked before people made changes.

4. Movement
Arab traders brought not only goods to Kuala Lumpur, Malaysia, but also Arab building styles and the Islamic religion.

5. Regions
Wheat farming is an important activity in Kansas. This means that Kansas is part of a farming region.

Understanding Movements of the Earth

Planet Earth is part of our solar system. The Earth revolves around the sun in a nearly circular path called an orbit. A revolution, or one complete orbit around the sun, takes 365 1/4 days, or a year. As the Earth revolves around the sun, it is also spinning around in space. This movement is called a rotation. The Earth rotates on its axis—an invisible line through the center of the Earth from the North Pole to the South Pole. The Earth makes one full rotation about every 24 hours. As the Earth rotates, it is daytime on the side facing the sun. It is night on the side away from the sun.

The Earth's axis is tilted at an angle. Because of this tilt, sunlight strikes different parts of the Earth at certain points in the year, creating different seasons.

Earth's Revolution and the Seasons

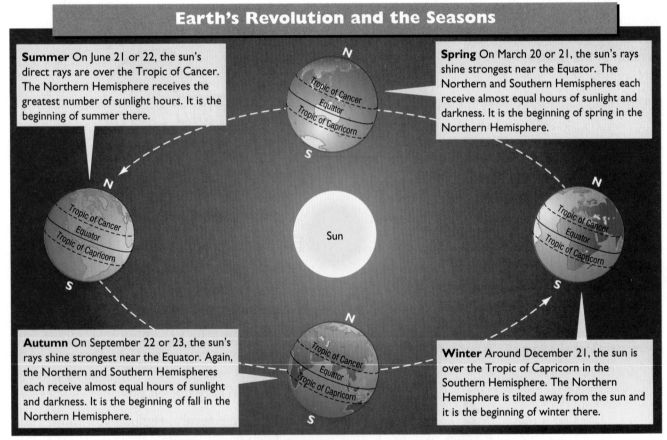

Summer On June 21 or 22, the sun's direct rays are over the Tropic of Cancer. The Northern Hemisphere receives the greatest number of sunlight hours. It is the beginning of summer there.

Spring On March 20 or 21, the sun's rays shine strongest near the Equator. The Northern and Southern Hemispheres each receive almost equal hours of sunlight and darkness. It is the beginning of spring in the Northern Hemisphere.

Autumn On September 22 or 23, the sun's rays shine strongest near the Equator. Again, the Northern and Southern Hemispheres each receive almost equal hours of sunlight and darkness. It is the beginning of fall in the Northern Hemisphere.

Winter Around December 21, the sun is over the Tropic of Capricorn in the Southern Hemisphere. The Northern Hemisphere is tilted away from the sun and it is the beginning of winter there.

▲ **Location** This diagram shows how the Earth's tilt and orbit around the sun combine to create the seasons. Remember, in the Southern Hemisphere the seasons are reversed.

PRACTICE YOUR WORLD EXPLORER SKILLS

1 What causes the seasons in the Northern Hemisphere to be the opposite of those in the Southern Hemisphere?

2 During which two months of the year do the Northern and Southern Hemispheres have about equal hours of daylight and darkness?

Maps and Globes Represent the Earth

Globes

A globe is a scale model of the Earth. It shows the actual shapes, sizes, and locations of all the Earth's landmasses and bodies of water. Features on the surface of the Earth are drawn to scale on a globe. This means a smaller unit of measure on the globe stands for a larger unit of measure on the Earth.

Because a globe is made in the true shape of the Earth, it offers these advantages for studying the Earth.

- The shape of all land and water bodies are accurate.
- Compass directions from one point to any other point are correct.
- The distance from one location to another is always accurately represented.

However, a globe presents some disadvantages for studying the Earth. Because a globe shows the entire Earth, it cannot show small areas in great detail. Also, a globe is not easily folded and carried from one place to another. For these reasons, geographers often use maps to learn about the Earth.

Maps

A map is a drawing or representation, on a flat surface, of a region. A map can show details too small to be seen on a globe. Floor plans, mall directories, and road maps are among the maps we use most often.

While maps solve some of the problems posed by globes, they have some disadvantages of their own. Maps flatten the real round world. Mapmakers cut, stretch, push, and pull some parts of the Earth to get it all flat on paper. As a result, some locations may be distorted. That is, their size, shape, and relative location may not be accurate. For example, on most maps of the entire world, the size and shape of the Antarctic and Arctic regions are not accurate.

PRACTICE YOUR WORLD EXPLORER SKILLS

1. What is the main difference between a globe and a map?

2. What is one advantage of using a globe instead of a map?

Global Gores

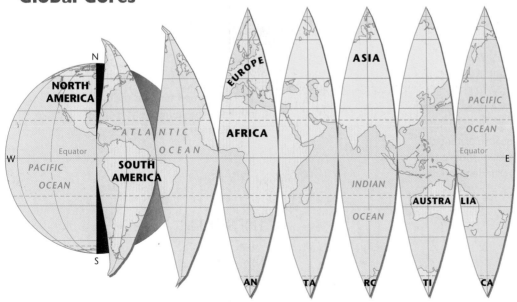

◀ **Location**
When mapmakers flatten the surface of the Earth, curves become straight lines. As a result, size, shape, and distance are distorted.

Locating Places on a Map or a Globe

The Hemispheres

Another name for a round ball like a globe is a sphere. The Equator, an imaginary line halfway between the North and South Poles, divides the globe into two hemispheres. (The prefix *hemi* means "half.") Land and water south of the Equator are in the Southern Hemisphere. Land and water north of the Equator are in the Northern Hemisphere.

Mapmakers sometimes divide the globe along an imaginary line that runs from North Pole to South Pole. This line, called the Prime Meridian, divides the globe into the Eastern and Western Hemispheres.

Northern Hemisphere

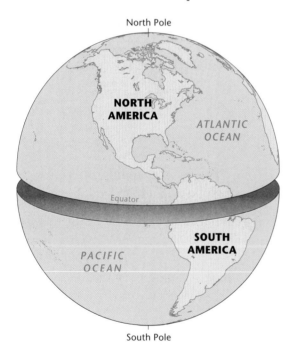

Southern Hemisphere

▲ The Equator divides the Northern Hemisphere from the Southern Hemisphere.

Western Hemisphere   **Eastern Hemisphere**

▲ The Prime Meridian divides the Eastern Hemisphere from the Western Hemisphere.

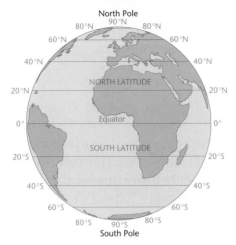

Parallels of Latitude

The Equator, at 0° latitude, is the starting place for measuring latitude or distances north and south. Most globes do not show every parallel of latitude. They may show every 10, 20, or even 30 degrees.

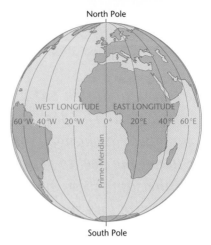

Meridians of Longitude

The Prime Meridian, at 0° longitude, runs from pole to pole through Greenwich, England. It is the starting place for measuring longitude or distances east and west. Each meridian of longitude meets its opposite longitude at the North and South Poles.

The Global Grid

Two sets of lines cover most globes. One set of lines runs parallel to the Equator. These lines, including the Equator, are called *parallels of latitude*. They are measured in degrees (°). One degree of latitude represents a distance of about 70 miles (112 km). The Equator has a location of 0°. The other parallels of latitude tell the direction and distance from the Equator to another location.

The second set of lines runs north and south. These lines are called *meridians of longitude*. Meridians show the degrees of longitude east or west of the Prime Meridian, which is located at 0°. A meridian of longitude tells the direction and distance from the Prime Meridian to another location. Unlike parallels, meridians are not the same distance apart everywhere on the globe.

Together the pattern of parallels of latitude and meridians of longitude is called the global grid. Using the lines of latitude and longitude, you can locate any place on Earth. For example, the location of 30° north latitude and 90° west longitude is usually written as 30°N, 90°W. Only one place on Earth has these coordinates—the city of New Orleans, in the state of Louisiana.

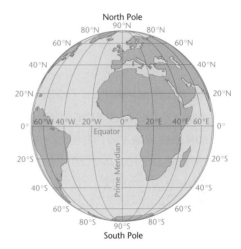

The Global Grid

By using lines of latitude and longitude, you can give the absolute location of any place on the Earth.

PRACTICE YOUR WORLD EXPLORER SKILLS

1. Which continents lie completely in the Northern Hemisphere? The Western Hemisphere?

2. Is there land or water at 20°S latitude and the Prime Meridian? At the Equator and 60°W longitude?

Map Projections

Imagine trying to flatten out a complete orange peel. The peel would split. The shape would change. You would have to cut the peel to get it to lie flat. In much the same way, maps cannot show the correct size and shape of every landmass or body of water on the Earth's curved surface. Maps shrink some places and stretch others. This shrinking and stretching is called distortion—*a change made to a shape.*

To make up for this disadvantage, mapmakers use different map projections. Each map projection is a way of showing the round Earth on flat paper. Each type of projection has some distortion. No one projection can accurately show the correct area, shape, distance, and direction for the Earth's surface. Mapmakers use the projection that has the least distortion for the information they are studying.

Same-Shape Maps

Some map projections can accurately show the shapes of landmasses. However, these projections often greatly distort the size of landmasses as well as the distance between them.

One of the most common same-shape maps is a Mercator projection, named for the mapmaker who invented it. The Mercator projection accurately shows shape and direction, but it distorts distance and size. In this projection, the northern and southern areas of the globe appear stretched more than areas near the Equator. Because the projection shows true directions, ships' navigators use it to chart a straight line course between two ports.

Mercator Projection

Equal-Area Maps

Some map projections can show the correct size of landmasses. Maps that use these projections are called equal-area maps. In order to show the correct size of landmasses, these maps usually distort shapes. The distortion is usually greater at the edges of the map and less at the center.

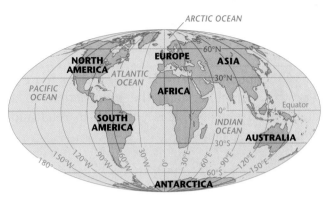

Equal-Area Projection

Robinson Maps

Many of the maps in this book use the Robinson projection. This is a compromise between the Mercator and equal-area projections. It gives a useful overall picture of the world. The Robinson projection keeps the size and shape relationships of most continents and oceans but does distort size of the polar regions.

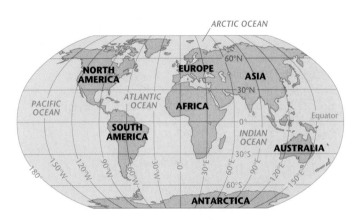

Robinson Projection

Azimuthal Maps

Another kind of projection shows true compass direction. Maps that use this projection are called azimuthal maps. Such maps are easy to recognize—they are usually circular. Azimuthal maps are often used to show the areas of the North and South Poles. However, azimuthal maps distort scale, area, and shape.

1. What feature is distorted on an equal-area map?

2. Would you use a Mercator projection to find the exact distance between two locations? Tell why or why not.

3. Which would be a better choice for studying the Antarctic—an azimuthal projection or a Robinson projection? Explain.

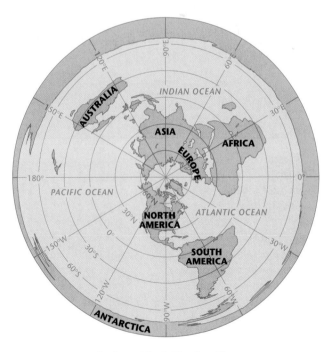

Azimuthal Projection

Parts of a Map

apmakers provide several clues to help you understand the information on a map. As an explorer, it is your job to read and interpret these clues.

Compass
Many maps show north at the top of the map. One way to show direction on a map is to use an arrow that points north. There may be an N shown with the arrow. Many maps give more information about direction by displaying a compass showing the directions, north, east, south, and west. The letters N, E, S, and W are placed to indicate these directions.

Title
The title of a map is the most basic clue. It signals what kinds of information you are likely to find on the map. A map titled *West Africa: Population Density* will be most useful for locating information about where people live in West Africa.

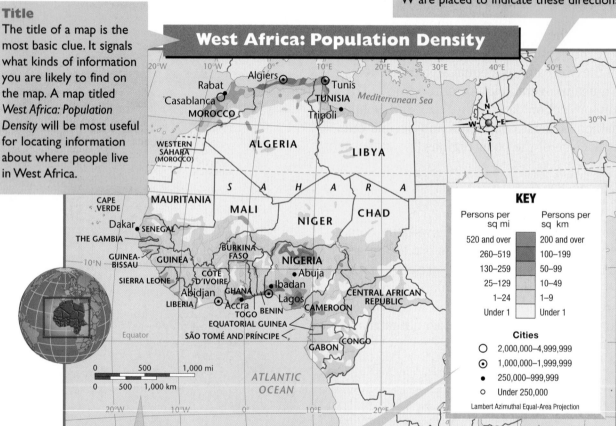

West Africa: Population Density

KEY

Persons per sq mi	Persons per sq km
520 and over	200 and over
260–519	100–199
130–259	50–99
25–129	10–49
1–24	1–9
Under 1	Under 1

Cities

- ○ 2,000,000–4,999,999
- ⊙ 1,000,000–1,999,999
- ● 250,000–999,999
- ○ Under 250,000

Lambert Azimuthal Equal-Area Projection

Scale
A map scale helps you find the actual distances between points shown on the map. You can measure the distance between any two points on the map, compare them to the scale, and find out the actual distance between the points. Most map scales show distances in both miles and kilometers.

Key
Often a map has a key, or legend, that shows the symbols used on the map and what each one means. On some maps, color is used as a symbol. On those maps, the key also tells the meaning of each color.

PRACTICE YOUR WORLD EXPLORER SKILLS

1. What part of a map tells you what the map is about?

2. Where on the map should you look to find out the meaning of this symbol? ●

3. What part of the map can you use to find the distance between two cities?

Comparing Maps of Different Scale

ere are three maps drawn to three different scales. The first map shows Moscow's location in the northeastern portion of Russia. This map shows the greatest area—a large section of northern Europe. It has the smallest scale (1 inch = about 900 miles) and shows the fewest details. This map can tell you what direction to travel to reach Moscow from Finland.

Find the red box on Map 1. It shows the whole area covered by Map 2. Study Map 2. It gives a closer look at the city of Moscow. It shows the fea-

tures around the city, the city's boundary, and the general shape of the city. This map can help you find your way from the airport to the center of town.

Now find the red box on Map 2. This box shows the area shown on Map 3. This map moves you closer into the city. Like the zoom on a computer or camera, Map 3 shows the smallest area but has the greatest detail. This map has the largest scale (1 inch = about 0.8 miles). This is the map to use to explore downtown Moscow.

Map 1

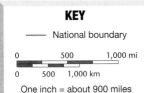

KEY

—— National boundary

0   500   1,000 mi
0   500 1,000 km

One inch = about 900 miles

Map 2

KEY

Built-up area

Road or street

0   5   10 mi
0   5   10 km

One inch = about 12.5 miles

Map 3

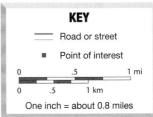

KEY

—— Road or street

■ Point of interest

0   .5   1 mi
0   .5   1 km

One inch = about 0.8 miles

PRACTICE
YOUR
WORLD EXPLORER
SKILLS

1 Which map would be best for finding the location of Red Square? Why?

2 Which map best shows Moscow's location relative to Poland? Explain.

3 Which map best shows the area immediately surrounding the city?

Political Maps

Mapmakers create maps to show all kinds of information. The kind of information presented affects the way a map looks. One type of map is called a political map. Its main purpose is to show continents, countries, and divisions within countries such as states or provinces. Usually different colors are used to show different countries or divisions within a country. The colors do not have any special meaning. They are used only to make the map easier to read.

Political maps also show where people have built towns and cities. Symbols can help you tell capital cities from other cities and towns. Even though political maps do not give information that shows what the land looks like, they often include some physical features such as oceans, lakes, and rivers.

Political maps usually have many labels. They give country names, and the names of capital and major cities. Bodies of water such as lakes, rivers, oceans, seas, gulfs, and bays are also labeled.

1. What symbol shows the continental boundary?

2. What symbol is used to indicate a capital city? A major city?

3. What kinds of landforms are shown on this map?

▲ The keys of political maps may include symbols. Study the key to learn what the symbols on this map mean.

Physical Maps

Like political maps, physical maps show country labels and labels for capital cities. However, physical maps also show what the land of a region looks like by showing the major physical features such as plains, hills, plateaus, or mountains. Labels give the names of features such as mountain peaks, mountains, plateaus, and river basins.

In order to tell one landform from another, physical maps often show elevation and relief.

Elevation is the height of the land above sea level. Physical maps in this book use color to show elevation. Browns and oranges show higher lands while blues and greens show lands that are at or below sea level.

Relief shows how quickly the land rises or falls. Hills, mountains, and plateaus are shown on relief maps using shades of gray. Level or nearly level land is shown without shading. Darkly shaded areas indicate steeper lands.

Hawaii: Physical

KEY
• City
Lambert Conformal Conic Projection

▲ On a physical map, shading is sometimes used to show relief. Use the shading to locate the mountains in Hawaii.

PRACTICE YOUR WORLD EXPLORER SKILLS

1. How is relief shown on the map to the left?

2. How can you use relief to decide which areas will be the most difficult to climb?

3. What information is given with the name of a mountain peak?

▼ Mauna Kea, an extinct volcano, is the highest peak in the state of Hawaii. Find Mauna Kea on the map.

Special Purpose Maps

As you explore the world, you will encounter many different kinds of special purpose maps. For example, a road map is a special purpose map. The title of each special purpose map tells the purpose and content of the map. Usually a special purpose map highlights only one kind of information. Examples of special purpose maps include land use, population distribution, recreation, transportation, natural resources, or weather.

The key on a special purpose map is very important. Even though a special purpose map shows only one kind of information, it may present many different pieces of data. This data can be shown in symbols, colors, or arrows. In this way, the key acts like a dictionary for the map.

Reading a special purpose map is a skill in itself. Look at the map below. First, try to get an overall sense of what it shows. Then, study the map to identify its main ideas. For example, one main idea of this map is that much of the petroleum production in the region takes place around the Persian Gulf.

1 What part of a special purpose map tells what information is contained on the map?

2 What part of a special purpose map acts like a dictionary for the map?

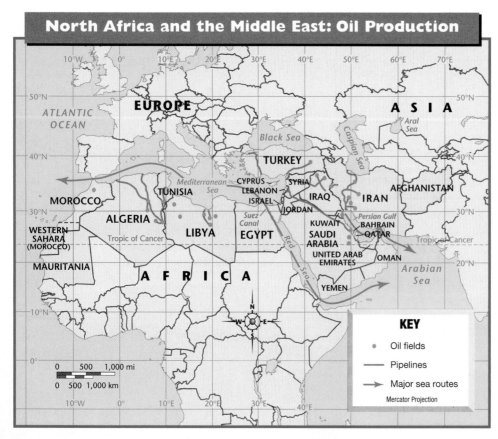

North Africa and the Middle East: Oil Production

KEY
- • Oil fields
- — Pipelines
- → Major sea routes

Mercator Projection

◀ The title on a special purpose map indicates what information can be found on the map. The symbols used on the map are explained in the map's key.

Landforms, Climate Regions, and Natural Vegetation Regions

aps that show landforms, climate, and vegetation regions are special purpose maps. Unlike the boundary lines on a political map, the boundary lines on these maps do not separate the land into exact divisions. A tropical wet climate gradually changes to a tropical wet and dry climate. A tundra gradually changes to an ice cap. Even though the boundaries between regions may not be exact, the information on these maps can help you understand the region and the lives of people in it.

Landforms

Understanding how people use the land requires an understanding of the shape of the land itself. The four most important landforms are mountains, hills, plateaus, and plains. Human activity in every region in the world is influenced by these landforms.

- **Mountains** are high and steep. Most are wide at the bottom and rise to a narrow peak or ridge. Most geographers classify a mountain as land that rises at least 2,000 feet (610 m) above sea level. A series of mountains is called a mountain range.

- **Hills** rise above surrounding land and have rounded tops. Hills are lower and usually less steep than mountains. The elevation of surrounding land determines whether a landform is called a mountain or a hill.
- A **plateau** is a large, mostly flat area of land that rises above the surrounding land. At least one side of a plateau has a steep slope.
- **Plains** are large areas of flat or gently rolling land. Plains have few changes in elevation. Many plains areas are located along coasts. Others are located in the interior regions of some continents.

▶ A satellite view of the Earth showing North and South America. What landforms are visible in the photograph?

Climate Regions

Another important influence in the ways people live their lives is the climate of their region. Climate is the weather of a given location over a long period of time. Use the descriptions in the table below to help you visualize the climate regions shown on maps.

Climate	Temperatures	Precipitation
Tropical		
Tropical wet	Hot all year round	Heavy all year round
Tropical wet and dry	Hot all year round	Heavy when sun is overhead, dry other times
Dry		
Semiarid	Hot summers, mild to cold winters	Light
Arid	Hot days, cold nights	Very light
Mild		
Mediterranean	Hot summers, cool winters	Dry summers, wet winters
Humid subtropical	Hot summers, cool winters	Year round, heavier in summer than in winter
Marine west coast	Warm summers, cool winters	Year round, heavier in winter than in summer
Continental		
Humid continental	Hot summers, cold winters	Year round, heavier in summer than in winter
Subarctic	Cool summers, cold winters	Light
Polar		
Tundra	Cool summers, very cold winters	Light
Ice cap	Cold all year round	Light
Highlands	Varies, depending on altitude and direction of prevailing winds	Varies, depending on altitude and direction of prevailing winds

Natural Vegetation Regions

Natural vegetation is the plant life that grows wild without the help of humans. A world vegetation map tells what the vegetation in a place would be if people had not cut down forests or cleared grasslands. The table below provides descriptions of natural vegetation regions shown on maps. Comparing climate and vegetation regions can help you see the close relationship between climate and vegetation.

Vegetation	Description
Tropical rain forest	Tall, close-growing trees forming a canopy over smaller trees, dense growth in general
Deciduous forest	Trees and plants that regularly lose their leaves after each growing season
Mixed forest	Both leaf-losing and cone-bearing trees, no type of tree dominant
Coniferous forest	Cone-bearing trees, evergreen trees and plants
Mediterranean vegetation	Evergreen shrubs and small plants
Tropical savanna	Tall grasses with occasional trees and shrubs
Temperate grassland	Tall grasses with occasional stands of trees
Desert scrub	Low shrubs and bushes, hardy plants
Desert	Little or no vegetation
Tundra	Low shrubs, mosses, lichens; no trees
Ice cap	Little or no vegetation
Highlands	Varies, depending on altitude and direction of prevailing winds

PRACTICE YOUR WORLD EXPLORER SKILLS

1 How are mountains and hills similar? How are they different?

2 What is the difference between a plateau and a plain?

Africa

KEY

— National boundary

⊛ National capital

• Other city

Lambert Azimuthal Equal Area Projection

Background photo: Mt. Kilimanjaro, Tanzania

Data compiled from the *Dorling Kindersley World Desk Reference*, the CIA Factbook, and the *Infoplease Internet Encyclopedia*.

GEOFACTS

Africa

Population: 697.3 million

Most Populated City: Cairo, Egypt (6.4 million)

Largest Country: Sudan (917,374 sq mi/ 2,376,000 sq km)

Smallest Country: Seychelles (104 sq mi/ 270 sq km)

Highest Point: Mt. Kilimanjaro (19,341 ft/5,895 m)

Lowest Point: Lac'Assal (-512 ft/-156 m)

Longest River: Nile River (4,160 mi/ 6,695 km)

Uganda

Johannesburg, South Africa

North Africa

ATLANTIC OCEAN

Strait of Gibraltar

Tangier
Rabat
Casablanca
Marrakech
Meknès
Fès
Oran
Constantine
Algiers
Annaba
Tunis
TUNISIA
Mediterranean Sea
Tripoli
Banghazi
Alexandria
Cairo
Giza

MOROCCO

WESTERN SAHARA (MOROCCO)

ALGERIA

LIBYA

EGYPT

Red Sea

Tropic of Cancer

0   400   800 mi
0   400   800 km

Capital: Algiers

Area: 919,590 sq mi/2,381,740 sq km

Population: 30.8 million

Ethnic Groups: Arab, Berber

Religions: Sunni Muslim, Christian, Jewish

Government: republic

Currency: Algerian dinar

Exports: petroleum, natural gas, petroleum products

Official Language: Arabic

Algeria
(AL jeer ee uh)

Capital: Cairo

Area: 384,343 sq mi/995,450 sq km

Population: 67.2 million

Ethnic Groups: Eastern Hamitic, Nubian, Armenian, Greek

Religions: Muslim (mostly Sunni), Coptic Christian

Government: republic

Currency: Egyptian pound

Exports: crude oil, petroleum products, cotton, textiles

Official Language: Arabic

Egypt
(EE jipt)

Background photo: City of the Dead, Cairo, Egypt

Capital: Tripoli/Benghazi

Area: 679,358 sq mi/1,759,540 sq km

Population: 5.5 million

Ethnic Groups: Arab, Berber

Religions: Sunni Muslim

Government: military dictatorship

Currency: Libyan dinar

Exports: crude oil, refined petroleum products, natural gas

Official Language: Arabic

Libya
(LIB ee uh)

Giza, Egypt

Capital: Rabat

Area: 172,316 sq mi/446,300 sq km

Population: 27.9 million

Ethnic Groups: Arab, Berber, Shluh, Tamazight, French, Spanish

Religions: Muslim, Christian, Jewish

Government: constitutional monarchy

Currency: Moroccan dirham

Exports: phosphates and fertilizers, food and beverages, minerals

Official Language: Arabic

Morocco
(mu ROK oh)

Capital: Tunis

Area: 59,984 sq mi/155,360 sq km

Population: 9.5 million

Ethnic Groups: Arab, Berber, French

Religions: Muslim, Christian, Jewish

Government: republic

Currency: Tunisian dinar

Exports: textiles, mechanical goods, phosphates and chemicals, agricultural products, hydrocarbons

Official Language: Arabic

Tunisia
(too NEE zhuh)

West Africa

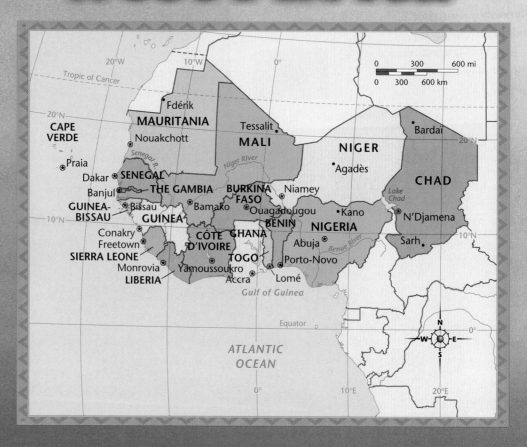

Tropic of Cancer
20°W   10°W   0°

0   300   600 mi
0   300   600 km

Fdérik
MAURITANIA   Tessalit
20°N   Bardaï
CAPE   Nouakchott   MALI   NIGER   20°N
VERDE
                   Senegal R.   Niger River   Agadès
Praia   CHAD
Dakar SENEGAL   Lake
Banjul THE GAMBIA   BURKINA   Niamey   Chad
                              FASO   N'Djamena
GUINEA-   Bissau   Bamako Ouagadougou   Kano
BISSAU   GUINEA   BENIN
Conakry   CÔTE GHANA   NIGERIA
Freetown   D'IVOIRE   Abuja   Sarh
SIERRA LEONE   TOGO   Porto-Novo   Benue River
         Monrovia Yamoussoukro   Lomé
         LIBERIA   Accra
                         Gulf of Guinea

                         Equator

ATLANTIC   N
OCEAN   W   E
                              S
0°   10°E   20°E

Capital: Porto-Novo

Area: 42,710 sq mi/110,620 sq km

Population: 5.9 million

Ethnic Groups: Fon, Adja, Yoruba, Bariba, Somba, French

Religions: traditional beliefs, Christian, Muslim

Government: republic

Currency: CFA franc

Exports: cotton, crude oil, palm products, cocoa

Official Language: French

Benin
(be NEEN)

Capital: Ouagadougou

Area: 105,714 sq mi/273,800 sq km

Population: 11.6 million

Ethnic Groups: Mossi, Gurunsi, Senufo, Lobi, Bobo, Mande, Fulani

Religions: traditional beliefs, Muslim, Roman Catholic

Government: parliamentary

Currency: CFA franc

Exports: cotton, animal products, gold

Official Language: French

Burkina Faso
(bur KEE nuh FAH soh)

Background photo: Accra, Ghana

Capital: Praia

Area: 1,556 sq mi/4,030 sq km

Population: 418,000

Ethnic Groups: Mestico, Portuguese Creole, European

Religions: Roman Catholic, Protestant

Government: republic

Currency: Cape Verde escudo

Exports: fuel, shoes, garments, fish, bananas, hides

Official Language: Portuguese

Cape Verde
(kayp vurd)

Capital: Yamoussoukro

Area: 122,780 sq mi/318,000 sq km

Population: 15.9 million

Ethnic Groups: Baoulé, Bete, Senufo, Malinke, Agni

Religions: Muslim, Christian

Government: republic

Currency: CFA franc

Exports: cocoa, coffee, tropical woods, petroleum, cotton, bananas, pineapples, palm oil, cotton, fish

Official Language: French

Cote D'Ivoire
(koht deev WAR)

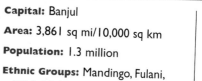

Capital: Banjul

Area: 3,861 sq mi/10,000 sq km

Population: 1.3 million

Ethnic Groups: Mandingo, Fulani, Wolof, Jola, Serahull

Religions: Muslim, Christian, traditional beliefs

Government: republic

Currency: Dalasi

Exports: peanuts and peanut products, fish, cotton lint, palm kernels

Official Language: English

The Gambia
(GAM bee uh)

Capital: N'Djamena

Area: 486,177 sq mi/1,259,200 sq km

Population: 7.5 million

Ethnic Groups: Arab, Toubou, Hadjerai, Sara, Ngambaye

Religions: Muslim, traditional beliefs, Christian

Government: republic

Currency: CFA franc

Exports: cotton, cattle, textiles

Official Languages: Arabic and French

Chad
(chad)

Capital: Accra

Area: 92,100 sq mi/238,540 sq km

Population: 19.7 million

Ethnic Groups: Akan, Mole-Dagbani, Ga-Adangbe, Ewe

Religions: Christian, traditional beliefs, Muslim

Government: constitutional democracy

Currency: Cedi

Exports: gold, cocoa, timber, tuna, bauxite, aluminum, manganese ore

Official Language: English

Ghana
(GAH nuh)

Capital: Conakry

Area: 94,926 sq mi/245,860 sq km

Population: 7.4 million

Ethnic Groups: Fila, Malinke, Soussou, Kissi

Religions: Muslim, Christian, traditional beliefs

Government: republic

Currency: Guinea franc

Exports: bauxite, alumina, gold, diamonds, coffee, fish

Official Language: French

Guinea
(GIN ee)

Capital: Monrovia

Area: 37,189 sq mi/96,320 sq km

Population: 2.9 million

Ethnic Groups: indigenous tribes, Americo Liberians

Religions: Christian, traditional beliefs, Muslim

Government: republic

Currency: Liberian dollar

Exports: diamonds, iron ore, rubber, timber, coffee, cocoa

Official Language: English

Liberia
(ly BEER ee uh)

Capital: Bissau

Area: 10,857 sq mi/28,120 sq km

Population: 1.2 million

Ethnic Groups: Balanta, Fula, Manjaca, Mandinga, European

Religions: traditional beliefs, Muslim, Christian

Government: republic

Currency: Guinea peso

Exports: cashew nuts, shrimp, peanuts, palm kernels, sawn lumber

Official Language: Portuguese

Guinea-Bissau
(GIN ee bi SOW)

Capital: Bamako

Area: 471,115 sq mi/1,220,190 sq km

Population: 11 million

Ethnic Groups: Mande, Peul, Voltaic, Songhai, Tuareg, Moor

Religions: Sunni Muslim, traditional beliefs, Christian

Government: republic

Currency: CFA franc

Exports: cotton, gold, livestock

Official Language: French

Mali
(MAH lee)

Capital: Nouakchott

Area: 395,953 sq mi/1,025,520 sq km

Population: 2.6 million

Ethnic Groups: Maur, black

Religion: Muslim

Government: republic

Currency: Ouguiya

Exports: fish and fish products, iron ore, gold

Official Languages: Arabic and French

Mauritania
(mawr i TAY nee uh)

Capital: Dakar

Area: 74,336 sq mi/192,530 sq km

Population: 9.2 million

Ethnic Groups: Wolof, Fulani, Serer, Diola, Mandinka

Religions: Muslim, traditional beliefs, Roman Catholic

Government: republic

Currency: CFA franc

Exports: fish, groundnuts (peanuts), petroleum products, phosphates

Official Language: French

Senegal
(sen uh GAWL)

Capital: Niamey

Area: 489,073 sq mi/1,266,700 sq km

Population: 10.4 million

Ethnic Groups: Hausa, Djerma, Songhai

Religions: Muslim, traditional beliefs, Christian

Government: republic

Currency: CFA franc

Exports: uranium ore, livestock products, cowpeas, onions

Official Language: French

Niger
(NYE jur)

Capital: Freetown

Area: 27,652 sq mi/71,620 sq km

Population: 4.7 million

Ethnic Groups: Temne, Mende, Creole

Religions: Muslim, traditional beliefs, Christian

Government: constitutional democracy

Currency: Leone

Exports: diamonds, rutile, cocoa, coffee, fish

Official Language: English

Sierra Leone
(see ER uh lee OH nee)

Capital: Abuja

Area: 351,648 sq mi/910,770 sq km

Population: 108 million

Ethnic Groups: Hausa, Fulani, Yoruba, Igbo

Religions: Muslim, Christian, traditional beliefs

Government: republic

Currency: Naira

Exports: petroleum and petroleum products, cocoa, rubber

Official Language: English

Nigeria
(ny JEER ee uh)

Capital: Lomé

Area: 21,000 sq mi/54,390 sq km

Population: 4.5 million

Ethnic Groups: native African, Ewe, Mina, Kabre

Religions: traditional beliefs, Christian, Muslim

Government: republic

Currency: CFA franc

Exports: cotton, phosphates, coffee, cocoa

Official Language: French

Togo
(TOH goh)

East Africa

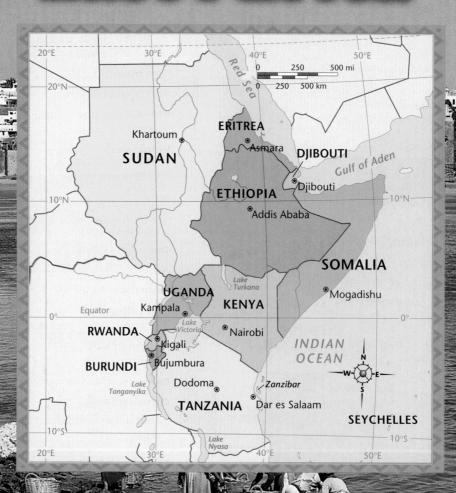

20°E · 30°E · 40°E · 50°E

Red Sea

250 · 500 mi
0 · 250 · 500 km

20°N

Khartoum

ERITREA

Asmara

DJIBOUTI

Gulf of Aden

SUDAN

Djibouti

10°N

ETHIOPIA

10°N

Addis Ababa

SOMALIA

Lake Turkana

UGANDA

Mogadishu

Equator

Kampala

KENYA

0°

0°

Lake Victoria

RWANDA

Nairobi

Kigali

INDIAN OCEAN

N

BURUNDI

Bujumbura

W · E

Lake Tanganyika

Dodoma

Zanzibar

S

10°S

TANZANIA

Dar es Salaam

10°S

Lake Nyasa

SEYCHELLES

20°E · 30°E · 40°E · 50°E

Capital: Bujumbura

Area: 9,903 sq mi/25,650 sq km

Population: 6.6 million

Ethnic Groups: Hutu, Tutsi, Twa

Religions: Roman Catholic, Protestant, traditional beliefs, Muslim

Government: republic

Currency: Burundi franc

Exports: coffee, tea, sugar, cotton, hides

Official Languages: French and Kirundi

Burundi
(boo RUN dee)

Background photo: Shores of Somalia

Capital: Djibouti

Area: 8,950 sq mi/23,180 sq km

Population: 629,000

Ethnic Groups: Issa, Afar

Religions: Muslim, Christian

Government: republic

Currency: Djibouti franc

Exports: reexports, hides and skins, coffee

Official Languages: Arabic and French

Djibouti
(ji BOO tee)

Capital: Addis Ababa

Area: 425,096 sq mi/1,101,000 sq km

Population: 61.1 million

Ethnic Groups: Oromo, Amhara Sidamo, Shankella, Somali, Afar

Religions: Muslim, Ethiopian Orthodox, traditional beliefs

Government: federal republic

Currency: Ethiopian birr

Exports: coffee, gold, leather products, oilseeds

Official Language: Amharic

Ethiopia
(ee thee OH pee uh)

Capital: Asmara

Area: 36,170 sq mi/93,680 sq km

Population: 3.7 million

Ethnic Groups: ethnic Tigrinya, Tigre, Kunama, Afar, Saho

Religions: Muslim, Christian

Government: transitional government

Currency: Nakfa

Exports: livestock, sorghum, textiles, food, small manufactures

Official Language: Tigrinya

Eritrea
(ayr uh TREE uh)

Capital: Nairobi

Area: 218,907 sq mi/566,970 sq km

Population: 29.5 million

Ethnic Groups: Kikuyu, Luhya, Luo, Kalenjin, Kamba, Kisii, Meru

Religions: Protestant, Roman Catholic, traditional beliefs, Muslim

Government: republic

Currency: Kenya shilling

Exports: tea, coffee, horticultural products, petroleum products

Official Languages: Swahili and English

Kenya
(KEN yuh)

Capital: Kigali

Area: 9,633 sq mi/ 24,950 sq km

Population: 7.2 million

Ethnic Groups: Hutu, Tutsi, Twa

Religions: Roman Catholic, Protestant, Muslim, traditional beliefs

Government: republic

Currency: Rwanda franc

Exports: coffee, tea, hides, tin ore

Official Languages: French and Rwandan

Rwanda
(roo AHN duh)

Capital: Victoria

Area: 104 sq mi/270 sq km

Population: 75,000

Ethnic Group: Seychellois

Religions: Roman Catholic, Anglican, Muslim

Government: republic

Currency: Seychelles rupee

Exports: fish, cinnamon bark, copra, petroleum products (reexports)

Official Language: Seselwa (French Creole)

Seychelles
(say SHELZ)

Capital: Mogadishu

Area: 242,216 sq mi/627,340 sq km

Population: 9.7 million

Ethnic Groups: Somali, Bantu, Arab

Religions: Sunni Muslim, Christian

Government: none

Currency: Somali shilling

Exports: livestock, bananas, hides, fish

Official Languages: Arabic and Somali

Somalia
(soh MAHL yuh)

Victoria, Seychelles

Capital: Khartoum

Area: 917,374 sq mi/2,376,000 sq km

Population: 28.9 million

Ethnic Groups: Arab, Dinka, Nuer, Beja

Religions: Sunni Muslim, traditional beliefs, Christian

Government: transitional

Currency: Sudanese pound or dinar

Exports: cotton, sesame, livestock, groundnuts, oil, gum arabic

Official Language: Arabic

Sudan
(soo DAN)

Tanzania

Capital: Dodoma

Area: 342,100 sq mi/886,040 sq km

Population: 32.8 million

Ethnic Group: Bantu

Religions: Muslim, Christian, traditional beliefs

Government: republic

Currency: Tanzanian shilling

Exports: coffee, manufactured goods, cotton, cashew nuts, minerals, tobacco, sisal

Official Languages: English and Swahili

Tanzania
(tan zuh NEE uh)

Capital: Kampala

Area: 77,046 sq mi/199,550 sq km

Population: 21.1 million

Ethnic Groups: Baganda, Karamojong

Religions: Roman Catholic, Protestant, traditional beliefs

Government: republic

Currency: New Uganda shilling

Exports: coffee, fish and fish products, tea, electrical products, iron

Official Languages: English and Swahili

Uganda
(yoo GAHN duh)

Central and Southern Africa

Capital: Luanda

Area: 434,235 sq mi/1,124,670 sq km

Population: 12.5 million

Ethnic Groups: Ovimbundu, Mbundu, Bakongo

Religions: traditional beliefs, Roman Catholic, Protestant

Government: transitional government

Currency: Readjusted kwanza

Exports: crude oil, diamonds, refined petroleum products, gas

Official Language: Portuguese

Angola
(an GOH luh)

Capital: Gaborone

Area: 218,814 sq mi/566,730 sq km

Population: 1.6 million

Ethnic Groups: Tswana

Religions: traditional beliefs, Christian

Government: parliamentary republic

Currency: Pula

Exports: diamonds, vehicles, copper, nickel, meat

Official Language: English

Botswana
(bot SWAH nuh)

Background photo: Cape Town, South Africa

Capital: Yaoundé

Area: 179,691 sq mi/465,400 sq km

Population: 14.7 million

Ethnic Groups: Cameroon Highlanders, Equatorial Bantu

Religions: Roman Catholic, traditional beliefs, Muslim, Protestant

Government: unitary republic

Currency: CFA Franc

Exports: crude oil and petroleum products, lumber, cocoa beans

Official Languages: English and French

Cameroon
(KAM uh ROON)

Capital: Kinshasa

Area: 875,520 sq mi/2,267,600 sq km

Population: 50.3 million

Ethnic Groups: Bantu, Hamitic

Religions: traditional beliefs, Roman Catholic, Protestant

Government: dictatorship

Currency: Congolese franc

Exports: diamonds, copper, coffee, cobalt, crude oil

Official Languages: French and English

Congo, Democratic Republic of
(KON goh)

Capital: Bangui

Area: 240,530 sq mi/622,980 sq km

Population: 3.6 million

Ethnic Groups: Baya, Banda, Sara, Mandjia, Mboum, M'Baka, Europeans

Religions: traditional beliefs, Protestant, Roman Catholic, Muslim

Government: republic

Currency: CFA franc

Exports: diamonds, timber, cotton, coffee, tobacco

Official Language: French

Central African Republic
(sen TRAWL AF ri kuhn)

Capital: Brazzaville

Area: 131,853 sq mi/341,500 sq km

Population: 2.9 million

Ethnic Groups: Bakongo, Sangha, Teke, Mbochi

Religions: Christian, traditional beliefs, Muslim

Government: republic

Currency: CFA franc

Exports: petroleum, lumber, plywood, sugar, cocoa, coffee, diamonds

Official Language: French

Congo, Republic of the
(KON goh)

Capital: Moroni

Area: 861 sq mi/2,230 sq km

Population: 676,000

Ethnic Groups: Antalote, Cafre, Makoa, Oimatsaha, Sakalava

Religions: Sunni Muslim, Roman Catholic

Government: independent republic

Currency: Comoros franc

Exports: vanilla, ylang-ylang, cloves, perfume oil, copra

Official Languages: Arabic and French

Comoros
(KAHM uh ROHZ)

Capital: Malabo

Area: 10,830 sq mi/28,050 sq km

Population: 442,000

Ethnic Groups: Bioko, Rio Muni

Religions: Roman Catholic

Government: republic

Currency: CFA franc

Exports: petroleum, timber, cocoa

Official Language: Spanish

Equatorial Guinea
(eh kwuh TOHR ee uhl GIN ee)

REGIONAL · DATABASE

Capital: Lilongwe

Area: 45,745 sq mi/118,480 sq km

Population: 10.6 million

Ethnic Groups: Chewa, Nyanja, Tumbuka, Yao, Lomwe

Religions: Protestant, Roman Catholic, Muslim, traditional beliefs

Government: multiparty democracy

Currency: Malawi kwacha

Exports: tobacco, tea, sugar, cotton, coffee, peanuts, wood products

Official Language: English

Malawi
(mah LAH wee)

Capital: Libreville

Area: 99,486 sq mi/257,670 sq km

Population: 1.2 million

Ethnic Groups: Fang, Bantu, Eshira, European, African, French

Religions: Christian, Muslim

Government: republic

Currency: CFA franc

Exports: crude oil, timber, manganese, uranium

Official Language: French

Gabon
(gah BOHN)

Capital: Maseru

Area: 11,718 sq mi/30,350 sq km

Population: 2.1 million

Ethnic Groups: Basotho, European

Religions: Christian, traditional beliefs

Government: parliamentary constitutional monarchy

Currency: Loti

Exports: clothing, footwear, road vehicles, wool, mohair, food

Official Languages: English and Sesotho

Lesotho
(le SOH thoh)

Capital: Port Louis

Area: 718 sq mi/1,860 sq km

Population: 1.2 million

Ethnic Groups: Indo-Mauritian, Creole, Sino-Mauritian

Religions: Hindu, Roman Catholic, Muslim, Protestant

Government: parliamentary democracy

Currency: Mauritian rupee

Exports: clothing, textiles, sugar

Official Language: English

Mauritius
(maw RISH us)

Capital: Antananarivo

Area: 224,533 sq mi/581,540 sq km

Population: 15.5 million

Ethnic Groups: Malayo-Indonesian, Cotiers, French, Indian, Creole

Religions: traditional beliefs, Christian, Muslim

Government: republic

Currency: Franc malagache

Exports: coffee, vanilla, cloves

Official Languages: French and Malagasy

Madagascar
(mad uh GAS kahr)

Capital: Maputo

Area: 302,737 sq mi/784,090 sq km

Population: 19.3 million

Ethnic Groups: Makua Lomwe, Thonga, Malawi, Shona, Yao

Religions: traditional beliefs, Christian, Muslim

Government: republic

Currency: Metical

Exports: prawns, cashews, cotton, sugar, copra, citrus, coconuts, timber

Official Language: Portuguese

Mozambique
(moh zahm BEEK)

210

Capital: Windhoek

Area: 318,260 sq mi/824,290 sq km

Population: 1.7 million

Ethnic Groups: Ovambo, Kavango, Herero, Damara

Religions: Christian, traditional beliefs

Government: republic

Currency: Namibian dollar

Exports: diamonds, copper, gold, zinc, lead, uranium, cattle, processed fish, karakul skins

Official Language: English

Namibia
(nuh MIB ee uh)

Capital: Mbabane

Area: 6,641 sq mi/17,200 sq km

Population: 980,000

Ethnic Groups: African, European

Religions: Christian, traditional beliefs

Government: monarchy

Currency: Lilangeni

Exports: soft drink concentrates, sugar, wood pulp, cotton yarn, refrigerates, citrus, canned fruit

Official Languages: English, Swazi

Swaziland
(SWAH zee land)

Capital: São Tomé

Area: 371 sq mi/960 sq km

Population: 135,000

Ethnic Groups: African, Portuguese, Creole

Religions: Roman Catholic, Evangelical Protestant, Seventh-Day Adventist

Government: republic

Currency: Dobra

Exports: cocoa, copra, coffee, palm oil

Official Language: Portuguese

São Tomé and Príncipe
(SOU taw ME and PRIN si puh)

Capital: Lusaka

Area: 285,992 sq mi/740,720 sq km

Population: 9 million

Ethnic Groups: African, European

Religions: Christian, traditional beliefs, Muslim, Hindu

Government: republic

Currency: Zambian kwacha

Exports: copper, cobalt, electricity, tobacco

Official Language: English

Zambia
(ZAM bee uh)

Capital: Pretoria

Area: 471,443 sq mi/1,221,040 sq km

Population: 39.9 million

Ethnic Groups: Zulu, white, mixed, Xhosa

Religions: Dutch Reformed, Roman Catholic, Methodist

Government: republic

Currency: Rand

Exports: gold, diamonds, other metals and minerals, machinery

Official Languages: Afrikaans and English

South Africa
(sowth AF ri kuh)

Capital: Harare

Area: 149,293 sq mi/ 390,580 sq km

Population: 11.5 million

Ethnic Groups: Shona, Ndebele, white, mixed, Asian

Religions: Syncretic, Christian, traditional beliefs, Muslim

Government: parliamentary democracy

Currency: Zimbabwe dollar

Exports: tobacco, gold, ferroalloys, cotton

Official Language: English

Zimbabwe
(zim BAH bway)

Atlas

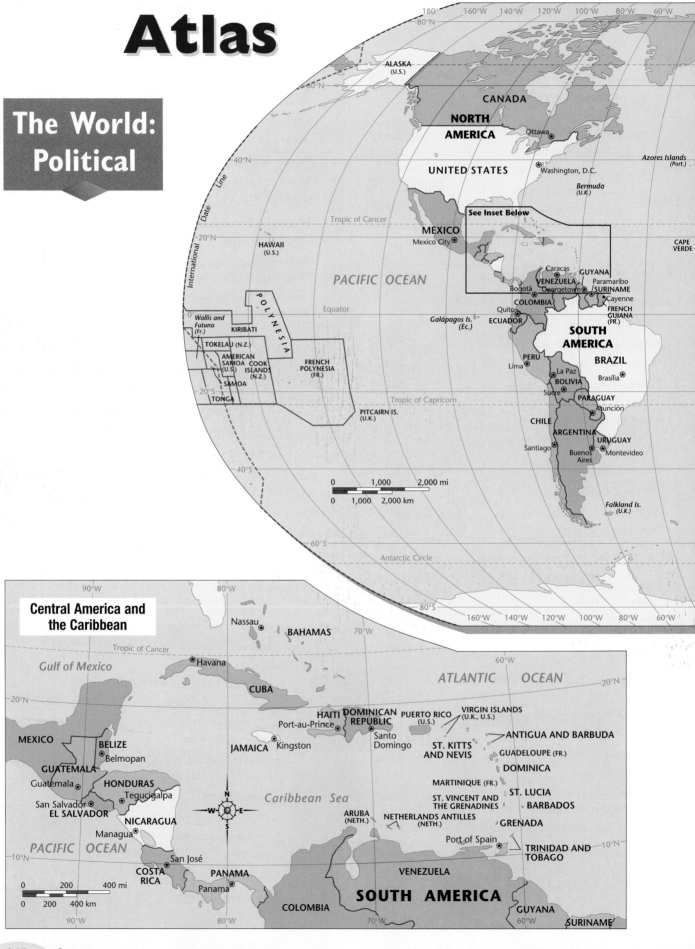

180° 160°W 140°W 120°W 100°W 80°W 60°W
80°N

ALASKA
(U.S.)

CANADA

NORTH
AMERICA

Ottawa ✹

UNITED STATES

Washington, D.C. ✹

Azores Islands
(Port.)

40°N

Bermuda
(U.K.)

CAPE
VERDE

Tropic of Cancer

See Inset Below

MEXICO

20°N

Mexico City ✹

HAWAII
(U.S.)

PACIFIC OCEAN

Caracas
VENEZUELA   GUYANA
Bogotá ✹   Georgetown ✹ Paramaribo ✹
COLOMBIA   SURINAME
Quito ✹   Cayenne
ECUADOR   FRENCH
Galápagos Is.   GUIANA
(Ec.)   (FR.)

P O L Y N E S I A

Equator

Wallis and
Futuna
(Fr.)   KIRIBATI

TOKELAU (N.Z.)

AMERICAN
SAMOA COOK
(U.S) ISLANDS
(N.Z.)

SAMOA

FRENCH
POLYNESIA
(FR.)

PERU

Lima ✹

SOUTH
AMERICA

BRAZIL

La Paz ✹
BOLIVIA   Brasília ✹

20°S

TONGA

Tropic of Capricorn

Sucre ✹   PARAGUAY
Asunción ✹

PITCAIRN IS.
(U.K.)

CHILE

ARGENTINA   URUGUAY

Santiago ✹   Buenos Montevideo
Aires

0   1,000   2,000 mi

0   1,000   2,000 km

40°S

Falkland Is.
(U.K.)

60°S

Antarctic Circle

International Date Line

60°N

40°N

20°N

Equator

20°S

80°S

160°W 140°W 120°W 100°W 80°W 60°W

Central America and the Caribbean

90°W   80°W

Nassau ✹

BAHAMAS

70°W

Tropic of Cancer

Gulf of Mexico

Havana ✹

ATLANTIC   OCEAN

60°W

20°N

20°N

CUBA

MEXICO

BELIZE
Belmopan ✹

GUATEMALA

Guatemala ✹

HONDURAS
Tegucigalpa ✹

San Salvador ✹
EL SALVADOR

NICARAGUA

Managua ✹

PACIFIC OCEAN

10°N

San José ✹

COSTA   PANAMA
RICA
Panama ✹

0   200   400 mi

0   200   400 km

JAMAICA   Kingston

HAITI DOMINICAN
REPUBLIC
Port-au-Prince ✹

PUERTO RICO
(U.S.)

Santo
Domingo
ST. KITTS
AND NEVIS

VIRGIN ISLANDS
(U.K., U.S.)

ANTIGUA AND BARBUDA

GUADELOUPE (FR.)

DOMINICA

MARTINIQUE (FR.)

ST. LUCIA

ST. VINCENT AND
THE GRENADINES

BARBADOS

Caribbean Sea

ARUBA
(NETH.)

NETHERLANDS ANTILLES
(NETH.)

GRENADA

Port of Spain

TRINIDAD AND
TOBAGO

10°N

VENEZUELA

SOUTH AMERICA

COLOMBIA

GUYANA

SURINAME

90°W   80°W   70°W   60°W

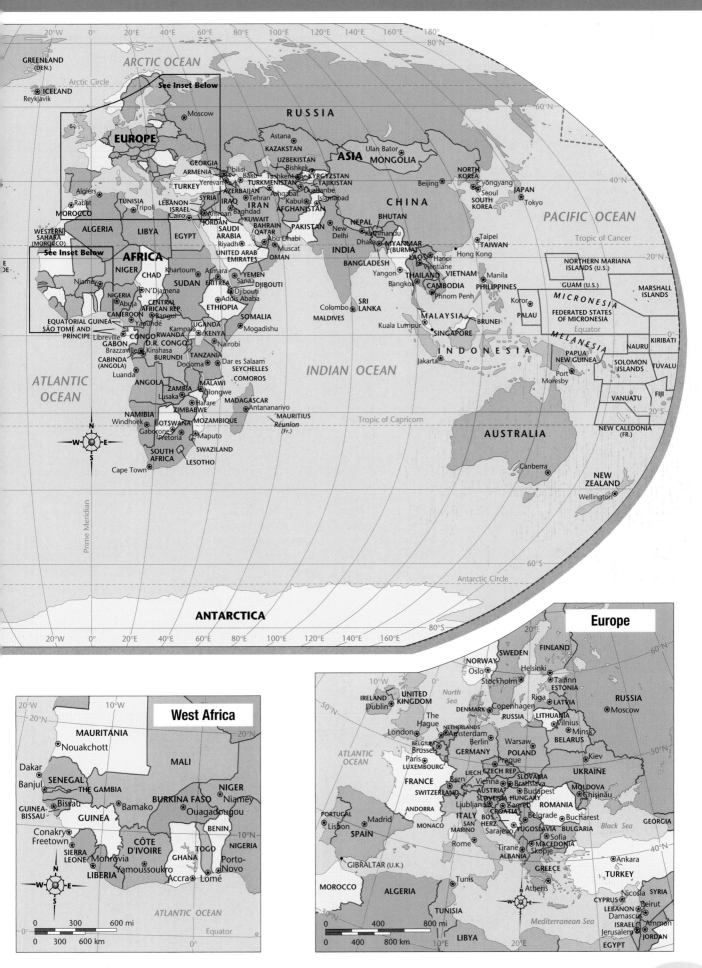

ARCTIC OCEAN

GREENLAND
(DEN.)

Arctic Circle

ICELAND
Reykjavik

Moscow

RUSSIA

EUROPE

Astana
KAZAKSTAN

ASIA
Ulan Bator
MONGOLIA

NORTH
KOREA
P'yŏngyang
Seoul
SOUTH
KOREA
Tokyo

JAPAN

PACIFIC OCEAN

GEORGIA
ARMENIA
TURKEY
Yerevan
Algiers
Rabat
MOROCCO

T'bilisi
Baku
UZBEKISTAN
Tashkent
Bishkek
TURKMENISTAN
AZERBAIJAN
Ashgabat
Tehran
SYRIA
IRAQ
LEBANON
ISRAEL
Cairo
Baghdad
JORDAN
Amman
KUWAIT
BAHRAIN
QATAR
SAUDI
ARABIA
Riyadh
Abu Dhabi
UNITED ARAB
EMIRATES
OMAN
Muscat

TUNISIA
Tripoli

KYRGYZSTAN
TAJIKISTAN
Dushanbe
Islamabad
AFGHANISTAN
Kabul
PAKISTAN

Beijing

CHINA

BHUTAN
NEPAL
New
Delhi
Kathmandu
Dhaka
INDIA

Taipei
TAIWAN
Hong Kong
Tropic of Cancer

NORTHERN MARIANA
ISLANDS (U.S.)

GUAM (U.S.)

WESTERN
SAHARA
(MOROCCO)

ALGERIA
LIBYA
EGYPT

See Inset Below

AFRICA
NIGER
CHAD
SUDAN
Khartoum
ERITREA
Asmara
YEMEN
Sanaa
DJIBOUTI
Djibouti

BANGLADESH
Yangon
MYANMAR
(BURMA)
LAOS
Hanoi
Vientiane
THAILAND
VIETNAM
Manila

Bangkok
CAMBODIA
Phnom Penh

PHILIPPINES

MICRONESIA
Koror
PALAU

MARSHALL
ISLANDS

FEDERATED STATES
OF MICRONESIA

Niamey
NIGERIA
Abuja
CENTRAL
AFRICAN REP.
N'Djamena
CAMEROON
Bangui
EQUATORIAL GUINEA
SÃO TOMÉ AND
PRÍNCIPE
Yaoundé
Libreville
GABON
CONGO
Brazzaville
Kinshasa
CABINDA
(ANGOLA)
Luanda

ETHIOPIA
SOMALIA
Addis Ababa
Mogadishu

UGANDA
Kampala
RWANDA
KENYA
BURUNDI
Nairobi
D.R. CONGO
TANZANIA
Dodoma
Dar es Salaam
SEYCHELLES
COMOROS

Colombo
SRI
LANKA
MALDIVES

Kuala Lumpur
MALAYSIA
BRUNEI
SINGAPORE

Equator

INDONESIA
Jakarta

MELANESIA
PAPUA
NEW GUINEA
Port
Moresby

NAURU
KIRIBATI

SOLOMON
ISLANDS
TUVALU

ATLANTIC
OCEAN

INDIAN OCEAN

ANGOLA
ZAMBIA
Lusaka
MALAWI
Lilongwe
ZIMBABWE
Harare
MADAGASCAR
Antananarivo
MAURITIUS
Réunion
(Fr.)
Tropic of Capricorn

VANUATU
FIJI

NEW CALEDONIA
(FR.)

NAMIBIA
Windhoek
BOTSWANA
Gaborone
Pretoria
Maputo
MOZAMBIQUE
SWAZILAND
SOUTH
AFRICA
LESOTHO
Cape Town

AUSTRALIA

Canberra

NEW
ZEALAND
Wellington

N
W E
S

Prime Meridian

ANTARCTICA

Antarctic Circle

West Africa

MAURITANIA
Nouakchott
MALI
Dakar
SENEGAL
Banjul
THE GAMBIA
NIGER
Niamey
GUINEA-
BISSAU
Bissau
BURKINA FASO
Bamako
Ouagadougou
GUINEA
BENIN
NIGERIA
Conakry
Freetown
SIERRA
LEONE
Monrovia
CÔTE
D'IVOIRE
GHANA
TOGO
Yamoussoukro
Accra
Lomé
Porto-
Novo
LIBERIA

N
W E
S

0   300   600 mi
0   300   600 km

ATLANTIC OCEAN
Equator

Europe

FINLAND
SWEDEN
NORWAY
Oslo
Helsinki
Stockholm
ESTONIA
Tallinn
RUSSIA
Moscow
IRELAND
UNITED
KINGDOM
North
Sea
Dublin
Riga
LATVIA
DENMARK
Copenhagen
LITHUANIA
The
Hague
London
RUSSIA
Vilnius
Minsk
NETHERLANDS
Amsterdam
Berlin
Warsaw
BELARUS
ATLANTIC
OCEAN
BELGIUM
Brussels
GERMANY
POLAND
Kiev
LUXEMBOURG
Paris
Prague
UKRAINE
LIECH.
CZECH REP.
SLOVAKIA
FRANCE
Bern
Vienna
Bratislava
MOLDOVA
SWITZERLAND
AUSTRIA
Budapest
Chişinău
SLOVENIA
HUNGARY
ANDORRA
Ljubljana
Zagreb
CROATIA
ROMANIA
PORTUGAL
ITALY
BOS.
HERZ.
Belgrade
Bucharest
SAN
MARINO
YUGOSLAVIA
BULGARIA
GEORGIA
Lisbon
Madrid
Rome
Sarajevo
Sofia
MONACO
SPAIN
Tiranë
MACEDONIA
Skopje
GIBRALTAR (U.K.)
ALBANIA
GREECE
Ankara
TURKEY
MOROCCO
Tunis
Athens
Nicosia
SYRIA
ALGERIA
CYPRUS
LEBANON
Beirut
TUNISIA
Mediterranean Sea
ISRAEL
Damascus
Amman
Jerusalem
JORDAN
LIBYA
EGYPT

Black Sea

N
W E
S

0   400   800 mi
0   400   800 km

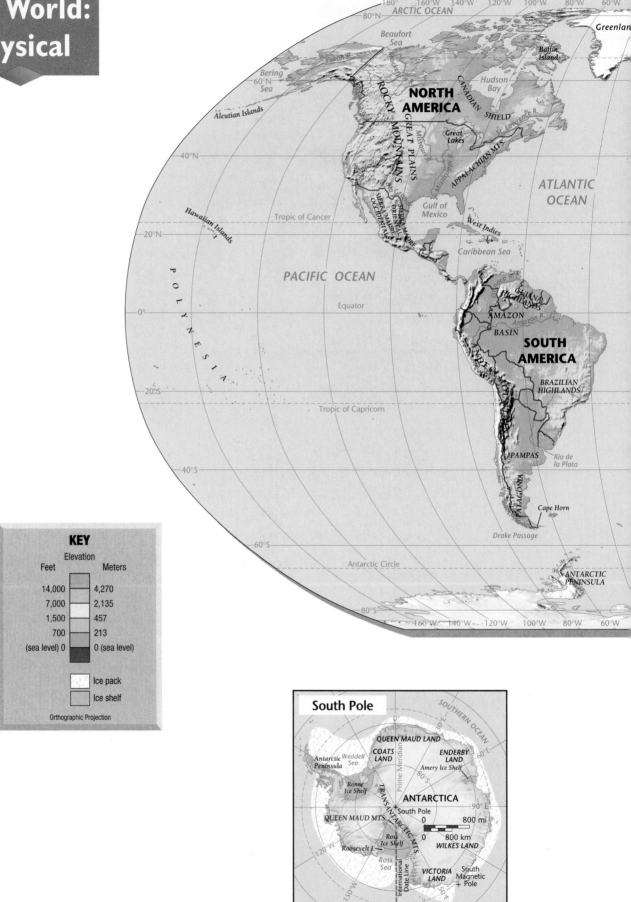

The World: Physical

KEY

Elevation

Feet		Meters
14,000		4,270
7,000		2,135
1,500		457
700		213
(sea level) 0		0 (sea level)

Ice pack

Ice shelf

Orthographic Projection

South Pole

SOUTHERN OCEAN

QUEEN MAUD LAND

COATS LAND

ENDERBY LAND

Antarctic Peninsula
Weddell Sea

Amery Ice Shelf

Ronne Ice Shelf

Prime Meridian

TRANSANTARCTIC MTS.

ANTARCTICA

South Pole

QUEEN MAUD MTS.

Ross Ice Shelf

Roosevelt I.

WILKES LAND

Ross Sea

VICTORIA LAND

South Magnetic Pole

International Date Line

0   800 mi

0   800 km

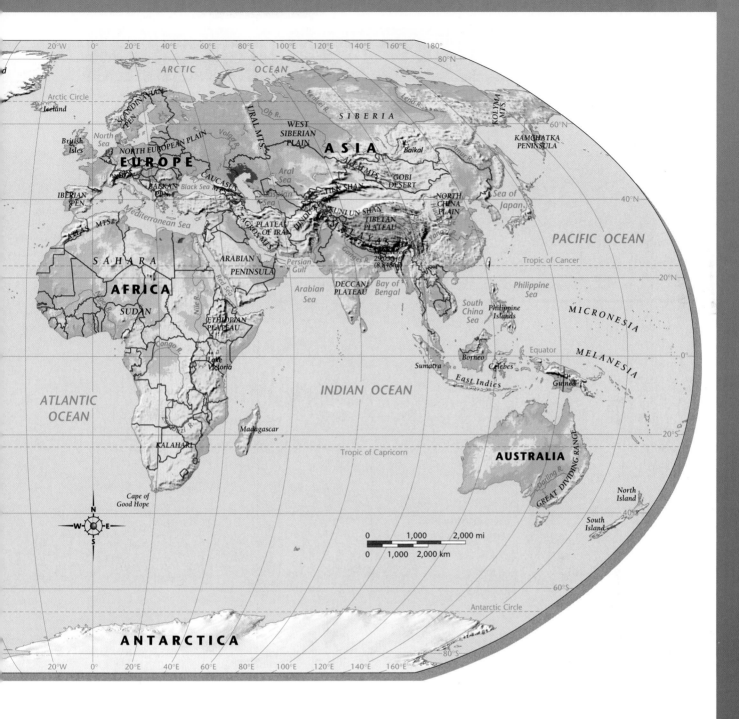

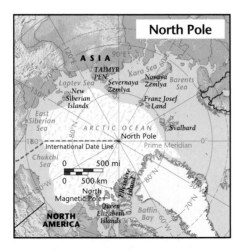

United States: Political

RUSSIA

ARCTIC OCEAN

ALASKA

CANADA

Bering Strait

Arctic Circle

70°N

70°N

60°N

60°N

Yukon River

Anchorage

Bering Sea

Gulf of Alaska

Juneau

0   250   500 mi

0   250   500 km

160°W   140°W

50°N

120°W   110°W

Seattle

Olympia

WASHINGTON

Spokane

Columbia

Portland

Salem

OREGON

Klamath Falls

Eureka

40°N

River

Helena

MONTANA

Billings

IDAHO

Boise

Snake River

Twin Falls

Jackson

WYOMING

Missouri River

Sheridan

Rapid C

Mino

Bismar

Winnemucca

Great
Salt Lake

Salt Lake City

Cheyenne

NEBRA

Sacramento

Carson City

NEVADA

UTAH

San Francisco

CALIFORNIA

Cedar
City

Las Vegas

Colorado River

Grand
Junction

COLORADO

Denver

Pueblo

Ark

Los Angeles

ARIZONA

Phoenix

Albuquerque

Santa Fe

NEW MEXICO

PACIFIC

OCEAN

San Diego

Tucson

Rio Grande

Roswell

El Paso

160°W   155°W

Honolulu

PACIFIC OCEAN

20°N   20°N

HAWAII

Hilo

0   50   100 mi

0   50   100 km

155°W

MEXICO

Tropic of Cancer

120°W   110°W

CANADA

Lake Superior

NORTH DAKOTA

Duluth

Sault Ste. Marie

MINNESOTA

MICHIGAN

Lake Huron

Presque Isle

MAINE

Augusta

Portland

Montpelier

VERMONT

NEW HAMPSHIRE

Concord

Boston

NEW YORK

MASSACHUSETTS

Lake Ontario

Albany

Providence

RHODE ISLAND

40°N

Hartford

CONNECTICUT

Minneapolis

St. Paul

WISCONSIN

Mississippi River

SOUTH DAKOTA

Milwaukee

Lansing

Lake Michigan

Buffalo

New Haven

Missouri

Madison

Detroit

Lake Erie

Cleveland

PENNSYLVANIA

Harrisburg

Pittsburgh

New York City

Trenton

NEW JERSEY

Philadelphia

Chicago

River

IOWA

Cedar Rapids

ILLINOIS

INDIANA

OHIO

Columbus

Baltimore

Dover

DELAWARE

Annapolis

Omaha

Des Moines

Indianapolis

Washington, D.C.

Lincoln

Cincinnati

WEST VIRGINIA

Richmond

MARYLAND

Springfield

Louisville

Frankfort

Charleston

VIRGINIA

Topeka

Kansas City

St. Louis

Ohio River

Norfolk

KANSAS

Jefferson City

KENTUCKY

River

MISSOURI

Tennessee River

Raleigh

Wichita

NORTH CAROLINA

Nashville

Charlotte

ATLANTIC

Tulsa

ARKANSAS

Memphis

TENNESSEE

OCEAN

OKLAHOMA

Columbia

Oklahoma City

Little Rock

Mississippi River

Atlanta

SOUTH CAROLINA

Red River

Pine Bluff

Birmingham

Charleston

Dallas

MISSISSIPPI

GEORGIA

ALABAMA

Columbus

Savannah

Shreveport

Jackson

Montgomery

30°N

Hattiesburg

Jacksonville

TEXAS

Tallahassee

Austin

Baton Rouge

FLORIDA

LOUISIANA

New Orleans

San Antonio

Houston

Tampa

Lake Okeechobee

Gulf of Mexico

Rio Grande

Miami

90°W

80°W

70°W

90°W

80°W

0   150   300 mi

0   150   300 km

N
W   E
S

KEY

— National boundary

— State boundary

⊛ National capital

⊙ State capital

• Other city

Transverse Mercator Projection

North and South America: Political

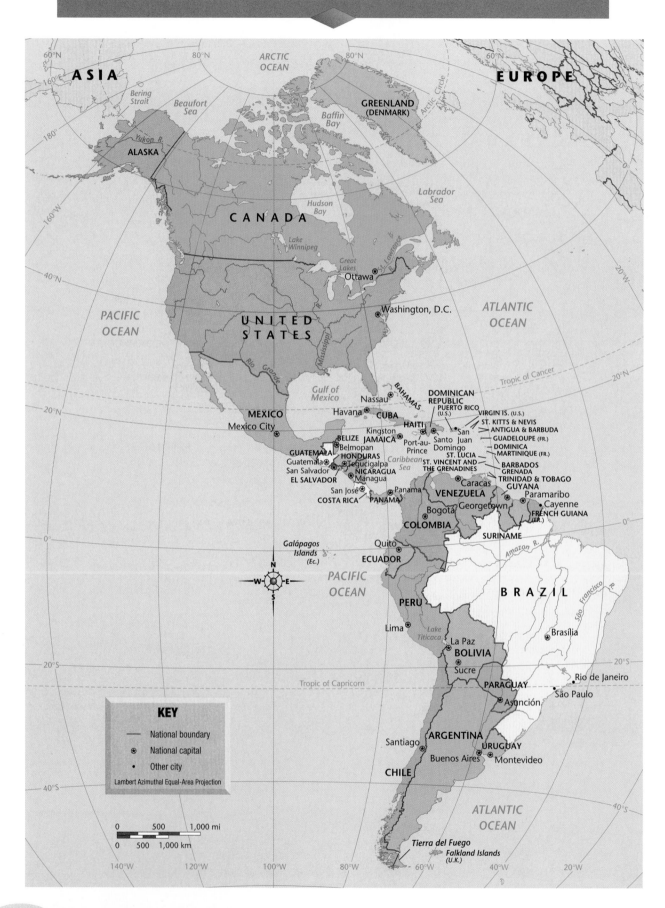

ASIA

EUROPE

ARCTIC OCEAN

Bering Strait

Beaufort Sea

GREENLAND (DENMARK)

Baffin Bay

Arctic Circle

ALASKA

Yukon R.

Labrador Sea

Hudson Bay

C A N A D A

Lake Winnipeg

Great Lakes

St. Lawrence

⊛ Ottawa

PACIFIC OCEAN

U N I T E D S T A T E S

⊛ Washington, D.C.

ATLANTIC OCEAN

Rio Grande

Mississippi

Tropic of Cancer

20°N

Gulf of Mexico

Nassau

BAHAMAS

DOMINICAN REPUBLIC

PUERTO RICO (U.S.)

VIRGIN IS. (U.S.)

MEXICO

Havana ⊛

CUBA

ST. KITTS & NEVIS

ANTIGUA & BARBUDA

Mexico City ⊛

Kingston

HAITI

San Juan

GUADELOUPE (FR.)

BELIZE

JAMAICA

Port-au-Prince

Santo Domingo

DOMINICA

MARTINIQUE (FR.)

Belmopan

HONDURAS

ST. LUCIA

BARBADOS

GUATEMALA ⊛

ST. VINCENT AND THE GRENADINES

GRENADA

Guatemala ⊛

Tegucigalpa ⊛

Caribbean Sea

TRINIDAD & TOBAGO

San Salvador ⊛

NICARAGUA

Caracas ⊛

GUYANA

EL SALVADOR

Managua ⊛

VENEZUELA

Paramaribo ⊛

San José ⊛

⊛ Panama

Georgetown ⊛

Cayenne •

COSTA RICA

PANAMA

FRENCH GUIANA (FR.)

Bogotá ⊛

SURINAME

COLOMBIA

Amazon R.

Galápagos Islands (Ec.)

Quito ⊛

ECUADOR

PACIFIC OCEAN

B R A Z I L

São Francisco R.

PERU

Lima ⊛

Lake Titicaca

La Paz ⊛

• Brasília

BOLIVIA

Sucre ⊛

Rio de Janeiro

Tropic of Capricorn

PARAGUAY

• São Paulo

Asunción ⊛

KEY

— National boundary

⊛ National capital

• Other city

Lambert Azimuthal Equal-Area Projection

ARGENTINA

URUGUAY

Santiago ⊛

Buenos Aires ⊛

Montevideo ⊛

CHILE

ATLANTIC OCEAN

| 0 | 500 | 1,000 mi |

| 0 | 500 | 1,000 km |

Tierra del Fuego

Falkland Islands (U.K.)

North and South America: Physical

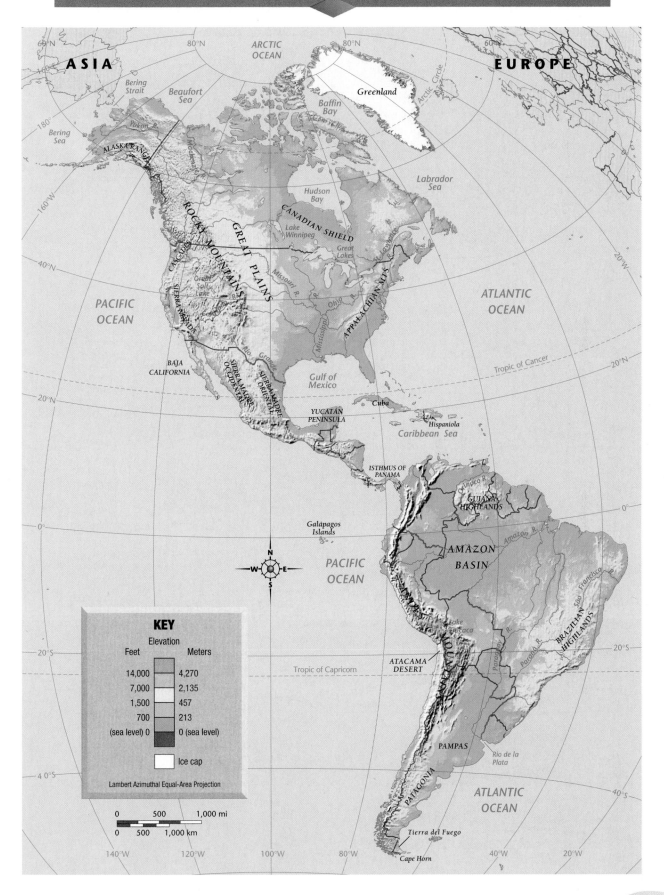

ASIA

ARCTIC OCEAN

EUROPE

Bering Strait

Beaufort Sea

Greenland

Bering Sea

Yukon R.

ALASKA RANGE

Baffin Bay

Labrador Sea

Hudson Bay

Mackenzie R.

CANADIAN SHIELD

ROCKY MOUNTAINS

GREAT PLAINS

CASCADES

Lake Winnipeg

Great Lakes

St. Lawrence

APPALACHIAN MTS.

PACIFIC OCEAN

SIERRA NEVADA

Great Salt Lake

Missouri R.

Ohio R.

Mississippi R.

ATLANTIC OCEAN

BAJA CALIFORNIA

SIERRA MADRE OCCIDENTAL

SIERRA MADRE ORIENTAL

Rio Grande

Gulf of Mexico

Tropic of Cancer

Cuba

YUCATÁN PENINSULA

Hispaniola

Caribbean Sea

ISTHMUS OF PANAMA

Orinoco R.

GUIANA HIGHLANDS

Galápagos Islands

AMAZON BASIN

Amazon R.

PACIFIC OCEAN

São Francisco R.

ANDES

Lake Titicaca

BRAZILIAN HIGHLANDS

ATACAMA DESERT

Tropic of Capricorn

Paraguay R.

Paraná R.

KEY

Elevation

Feet		Meters
14,000		4,270
7,000		2,135
1,500		457
700		213
(sea level) 0		0 (sea level)

☐ Ice cap

Lambert Azimuthal Equal-Area Projection

```
0      500    1,000 mi
0      500  1,000 km
```

PAMPAS

Rio de la Plata

PATAGONIA

ATLANTIC OCEAN

Tierra del Fuego

Cape Horn

Europe: Political

KEY

— National boundary
⊛ National capital
• Other city

Lambert Azimuthal Equal-Area Projection

ARCTIC OCEAN

30°W 20°W 10°W 0° 10°E 20°E 30°E 40°E 50°E

Arctic Circle

Reykjavik ⊛ **ICELAND**

ATLANTIC OCEAN

60°N

Faeroe Is. (Den.)

Prime Meridian

Shetland Is. (U.K.)

60°N

FINLAND

Gulf of Bothnia

SWEDEN

NORWAY
Lillehammer •

Turku • Helsinki ⊛ • St. Petersburg

Oslo ⊛ • Stockholm Tallinn ⊛

ESTONIA

RUSSIA

Moscow ⊛

North Sea

• Göteborg

Baltic Sea

Riga ⊛ **LATVIA**

DENMARK
Copenhagen ⊛

LITHUANIA
Vilnius ⊛

BELARUS

RUSSIA

Minsk •

IRELAND
Dublin ⊛

UNITED KINGDOM

• Manchester

Gdańsk •

POLAND
Warsaw ⊛
Łódź •

Kiev ⊛

50°N

Amsterdam Berlin •
The Hague ⊛ **GERMANY**
NETHERLANDS

London •

English Channel

Brussels ⊛
BELGIUM
Cologne •
Bonn •

Katowice • Kraków •

UKRAINE

LUXEMBOURG
Luxembourg ⊛ Frankfurt •
Prague ⊛ **CZECH REPUBLIC**
Brno • **SLOVAKIA**

• Paris

Danube R.

Munich • • Bratislava ⊛
Vienna ⊛

MOLDOVA
Chişinău ⊛

Bay of Biscay

FRANCE

LIECHTENSTEIN
Bern ⊛
SWITZERLAND

AUSTRIA • Budapest ⊛ **HUNGARY**

• Cluj-Napoca
ROMANIA

Milan •

Ljubljana ⊛ • Zagreb ⊛
SLOVENIA

Bucharest ⊛

Black Sea

CROATIA

BOSNIA-HERZEGOVINA Belgrade ⊛

SAN MARINO

Marseille • **MONACO**

ITALY

Adriatic Sea

Sarajevo ⊛ **YUGOSLAVIA**
Podgorica •

BULGARIA

Sofia ⊛

PORTUGAL

ANDORRA

Corsica

Rome ⊛

Skopje ⊛
ALBANIA **MACEDONIA**

40°N

Lisbon ⊛ • Madrid ⊛

• Barcelona

VATICAN CITY

Tiranë •

Aegean Sea

SPAIN

Sardinia

Naples •

Balearic Is.

Tyrrhenian Sea

Ionian Sea

GREECE

Athens ⊛

Mediterranean

Strait of Gibraltar

GIBRALTAR (U.K.)

Sicily

Crete

Sea

N
W E
S

AFRICA

MALTA

0 250 500 mi
0 250 500 km

10°E 0° 20°E

Europe: Physical

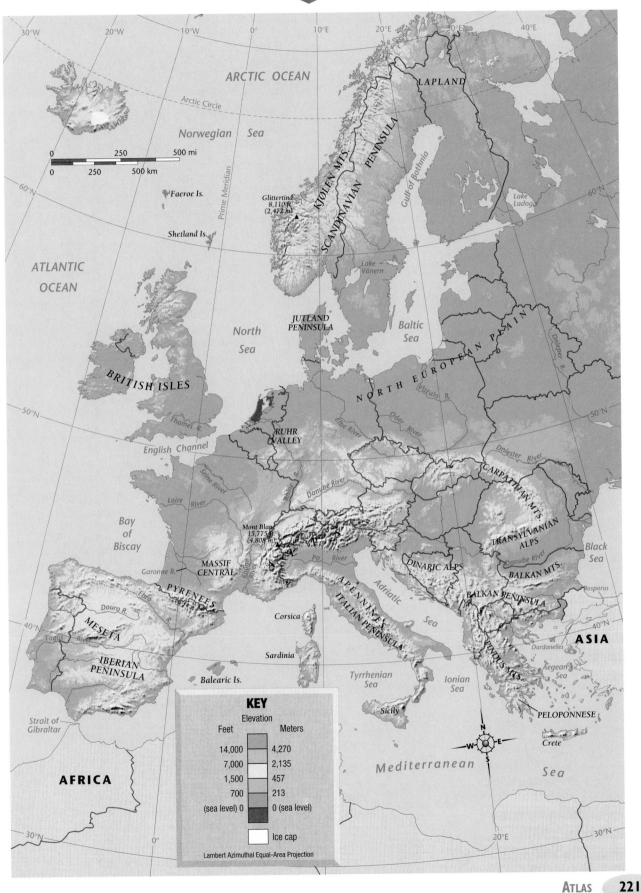

ARCTIC OCEAN

LAPLAND

Norwegian Sea

Arctic Circle

Faeroe Is.

Glittertind
8,110 ft
(2,472 m)

KJØLEN MTS.

SCANDINAVIAN PENINSULA

Gulf of Bothnia

Lake Ladoga

Shetland Is.

ATLANTIC OCEAN

Lake Vänern

Prime Meridian

JUTLAND PENINSULA

Baltic Sea

North Sea

NORTH EUROPEAN PLAIN

Dnieper R.

BRITISH ISLES

Vistula R.

Thames R.

RUHR VALLEY

Elbe River

Oder River

50°N

English Channel

Seine River

Dniester River

Rhine R.

CARPATHIAN MTS.

Loire River

Danube River

Bay of Biscay

Mont Blanc
15,775 ft
(4,808 m)

A L P S

Po River

TRANSYLVANIAN ALPS

Black Sea

MASSIF CENTRAL

Garonne R.

DINARIC ALPS

Danube River

BALKAN MTS.

Bosporus

PYRENEES

Ebro R.

A P E N N I N E S

Adriatic Sea

BALKAN PENINSULA

Douro R.

ITALIAN PENINSULA

MESETA

Corsica

PINDUS MTS.

ASIA

Tagus River

Dardanelles

Aegean Sea

IBERIAN PENINSULA

Sardinia

Tyrrhenian Sea

Ionian Sea

PELOPONNESE

Balearic Is.

Strait of Gibraltar

Sicily

Crete

AFRICA

Mediterranean Sea

KEY
Elevation

Feet	Meters
14,000	4,270
7,000	2,135
1,500	457
700	213
(sea level) 0	0 (sea level)

Ice cap

Lambert Azimuthal Equal-Area Projection

500 mi
500 km

Africa: Political

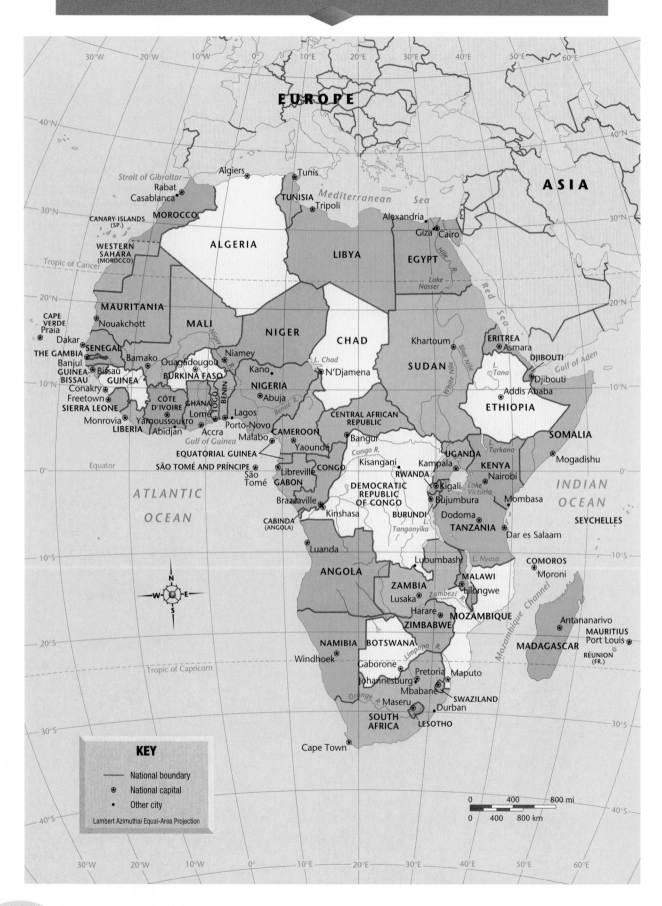

EUROPE

ASIA

Strait of Gibraltar
Algiers ⊛
Tunis
Rabat ⊛
Casablanca •
TUNISIA
Tripoli •
Mediterranean Sea
MOROCCO
Alexandria •
Giza • Cairo ⊛
CANARY ISLANDS (SP.)
30°N
WESTERN SAHARA (MOROCCO)
ALGERIA
LIBYA
EGYPT
Tropic of Cancer
Nile R.
Lake Nasser
20°N
MAURITANIA
MALI
NIGER
CHAD
Khartoum •
ERITREA
Asmara •
CAPE VERDE
Praia ⊛
Nouakchott ⊛
DJIBOUTI
Red Sea
Gulf of Aden
Dakar •
SENEGAL ⊛
Niger R.
Niamey ⊛
L. Chad
SUDAN
White Nile
Blue Nile
L. Tana
Djibouti •
THE GAMBIA
Bamako ⊛
Ouagadougou ⊛
Kano •
N'Djamena •
Banjul ⊛
GUINEA BISSAU
Bissau ⊛
BURKINA FASO
NIGERIA
Addis Ababa •
GUINEA
Conakry ⊛
CÔTE D'IVOIRE
GHANA
Abuja ⊛
CENTRAL AFRICAN REPUBLIC
ETHIOPIA
Freetown ⊛
BENIN
TOGO
Benue R.
SOMALIA
SIERRA LEONE
Yamoussoukro ⊛
Lomé
Lagos •
Monrovia ⊛
Accra ⊛
Porto-Novo ⊛
LIBERIA
Abidjan •
Malabo ⊛
CAMEROON
Bangui ⊛
L. Turkana
Mogadishu •
EQUATORIAL GUINEA
Gulf of Guinea
Yaoundé ⊛
UGANDA
KENYA
SÃO TOMÉ AND PRÍNCIPE ⊛
Kisangani •
Kampala ⊛
Nairobi ⊛
INDIAN OCEAN
Equator
São Tomé
Libreville ⊛
CONGO
RWANDA
Kigali ⊛
Lake Victoria
GABON
DEMOCRATIC REPUBLIC OF CONGO
Bujumbura ⊛
Mombasa •
ATLANTIC OCEAN
Brazzaville ⊛
BURUNDI
Dodoma •
SEYCHELLES
Kinshasa ⊛
L. Tanganyika
TANZANIA
Dar es Salaam •
CABINDA (ANGOLA)
Luanda ⊛
Lubumbashi •
L. Nyasa
COMOROS
Moroni •
ANGOLA
MALAWI
ZAMBIA
Lilongwe ⊛
Zambezi R.
Lusaka ⊛
Mozambique Channel
Antananarivo •
Harare ⊛
MOZAMBIQUE
MAURITIUS
Port Louis •
NAMIBIA
BOTSWANA
ZIMBABWE
MADAGASCAR
RÉUNION (FR.)
Windhoek ⊛
Limpopo R.
Gaborone ⊛
Pretoria ⊛
Maputo ⊛
Tropic of Capricorn
Johannesburg •
Mbabane ⊛
SWAZILAND
Orange R.
Maseru ⊛
• Durban
SOUTH AFRICA
LESOTHO
Cape Town •

KEY

⎯⎯ National boundary

⊛ National capital

• Other city

Lambert Azimuthal Equal-Area Projection

0   400   800 mi

0   400   800 km

Africa: Physical

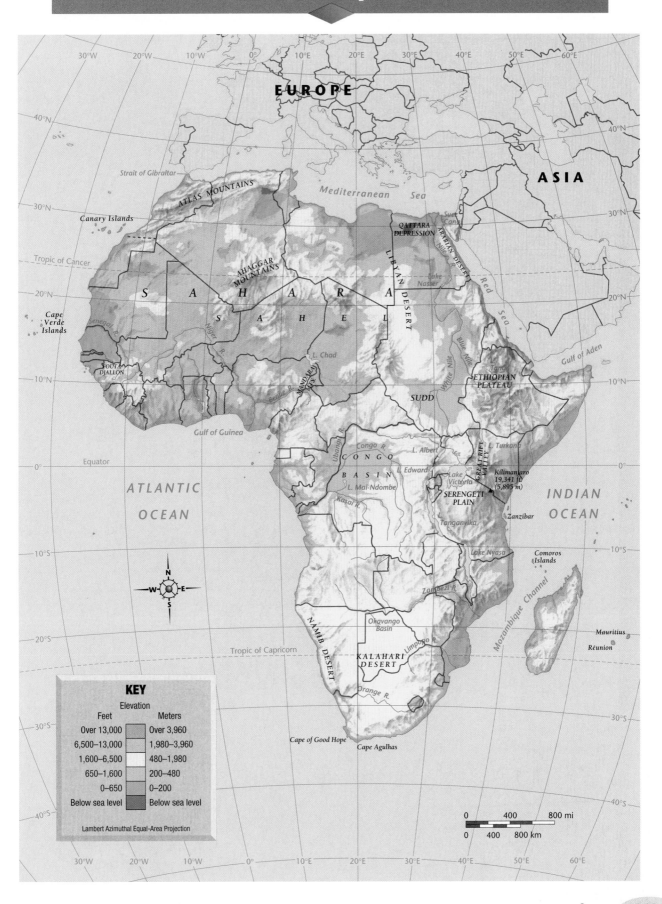

30°W · 20°W · 10°W · 0° · 10°E · 20°E · 30°E · 40°E · 50°E · 60°E

EUROPE

ASIA

40°N

Strait of Gibraltar

ATLAS MOUNTAINS

Mediterranean Sea

Canary Islands

30°N

QATTARA
DEPRESSION

Suez Canal

Tropic of Cancer

AHAGGAR
MOUNTAINS

Nile R.

ARABIAN DESERT

Lake Nasser

S   A   H   A   R   A

20°N

Cape Verde Islands

Senegal R.

S   A   H   E   L

LIBYAN DESERT

Red Sea

Niger R.

L. Chad

Gulf of Aden

10°N

FOUTA
DJALLON

Benue R.

MANDARA MTS.

White Nile

Blue Nile

ETHIOPIAN
PLATEAU

SUDD

Gulf of Guinea

Ubangi R.

Congo R.

C   O   N   G   O

L. Albert

L. Turkana

Tana

GREAT RIFT VALLEY

Equator   0°

ATLANTIC

OCEAN

B   A   S   I   N

L. Edward

Lake Victoria

Kilimanjaro
19,341 ft
(5,895 m)

INDIAN

OCEAN

L. Mai-Ndombe

SERENGETI
PLAIN

Kasai R.

Tanganyika

Zanzibar

10°S

Lake Nyasa

Comoros Islands

Zambezi R.

Mozambique Channel

Mauritius

Okavango Basin

Réunion

NAMIB DESERT

Tropic of Capricorn

Limpopo R.

KALAHARI
DESERT

30°S

Orange R.

Cape of Good Hope

Cape Agulhas

KEY

Elevation

Feet	Meters
Over 13,000	Over 3,960
6,500–13,000	1,980–3,960
1,600–6,500	480–1,980
650–1,600	200–480
0–650	0–200
Below sea level	Below sea level

Lambert Azimuthal Equal-Area Projection

N
W · E
S

0   400   800 mi

0   400   800 km

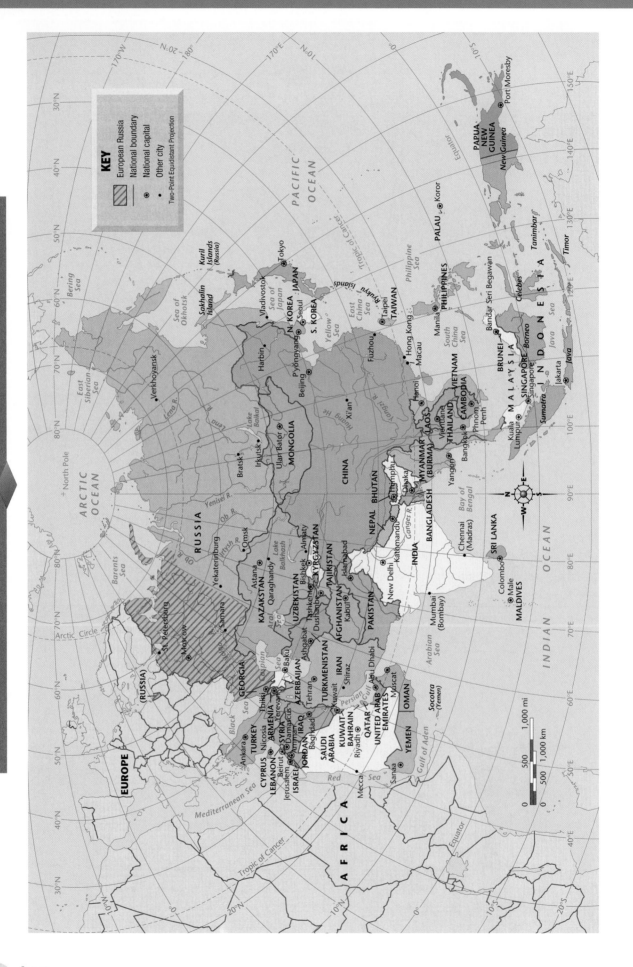

Asia: Political

KEY

- European Russia
- National boundary
- ⊛ National capital
- • Other city

Two-Point Equidistant Projection

EUROPE

AFRICA

RUSSIA

(RUSSIA)

North Pole

ARCTIC OCEAN

Arctic Circle

PACIFIC OCEAN

INDIAN OCEAN

Bering Sea

East Siberian Sea

Barents Sea

Sea of Okhotsk

Kuril Islands (Russia)

Sakhalin Island

Sea of Japan

JAPAN

Tokyo

Vladivostok

N. KOREA

Pyŏngyang

Seoul

S. KOREA

Yellow Sea

East China Sea

Ryūkyū Islands

Fuzhou

TAIWAN

Taipei

Hong Kong

Macau

South China Sea

Philippine Sea

PHILIPPINES

Manila

PALAU

Koror

Bandar Seri Begawan

BRUNEI

MALAYSIA

Kuala Lumpur

SINGAPORE

Singapore

Borneo

Celebes

INDONESIA

Sumatra

Java

Jakarta

Java Sea

Timor

Tanimbar

PAPUA NEW GUINEA

New Guinea

Port Moresby

Equator

Verkhoyansk

Harbin

Beijing

Xi'an

CHINA

Huang He

Chang Jiang

Yangtze R.

VIETNAM

Hanoi

LAOS

Vientiane

THAILAND

Bangkok

CAMBODIA

Phnom Penh

MYANMAR (BURMA)

Yangon

Bratsk

Irkutsk

Ulan Bator

MONGOLIA

Lake Baikal

Lena R.

Yenisei R.

Ob R.

Irtysh R.

Omsk

Yekaterinburg

Samara

St. Petersburg

Moscow

Volga R.

Caspian Sea

Black Sea

GEORGIA

Tbilisi

ARMENIA

Yerevan

AZERBAIJAN

Baku

TURKEY

Ankara

Nicosia

CYPRUS

LEBANON

Beirut

SYRIA

Damascus

ISRAEL

Jerusalem

Amman

JORDAN

IRAQ

Baghdad

SAUDI ARABIA

Riyadh

Mecca

KUWAIT

Kuwait

BAHRAIN

QATAR

UNITED ARAB EMIRATES

Abu Dhabi

Persian Gulf

Gulf of Oman

OMAN

Muscat

YEMEN

Sanaa

Socotra (Yemen)

Gulf of Aden

Red Sea

Mediterranean Sea

KAZAKHSTAN

Astana

Qaraghandy

Aral Sea

Lake Balkhash

UZBEKISTAN

Tashkent

Almaty

KYRGYZSTAN

Bishkek

TAJIKISTAN

Dushanbe

TURKMENISTAN

Ashgabat

IRAN

Tehran

Shiraz

AFGHANISTAN

Kabul

PAKISTAN

Islamabad

Arabian Sea

NEPAL

Kathmandu

BHUTAN

Thimphu

INDIA

New Delhi

Mumbai (Bombay)

Chennai (Madras)

Ganges R.

BANGLADESH

Dhaka

Bay of Bengal

SRI LANKA

Colombo

MALDIVES

Male

Tropic of Cancer

Equator

80°N

70°N

60°N

50°N

40°N

30°N

20°N

10°N

0°

10°S

20°S

180°

170°W

170°E

160°E

150°E

140°E

130°E

120°E

110°E

100°E

90°E

80°E

70°E

60°E

50°E

40°E

30°E

20°E

10°E

0°

1,000 mi

500 1,000 km

500

0

0

N

W E

S

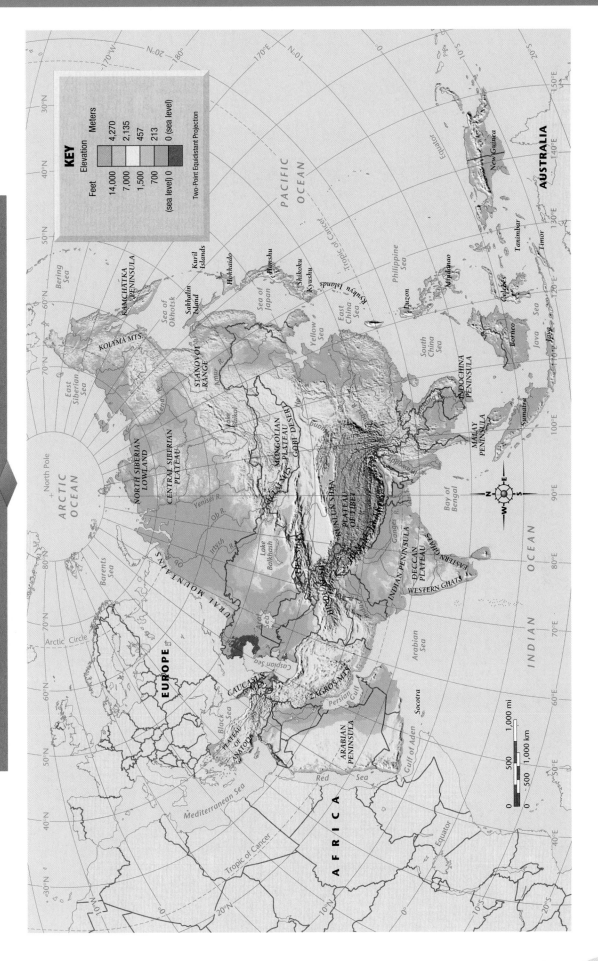

Asia: Physical

KEY

Elevation

Feet	Meters
14,000	4,270
7,000	2,135
1,500	457
700	213
(sea level) 0	0 (sea level)

Two-Point Equidistant Projection

North Pole

ARCTIC OCEAN

Arctic Circle

EUROPE

AFRICA

Bering Sea

East Siberian Sea

Barents Sea

KOLYMA MTS.

KAMCHATKA PENINSULA

Sea of Okhotsk

NORTH SIBERIAN LOWLAND

CENTRAL SIBERIAN PLATEAU

STANOVOY RANGE

Amur R.

Sakhalin Island

Kuril Islands

Hokkaido

Sea of Japan

Honshu

Shikoku

Kyushu

Ryukyu Islands

East China Sea

Yellow Sea

PACIFIC OCEAN

URAL MOUNTAINS

Ob R.

Yenisei R.

Lake Baikal

Lake Balkhash

Ob R.

Irtysh

MONGOLIAN PLATEAU

GOBI DESERT

Huang

TIEN SHAN

KUNLUN SHAN

PLATEAU OF TIBET

HIMALAYAS

Mekong

South China Sea

Philippine Sea

Luzon

Mindanao

Celebes

Borneo

Java Sea

Java

Sumatra

INDOCHINA PENINSULA

MALAY PENINSULA

Ganges R.

INDIAN PENINSULA

DECCAN PLATEAU

WESTERN GHATS

EASTERN GHATS

Bay of Bengal

Aral Sea

Caspian Sea

CAUCASUS MTS.

Black Sea

PLATEAU OF ANATOLIA

ZAGROS MTS.

Persian Gulf

ARABIAN PENINSULA

Arabian Sea

Socotra

Gulf of Aden

Red Sea

Mediterranean Sea

Tropic of Cancer

Equator

INDIAN OCEAN

Tropic of Cancer

New Guinea

Tanimbar

Timor

AUSTRALIA

Equator

N E S W

0 500 1,000 mi

0 500 1,000 km

Australia, New Zealand, and the Pacific Islands: Physical–Political

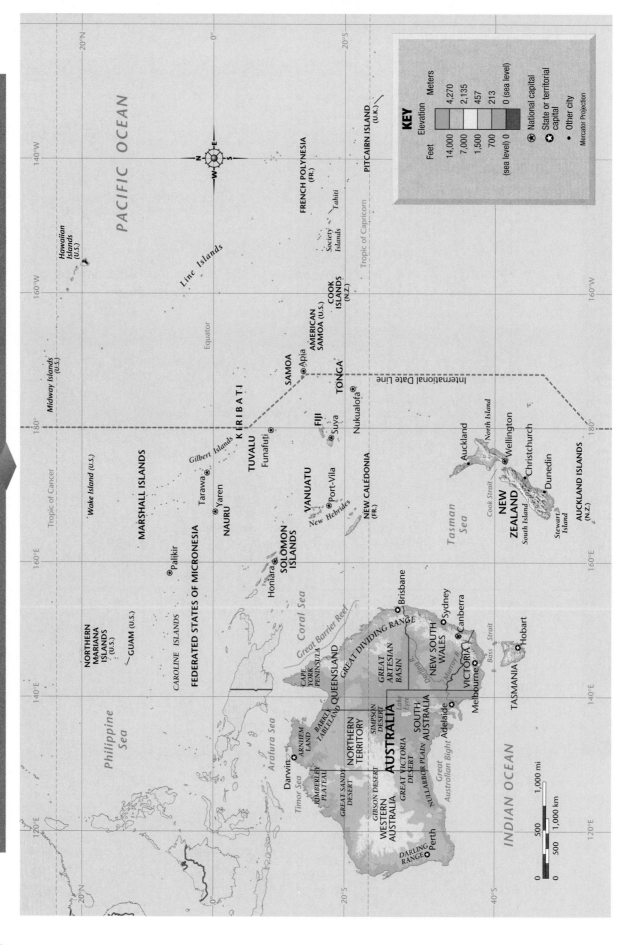

KEY

Elevation

Feet	Meters
14,000	4,270
7,000	2,135
1,500	457
700	213
(sea level) 0	0 (sea level)

⊗ National capital
⊛ State or territorial capital
• Other city

Mercator Projection

PACIFIC OCEAN

Hawaiian Islands (U.S.)

Line Islands

FRENCH POLYNESIA (FR.)

Society Islands
Tahiti

Tropic of Capricorn

PITCAIRN ISLAND (U.K.)

Midway Islands (U.S.)

Equator

AMERICAN SAMOA (U.S.)

COOK ISLANDS (N.Z.)

SAMOA
⊗ Apia

TONGA
⊗ Nukualofa

International Date Line

KIRIBATI

TUVALU
⊗ Funafuti

FIJI
⊗ Suva

Wake Island (U.S.)

Tropic of Cancer

Gilbert Islands

MARSHALL ISLANDS

Tarawa ⊗

NAURU
⊗ Yaren

VANUATU
⊗ Port-Vila

New Hebrides

NEW CALEDONIA (FR.)

Auckland
North Island

⊗ Wellington
Christchurch

Dunedin

AUCKLAND ISLANDS (N.Z.)

Tasman Sea

NEW ZEALAND
South Island

Cook Strait

Stewart Island

Palikir ⊗

FEDERATED STATES OF MICRONESIA

CAROLINE ISLANDS

NORTHERN MARIANA ISLANDS (U.S.)

GUAM (U.S.)

SOLOMON ISLANDS
Honiara ⊗

Coral Sea

Great Barrier Reef

Brisbane

GREAT DIVIDING RANGE

NEW SOUTH WALES
Sydney ⊛
Canberra ⊗

GREAT ARTESIAN BASIN

Murray R.
Darling R.

VICTORIA
Melbourne ⊛

Bass Strait

TASMANIA
Hobart ⊛

Philippine Sea

Arafura Sea

Timor Sea

Darwin ⊛

ARNHEM LAND

KIMBERLEY PLATEAU

NORTHERN TERRITORY

BARKLY TABLELAND

CAPE YORK PENINSULA

QUEENSLAND

SIMPSON DESERT

AUSTRALIA

Lake Eyre

GREAT SANDY DESERT

GIBSON DESERT

WESTERN AUSTRALIA

GREAT VICTORIA DESERT

SOUTH AUSTRALIA

NULLARBOR PLAIN

Adelaide ⊛

Great Australian Bight

DARLING RANGE
Perth ⊛

INDIAN OCEAN

| 0 | 500 | 1,000 mi |
| 0 | 500 | 1,000 km |

The Arctic

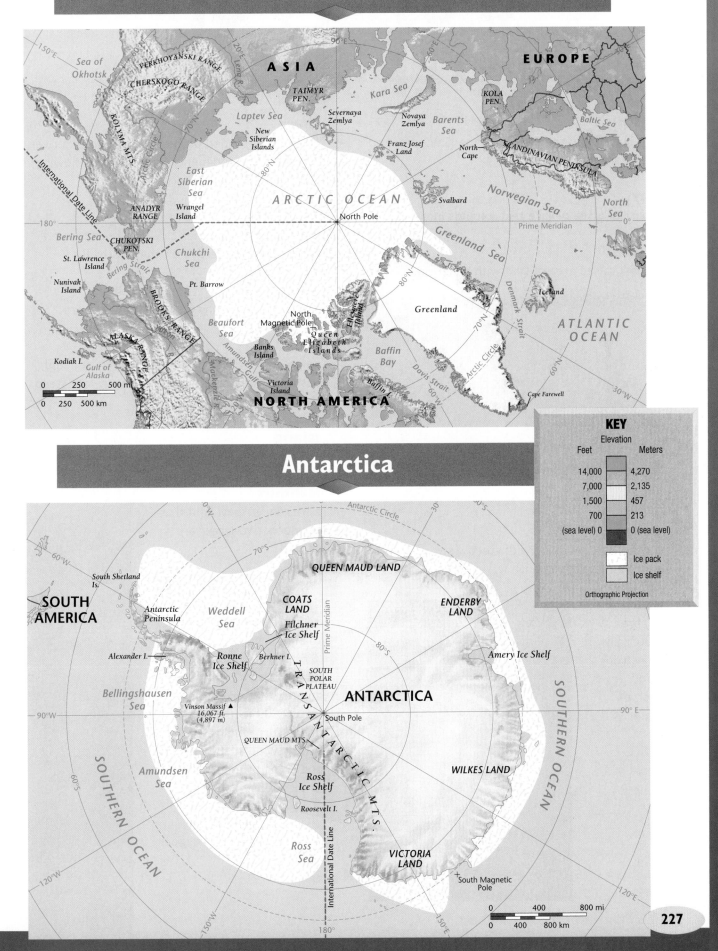

ASIA

Sea of Okhotsk

VERKHOYANSKI RANGE

CHERSKOGO RANGE

TAIMYR PEN.

Kara Sea

EUROPE

KOLA PEN.

KOLYMA MTS.

Laptev Sea

Severnaya Zemlya

Novaya Zemlya

Barents Sea

Baltic Sea

Lena R.

New Siberian Islands

Franz Josef Land

North Cape

SCANDINAVIAN PENINSULA

East Siberian Sea

Arctic Circle

ARCTIC OCEAN

North Pole

Svalbard

Norwegian Sea

North Sea

International Date Line

ANADYR RANGE

Wrangel Island

Prime Meridian

Bering Sea

CHUKOTSKI PEN.

Chukchi Sea

Greenland Sea

St. Lawrence Island

Bering Strait

Pt. Barrow

Denmark Strait

Iceland

Nunivak Island

BROOKS RANGE

Beaufort Sea

North Magnetic Pole

Ellesmere Island

Greenland

ATLANTIC OCEAN

ALASKA RANGE

Queen Elizabeth Islands

Arctic Circle

Kodiak I.

Gulf of Alaska

Banks Island

Amundsen Gulf

Mackenzie R.

Baffin Bay

Davis Strait

Victoria Island

Baffin I.

Cape Farewell

NORTH AMERICA

0 250 500 mi

0 250 500 km

Antarctica

KEY

Elevation

Feet		Meters
14,000		4,270
7,000		2,135
1,500		457
700		213
(sea level) 0		0 (sea level)

Ice pack

Ice shelf

Orthographic Projection

Antarctic Circle

QUEEN MAUD LAND

South Shetland Is.

SOUTH AMERICA

Antarctic Peninsula

Weddell Sea

COATS LAND

ENDERBY LAND

Filchner Ice Shelf

Prime Meridian

Amery Ice Shelf

Alexander I.

Ronne Ice Shelf

Berkner I.

SOUTH POLAR PLATEAU

ANTARCTICA

SOUTHERN OCEAN

Bellingshausen Sea

TRANSANTARCTIC MTS.

Vinson Massif
16,067 ft
(4,897 m)

South Pole

Amundsen Sea

QUEEN MAUD MTS.

WILKES LAND

Ross Ice Shelf

Roosevelt I.

VICTORIA LAND

SOUTHERN OCEAN

Ross Sea

International Date Line

South Magnetic Pole

0 400 800 mi

0 400 800 km

Glossary of Geographic Terms

basin
a depression in the surface of the land; some basins are filled with water

bay
a part of a sea or lake that extends into the land

butte
a small raised area of land with steep sides

▲ butte

canyon
a deep, narrow valley with steep sides; often has a stream flowing through it

cataract
a large waterfall; any strong flood or rush of water

◀ cataract

delta
a triangular-shaped plain at the mouth of a river, formed when sediment is deposited by flowing water

flood plain
a broad plain on either side of a river, formed when sediment settles on the riverbanks

glacier
a huge, slow-moving mass of snow and ice

hill
an area that rises above surrounding land and has a rounded top; lower and usually less steep than a mountain

island
an area of land completely surrounded by water

isthmus
a narrow strip of land that connects two larger areas of land

mesa
a high, flat-topped landform with cliff-like sides; larger than a butte

mountain
an area that rises steeply at least 2,000 feet (610 m) above surrounding land; usually wide at the bottom and rising to a narrow peak or ridge

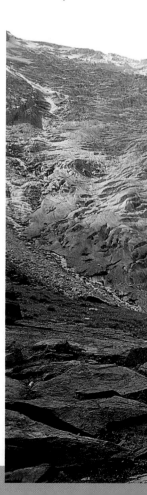

▶ glacier

◀ delta

mountain pass
a gap between mountains

peninsula
an area of land almost completely surrounded by water and connected to the mainland by an isthmus

plain
a large area of flat or gently rolling land

plateau
a large, flat area that rises above the surrounding land; at least one side has a steep slope

river mouth
the point where a river enters a lake or sea

strait
a narrow stretch of water that connects two larger bodies of water

tributary
a river or stream that flows into a larger river

volcano
an opening in the Earth's surface through which molten rock, ashes, and gasses from the Earth's interior escape

▶ volcano

Gazetteer

A

Abuja (9°N, 7°E) the federal capital of Nigeria, p. 110

Addis Ababa (9°N, 38°E) the capital city of Ethiopia, p. 139

Aksum an ancient city in northern Ethiopia, a powerful kingdom and trade center from about A.D. 200 to A.D. 600, p. 35

B

Belgian Congo name for a Belgian colony in central Africa in the early 1900s, oficially the Congo Free State; gained independence and became Zaire; now known as the Democratic Republic of Congo, p. 46

C

Cairo (30°N, 31°E) the capital of Egypt and most populous city in Africa, p. 66

Cape of Good Hope (34°S, 18°E) a province of the Republic of South Africa; the cape at the southern end of Cape Peninsula, South Africa, p. 42

Cape Town (33°S, 18°E) the legislative capital of the Republic of South Africa; the capital of Cape Province, p. 170

Central and Southern Africa countries in the central and southern region of Africa, p. 84

Congo, Democratic Republic of (1°S, 22°E) a country in Central Africa, formerly known as Zaire, p. 12

Congo River a river in Central Africa that flows into the Atlantic Ocean, p. 12

D

Dar es Salaam (6°S, 39°E) the capital and largest city in Tanzania, an industrial center and major port on the Indian Ocean, p. 79

E

East Africa countries in the eastern region of Africa, p. 76

Egypt (27°N, 30°E) a country in North Africa, officially Arab Republic of Egypt, p. 33

G

Ghana (8°N, 2°W) a country in West Africa, officially Republic of Ghana, p. 37

Gorée (16°N, 17°E) an island off the coast of Senegal, p. 41

Great Rift Valley the major branch of the East African Rift System, p. 11

K

Kalahari Desert a desert region in Southern Africa, p. 10

Kano (12°N, 8°E) a city and the capital of Kano state in northern Nigeria; a historic kingdom in northern Nigeria, p. 111

Katanga a southern province in Congo, p. 163

Kilwa late tenth-century Islamic city-state located on an island off the coast of present-day Tanzania, p. 39

L

Lagos (6°N, 3°E) a city and chief Atlantic port of Nigeria; a state in Nigeria, p. 110

Lalibela a town in Ethiopia famous for its stone churches carved in the 1100s, p. 139

M

Mali (15°N, 0.15°W) an early African empire; a present-day country in West Africa, officially Republic of Mali, p. 37

Mediterranean Sea (36°N, 13°E) the large sea separating Europe and Africa, p. 12

Mount Kenya (0.10°S, 37°E) a volcano in central Kenya, p. 146

N

Nairobi (1°S, 36°E) the capital of Kenya, p. 152

Namib Desert a desert extending along the Atlantic Coast of South Africa, p. 10

Niger (18°N, 8°E) a country in West Africa, officially Republic of Niger, p. 53

Niger River the river in West Africa that flows from Guinea into the Gulf of Guinea, p. 11

Nile River the longest river in the world, flows through northeastern Africa into the Mediterranean Sea, p. 11

North Africa countries in the northern region of Africa, p. 63

Nubia an ancient region in North Africa, p. 33

R

Republic of South Africa (28°S, 24°E) southernmost country in Africa, p. 81

S

Sahara largest tropical desert in the world, covers almost all of North Africa, p. 9

Sahel the region in West and Central Africa that forms a changing climate zone between the dry Sahara to the north and humid savannas to the south, p. 19

Senegal (14°N, 14°W) a country in West Africa, officially Republic of Senegal, p. 41

Songhai an empire and trading state in West Africa founded in the 1400s, p. 38

Southern Africa countries in the southern region of Africa, p. 82

T

Tombouctou (16°N, 3°W) city in Mali near the Niger River; in the past an important center of Islamic education and a trans-Saharan caravan stop (also spelled Timbuktu), p. 38

W

West Africa countries in the western region of Africa, p. 69

Z

Zaire former name of the Democratic Republic of Congo, p. 164

Zambezi River a river in Central and Southern Africa that flows into the Indian Ocean, p. 13

Zanzibar (6°S, 39°E) an island in the Indian Ocean off the coast of East Africa, part of Tanzania, p. 140

Zimbabwe (17°S, 29°E) a country in Southern Africa, officially Republic of Zimbabwe, p. 40

Glossary

This glossary lists key terms and other useful terms from the book.

A

apartheid the South African system in which racial groups were separated and racial discrimination was legal, p. 170

authoritarian controlled by one person or a small group, p. 164

B

bazaar a traditional open-air market with rows of shops or stalls, p. 97

boycott a refusal to buy or use certain products or services, p. 51

C

casbah an old, crowded section of a North African city, p. 103

cash crop a crop that is raised for sale, p. 23

cataract a rock-filled rapid, p. 11

census a count of the people in a country, p. 113

city-state a city that controls much of the land around it and has its own government, p. 39

civilization a society with cities, a central government, social classes, and usually, writing, art, and architecture, p. 32

clan a group of lineages, p. 72

colonize to settle an area and take over or create a government, p. 46

commercial farming the large-scale production of crops for sale, often coffee, cocoa, or bananas, p. 54

coup the takeover of a government, often done by military force, p. 119

Cultural

cultural diffusion the movement of customs and ideas from one culture to another, p. 67

cultural diversity a wide variety of cultures, p. 69

culture the way of life of people who share similar customs and beliefs, p. 63

D

democracy a government in which citizens have power through their elected representatives, p. 51

desertification the changing of fertile land into land that is too dry for crops, p. 123

discriminate to treat people unfairly based on race, religion, or gender, p. 170

diversify to add variety; a country can diversify its economy by producing more products, p. 25

domesticate to adapt wild plants and animals for human use, p. 32

drought a long period of little or no rainfall, p. 124

E

economy a system for producing, distributing, consuming, and owning goods, services, and wealth, p. 24

elevation the height of land above sea level, p. 10

erode to wear away slowly, p. 124

escarpment a steep cliff about 100 stories high, p. 11

ethnic group a group of people who share the same ancestors, culture, language, or religion, p. 34

extended family a family that includes relatives other than parents and children, p. 71

F

fellaheen peasants or agricultural workers in an Arab country, p. 97

fertile containing substances that plants need in order to grow well, p. 12

foreign debt money owed to foreign countries, p. 144

G

griot an African storyteller, p. 73

H

harambee the Swahili word for "let's pull together"; the campaign in Kenya begun by President Jomo Kenyatta in 1963, after the country became independent, p. 150

homeland South African lands where blacks were forced to live during apartheid; driest and least fertile parts of the country, p. 171

hunter-gatherer person who gathers wild food and hunts animals to survive, p. 31

hybrid a plant that is a combination of two or more types of the same plant, p. 55

I

irrigate to artificially water crops, p. 17

K

kinship a family relationship, p. 71

L

life expectancy how long an average person will live, p. 56

lineage a group of families with a common ancestor, p. 72

lingua franca a common language shared by different peoples, p. 142

literacy the ability to read and write, p. 56

M

migrant worker a person who moves from place to place to find work, p. 82

migrate to move from one place to another, p. 33

monastery a place where monks or nuns live, work, and study, p. 135

multiethnic containing many ethnic groups, p. 109

multiparty system two or more political parties in one country, p. 144

N

nationalism a feeling of pride in one's homeland; a group's identity as members of a nation, p. 47

nationalize to put a once-private industry under national control, p. 164

nomad a person who moves around to make a living, usually by herding animals, trading, hunting, or gathering food, p. 19

nuclear family a family that includes parents and children, p. 71

O

oasis a fertile place in a desert where there is water and vegetation, p. 17

P

Pan-Africanism a movement that stressed unity among all Africans, p. 48

pilgrimage a religious journey; for Muslims, the journey to Mecca, p. 38

plantation a large farm where cash crops are grown, p. 78

plateau a large, mostly flat area that rises above the surrounding land, p. 10

Q

Quran the holy book of the religion of Islam, p. 38

R

rift a deep crack in the Earth's surface, p. 11

S

savanna region of tall grasses, p. 18

silt bits of rock and dirt on river bottoms, p. 12

souq an open-air marketplace, p. 103

sovereignty political independence, p. 118

subsistence farming raising just enough crops to support one's family, p. 22

surplus more than is needed, p. 32

Swahili an African language that includes some Arabic words, p. 38

T

terrace a platform cut into the side of a mountain, used for growing crops in steep places, p. 101

tributary a small stream or river that flows into a larger river, p. 13

Index

separation from Africa, 9
Southern Africa, 208–211, 231
  countries of, *m 160*
  geography of, 10
sovereignty, 118, 234
  of Ghana, 118
Soviet Union, 49–50
Soweto, South Africa, *p 172*
Soyinka, Wole, 74
Spain, 43, *m 45*
specialized economy, 25
Statue of Liberty, 115
Stone Age, 31
strait, 229
subsistence farming, 22, *p 22,* 54, 234
Sudan, 12, *m 134,* 207, 228
Suez Canal, 97
sunscreen, 19
surplus, 32, 234
Swahili, 76–77
  language, 38–39, 77, 142, 150, 163
Swaziland, *m 160,* 211

T

talking drums, 120, 132–133
Tanganyika, 140
Tanzania, *m 134*
  ANC in, 81
  cities of, 79, *p 140*
  country profile, *m 141, c 141*
  crops of, 23
  economy of, 142–143
  farming in, 23, *p 143,* 145, *p 145*
  history of, 140
  language of, 77, 142
  literacy in, 56
  political systems of, 142, 144–145
  population of 141, *m 141, c 141*
  present-day, 144–145
  Regional Database, 207
  ujamaa villages of, *p 143*
  women in, *p 143*
terrace, 101
terrace farming, 236
Thirst Zone, 32
"The Smoke That Thunders." See
  Victoria Falls
time management, 166–167
Togo, *m 108,* 203, 229
Tombouctou, Mali, 38, *p 72, p 121,*
  m 122, 231
tools, 32, *p 32*
topsoil, 22

Torah, 94
trade
  Atlantic slave, 43–45
  and Askum, 35–36
  European, 41–42
  importance of, 37
  routes, *m 38*
  West African routes, *m 36*
tributaries, 13, 229, 234
tropical rain forest. See rain forest
Tropic of Cancer, 15, *m 16*
Tropic of Capricorn, 15, *m 16*
tsetse fly, 20
Tuareg, *p 1,* 65–66, *p 66,* 99–100, *p 99,*
  123–124
  and the practice of Islam, *p 124*
Tunisia, *p 66, m 92,* 199
  Great Mosque of, *p 68*
Tutankhamen, 96

U

Uganda, 20, *m 134,* 207
  Kampala, *p 77*
ujamaa, 143, *p 143,* 144
unification, of North Africa, 65–66
union, of workers, 83
United Kingdom. See also Great
  Britain
United Nations, 124–125
United States
  African Americans and the right to
    vote, 48
  African independence and, 49–50
  and Congo, 165
  slave trade and, 43
  in World War II, 49
urbanization, 72

V

vegetation, *m 5,* 193, 195
  in Mali, *m 122*
veil, importance of, in Egypt, 96, *p 96*
Victoria Falls, 14, *p 14*
volcanoes, 229, *p 229*
Volta River, 119
voting rights, 48

W

water, need for, 32
West Africa, 231
  coastal plain in, *p 11*

countries of, *m 108*
crops of, 21, *p 71*
cultures of, 69–74
ethnic groups in, 69, 71–72
family structure in, 71
farming in, 23
fishing industry in, *p 70*
folk tales of, 73
geography of, 10
Ghana, 115–120
kingdoms of, *m 36,* 37–38
languages of, 70
Mali, 121–125
Nigeria, 109–114
population density of, *m 188*
Portuguese exploration of, 42
Regional Bank, *p 125*
Regional Database, 200–203
trade routes of, *m 36,* 37
West African National Congress, 48
Western Sahara, *m 92*
White Nile, 12
women
  Berber, 101
  in East Africa, 78
  in Egypt, 96, *p 96, p 98*
  in Ghana, 117
  in Kenya, 78, 152–153
  in Mali, 123, *p 123*
  in matrilineal society, 72
  in South Africa, *p 171*
  in Tanzania, *p 143*
world
  physical map of, *m 214–215*
  political map of, *m 212–213*
World Health Organization, 56
World War II, African response to,
  49, *p 49*

Y

Yoruba, 73, 109, 110, 112, *p 113*

Z

Zaire, 231
  economic collapse of in the 1970s,
    164
  naming of by Mobutu, 164
  rebel takeover of, 165
  See also Congo, Democratic
    Republic of
Zambezi River, 13–14, 231
  length of, 13

Acknowledgments

Cover Design

Bruce Bond, Suzanne Schineller, and Olena Serbyn

Cover Photo

Jon Chomitz

Maps

MapQuest.com, Inc.
Map information sources: Columbia Encyclopedia, Encyclopaedia Britannica, Microsoft® Encarta®, National Geographic Atlas of the World, Rand McNally Commercial Atlas, The Times Atlas of the World.

Staff Credits

The people who made up the **World Explorer** team—representing editorial, editorial services, design services, on-line services/multimedia development, product marketing, production services, project office, and publishing processes—are listed below. Bold type denotes core team members.

Joyce Barisano, Margaret Broucek, **Paul Gagnon, Mary Hanisco, Dotti Marshall,** Kirsten Richert, Susan Swan, and Carol Signorino.

Additional Credits

Art and Design: Emily Soltanoff. Editorial: Debra Reardon, Nancy Rogier. Market Research: Marilyn Leitao. Publishing Processes: Wendy Bohannan.

Program Development and Production

Editorial and Project Management: Summer Street Press
Production: Pronk&Associates

Text

19, From *Sand and Fog: Adventures in Southern Africa,* by Jim Brandenburg. Copyright © 1994 by Jim Brandenburg. Reprinted with permission of Walker Publishing Company, Inc. **21,** From *Cocoa Comes to Mampong,* by Dei Anang. Copyright © 1949. Reprinted with the permission of Methodist Book Depot. **80,** From "African Statesman Still Sowing Seeds for Future," by James C. McKinley, Jr., *New York Times,* September 1, 1996. Copyright © 1996 by *The New York Times.* Reprinted by permission. **87,** From *The Africans,* by David Lamb. Copyright © 1982 by David Lamb. Reprinted with the permission of Random House, Inc. **99,** From "The World in Its Extreme," by William Langewiesche. Copyright © 1991 by William Langewiesche as first published in *The Atlantic Monthly,* November 1991. **117,** From *Ghana in Transition,* by David E. Apter. Copyright © 1955, '63, and '72 by Princeton University Press. Used with permission. **132,** "My Village" from *The Distant Talking Drum.* Text copyright © 1995 by Isaac Olaleye. Reprinted with permission of Wordsong/Boyds Mills Press, Inc. **133,** "Village Weavers" from *The Distant Talking Drum.* Text copyright © 1995 by Isaac Olaleye. Reprinted with permission of Wordsong/Boyds Mills Press, Inc. **141, 143,** From "Three Leaders," by Andrew Meldrum, *Africa Report,* September–October 1994. Copyright © 1994 by *Africa Report.* Reprinted by permission. **150,** From *Baricho - A Village in Kenya,* by Richard Wright. Copyright © 1993 by Warwickshire World Studies Centre. Distributed by DEDU, **153,** Cardigan Road, Leeds, LS6 1LJ, United Kingdom. Reprinted with permission of Warwickshire World Studies Centre. **153,** From "Back to No Man's Land," by George Monbiot, *Geographical Magazine,* July 1994. Copyright © 1994 by *Geographical Magazine.* Reprinted by permission. **156,** From *A Promise to the Sun* by Tololwa M. Mollel. Text Copyright © 1991 by Tololwa M. Mollel; Illustrations Copyright © 1991 by Beatriz Vidal. By permission of Little, Brown and Company.

Photos

iv bottom left, © J. Highet/Trip Photographic, **iv center left,** © M. & V. Birley/Tropix Photographic Library, **v top right,** © Boyd Norton/Boyd Norton, **v bottom left,** © B. Mnguni/Trip Photographic, **v bottom right,** © Nicholas Parfitt/Tony Stone Images, **1 center left,** Reuters/Corbis-Bettman, **1 top left,** Comstock, **1 center,** © Robert, Frerck/Odyssey Productions, **1 top right,** © Courtsey of Museum of Fine Arts Boston, **1 center right,** © Betty Press/Woodfin Camp & Associates, **1 background,** Artbase Inc., **5 center right,** © Mark Thayer, Boston, **9 bottomright,** © Paul C. Sereno/Paul C. Sereno, **10 bottom,** © Robert Frerck/Odyssey Productions, **10 center left,** © Wendy Stone/Odyssey Productions, **11 top right,** © G. Winters/Trip Photographic, **12 top left,** © SuperStock International, **13 center left,** © Comstock, **14 top right,** © Steve McCutcheon/Visuals Unlimited, **15 bottom right,** © Frans Lanting/Minden Pictures, **17 bottom right,** © Don W. Fawcett/Visuals Unlimited, **19 top right,** © Nicholas Parfitt/Tony Stone Images, **20 top right,** © Penny Tweedle/Tony Stone Images, **21 bottom right,** © Victor Englebert/Victor Englebert Photography, **21 bottom center,** © Cabisco/Visuals Unlimited, **22 bottom left,** © Victor Englebert/Victor Englebert Photography, **22 bottom right,** © Wendy Stone/Odyssey Productions, **22 bottom center,** © Brian Seed/Tony Stone Images, **25 center right,** © Ian Murphy/Tony Stone Images, **26 bottom,** © David Young-Wolff/PhotoEdit, **31 bottom right,** © The Granger Collection, **32 center,** © Lee Boltin/Boltin Picture Library, **32 top center,** © Lee Boltin/Boltin Picture Library, **32 top left,** © Lee Boltin/Boltin Picture Library, **33 top left,** © Courtesy of Museum of Fine Arts Boston, **35 bottom right,** © H. Rogers/Trip Photographic, **37 top center,** © The Granger Collection, **39 center,** © The Granger Collection, **39 top left,** © SuperStock International, **40 top left,** © Jason Laure'/Laure' Communications, **41 bottom right,** © Erich Lessing/Art Resource, **42 bottom,** © Robert Frerck/Odyssey Productions, **44 bottom left,** © The Granger Collection, **44 bottom right,** © The Granger Collection, **47 bottom right,** © Jason Laure'/Laure' Communications, **48 bottom right,** © L. P. Winfrey/Woodfin Camp & Associates, **49 top left,** © UPI/Corbis-Bettmann, **51 bottom right,** © UPI/Corbis-Bettmann, **52 top right,** © Wolfgang Kaehler/Wolfgang Kaehler Photography, **53 bottom right,** © W. Jacobs/Trip Photographic, **56 top,** © Jason Laure'/Laure' Communications, **57 top left,** © Marc & Evelyn Bernheim/Woodfin Camp & Associates, **58 bottom,** © Bill Aron/PhotoEdit, **62 center**

right, © M. & E. Bernheim/Woodfin Camp & Associates, **63 bottom right,** © Glen Allison/Tony Stone Images, **64 bottom,** © Robert Frerck/Woodfin Camp & Associates, **65 center right,** © Robert Azzi/Woodfin Camp & Associates, **66 top left,** © Bob Smith/Trip Photographic, **66 top right,** © Ben Nakayama/Tony Stone Images, **68 top right,** © Lorne Resnick/Tony Stone Images, **69 bottom right,** © Jason Laure'/Laure' Communications, **70 bottom right,** © Wolfgang Kaehler/Wolfgang Kaehler Photography, **71 top left,** © Wolfgang Kaehler/Wolfgang Kaehler Photography, **71 top right,** © M. & V. Birley/Tropix Photographic Library, **72 bottom,** © Wolfgang Kaehler/Wolfgang Kaehler Photography, **73 top left,** © Betty Press/Woodfin Camp & Associates, **74 top right,** © M. & E. Bernheim/Woodfin Camp & Associates, **75 bottom right,** © Victor Englebert/Victor Englebert Photography, **76 center,** © Robert Frerck/Odyssey Productions, **77 top left,** © P. Joynson-Hicks/Trip Photographic, **78–79 center,** © D. Saunders/Trip Photographic, **80 top left,** © Boyd Norton/Boyd Norton, **81 bottom right,** © Jason Laure'/Laure' Communications, **82 center left,** © Jason Laure'/Laure' Communications, **83 top center,** © Jason Laure'/Laure' Communications, **84 bottom right,** © D. Davis/Tropix Photographic Library, **85 top left,** © Robert Caputo/Aurora & Quanta Productions, **86 bottom left,** © Betty Press/Woodfin Camp & Associates, **87 center left,** © Michael Newman/PhotoEdit, **90 center right,** © M. & E. Bernheim/Woodfin Camp & Associates, **91 bottom left,** © Adam Novick/Village Pulse, **93 bottom right,** © P. Mitchell/Trip Photographic, **94, center left,** © Carmen Redondo/CORBIS/MAGMA, **95 top left,** © Roland & Sabrina Michaud/Woodfin Camp & Associates, **96 bottom,** © Donna DeCesare/Impact Visuals, **97 top left,** © Israel Talby/Woodfin Camp & Associates, **98 top,** © Don Smetzer/Tony Stone Images, **99 bottom left,** © Victor Englebert/Victor Englebert Photography, **100 center left,** © Andrea Jemolo/CORBIS/MAGMA, **101 bottom center,** © Sylvain Grandadam/Tony Stone Images, **102 top left,** © Sean Sprague/Impact Visuals, **103 top right,** © Victor Englebert/Victor Englebert Photography, **103 top left,** © Wendy Stone/Odyssey Productions, **110 center left,** ©Paul Almasy/CORBIS/MAGMA, **111 bottom right,** © Marc & Evelyn Bernheim/Woodfin Camp & Associates, **112 top right,** © Robert Frerck/Odyssey Productions, **113 bottom,** © J. Highet/Trip Photographic, **113 top right,** © Sylvan Wittwer/Visuals Unlimited, **114 top center,** © Trip/Trip Photographic, **115 bottom right,** © AP/Wide World Photos, **116 center left,** Milepost 92 1/2/Corbis/Magma, **117 bottom center,** © Frank Fournier/Woodfin Camp & Associates, **118 top left,** © Tim Beddow/Tony Stone Images, **119 center right,** © AP/Wide World Photos, **120 center left,** © M. & V. Birley/Tropix Photographic Library, **120 center right,** © M. & V. Birley/Tropix Photographic Library, **121 bottom right,** © M. Jelliffe/Trip Photographic, **123 bottom left,** © Norman Myers/Bruce Coleman Inc., **124 bottom center,** © Wolfgang Kaehler/Wolfgang Kaehler Photography, **125 top left,** © Betty Press/Woodfin Camp & Associates, **126 bottom left,** © Michael Newman/PhotoEdit, **130 bottom right,** © David Young-Wolff/PhotoEdit, **131 top right,** © David Young-Wolff/PhotoEdit, **132 bottom center,** © Betty Press/Woodfin Camp & Associates, **133 center,** © Lawrence Manning/Tony Stone Images, **135 bottom right,** © Robert Caputo/Aurora & Quanta Productions, **137 bottom right,** © The Granger Collection, **137 bottom left,** © The Granger Collection, **139 top right,** © R. Ashford/Tropix Photographic Library, **140 bottom left,** © AP/Wide World Photos, **141 center left,** © Miller Photography/Animals Animals, **142 top right,** © Reuters/Corbis-Bettmann, **143 bottom,** © M. & V. Birley/Tropix Photographic Library, **144 bottom right,** © Gerald Cubitt/Gerald Cubitt Photographer, **144 bottom left,** © Gerald Cubitt/Gerald Cubitt Photographer, **145 top,** © AP/Wide World Photos, **146 bottom left,** © James P. Rowan/Tony Stone Images, **148 bottom left,** © M. & E. Bernheim/Woodfin Camp & Associates, **149,** Dorling Kindersley Picture Library, **150 top left,** © Betty Press/Woodfin Camp & Associates, **151 bottom left,** © Victor Englebert/Victor Englebert Photography, **152 bottom right,** Matutu Ride, by Ian Kamau, Kenya. Courtesy of the International Children's Art Museum, **157 top right,** © Marc Chamberlain/Tony Stone Images, **158 bottom left,** © Tim Davis/Tony Stone Images, **161 bottom left,** © Jason Laure'/Laure' Communications, **162 center left,** Paul Almasy/Corbis/Magma, **163 bottom right,** © M. Jelliffe/Trip Photographic, **164 bottom left,** © Betty Press/Woodfin Camp & Associates, **166 bottom left,** © Michael Newman/PhotoEdit, **168 bottom left,** © B. Mnguni/Trip Photographic, **169 center left,** © Paul Almasy/CORBIS/MAGMA, **170 bottom left,** © Jason Laure'/Laure' Communications, **171 top right,** © Paula Bronstein/Impact Visuals, **172 bottom right,** © African Institute of Art, Funda Art Centre in Soweto, **173 center right,** © Reuters/Corbis-Bettman, **176 bottom left,** © Mark Thayer, Boston, **177 center right,** © Betty Press/Woodfin Camp & Associates, **179 left,** © Mark Thayer, Boston, **180 center left,** © Steve Leonard/Tony Stone Images, **180 bottom,** Robert Frerck/Odyssey Productions, **181 center left,** © Wolfgang Kaehler/Wolfgang Kaehler Photography, **181 bottom left,** © John Elk/Tony Stone Images, **181 bottom right,** Will & Deni McIntyre/Tony Stone Images, **191 bottom,** © G. Brad Lewis/Tony Stone Images, **193 bottom right,** © Nigel Press/Tony Stone Images, **196–197 background,** Artbase Inc., **197 center,** Artbase Inc., **197 bottom right,** Artbase Inc., **198–199 background,** Artbase Inc., **199 center,** Artbase Inc., **200–201 background,** Artbase Inc., **201–202 background,** Artbase Inc., **202–203 background,** Artbase Inc., **204–205 background,** Artbase Inc., **206 bottom right,** Artbase Inc., **206–207 background,** Artbase Inc., **207 center right,** Artbase Inc., **208–209 background,** Artbase Inc., **208–227,** Flags, The Flag Institute, Chester, **210–211 background,** Artbase Inc., **228 bottom center,** © Spencer Swanger/Tom Stack & Associates, **228 bottom left,** © John Beatty/Tony Stone Images, **228 center left,** © A. & L. Sinibaldi/Tony Stone Images, **229 center right,** © Hans Strand/Tony Stone Images, **229 top left,** © Paul Chesley/Tony Stone Images.